D1171704

WHITEWATER!

Other Books by the Authors

The Fisherman's Almanac, by Dan Morris and Norman Strung

The Hunter's Almanac, by Norman Strung

Family Fun Around the Water, by Norman Strung and Dan Morris

Camping in Comfort, by Norman and Sil Strung

Deer Hunting, by Norman Strung

Spinfishing, by Norman Strung and Milt Rosko

Misty Mornings and Moonless Nights:
   A Waterfowler's Guide, by Norman Strung

Communicating the Outdoor Experience, edited by Norman Strung

Norman Strung
Sam Curtis
Earl Perry

WHITEWATER!

MACMILLAN PUBLISHING CO., INC. / COLLIER MACMILLAN PUBLISHERS
New York   **London**

To the late Walter Kirschbaum: best of kayakers, best of men

Line drawings by C. W. "Wally" Hansen

Macmillan Publishing Co., Inc.
866 Third Avenue, New York, N.Y. 10022
Collier Macmillan Canada, Ltd.

Library of Congress Cataloging in Publication Data
Strung, Norman.
  Whitewater!
  Bibliography: p.
  Includes index.
  1. White-water canoeing. 2. Rafting (Sports)
I. Curtis, Sam, joint author. II. Perry, Earl,
joint author. III. Title.
GV788.S85   797.1'22   75-26912
ISBN 0-02-615110-3

First Printing 1976

Printed in the United States of America

Contents

Preface

Whitewater! The sound of the word conjures up spray-spangled cataracts and the silky coolness of smooth pools. My ears recall the roar of rapids, and the muted tinkle of riffles. I feel warm sand between my toes, cold water on my face, and my nostrils flare to whiff the pungent smell of river moss.

It's impossible to find the one word, or even several, that defines whitewater floating and its attraction for the hundreds of thousands of river rats who risk their boats and their lives on wild rivers each year. It is a complex undertaking, with equally complex rewards, and perhaps that, in part, explains the lure: its richness. Dealing effectively with water driven mad by gravity and geology requires a wealth of knowledge, skill and no small amount of courage. Coupled with the kind of environment that surrounds a free-flowing river—raw nature, pristine yet ever changing—the combinations of challenges, scenes and situations are infinite . . . as are the pleasures.

Besides, there's no real need to go into the "whys" of whitewater floating. As with humor, when you dissect such subjective joys you risk losing the patient on the operating table. The "hows," however, are a different matter.

There is a more than substantial body of knowledge that should belong to anyone who plans to float fast water, and the depth of needed savvy increases as the pace of the river quickens. Make no mistake: the crowning turbulence of froth and foam called whitewater is no "safe" ally. You meet it on its own terms, not in battle, but ballet. To survive the dance you have to know the steps: the equipment best suited to the type of river you're floating, how to use it, and a great deal about the workings of water on the move. It is in explanation of these skills that *Whitewater!* is written.

The book begins with a chapter entitled "Whitewater," one in which we all had a hand.

Whether your floating inclinations lie in rafts, canoes or kayaks, the river is the common denominator. Be it a serpentine giant like the Colorado or a stippled rock garden like the Allagash, water flow is governed by hydrological rules. Rivers respond to their bed in predictable patterns. Identifying these patterns required the sum of our experiences. The product is a kind of universal river: one that will familiarize you with whitewater, no matter what river you float or what craft you choose.

Whitewater craft, on the other hand, have individual personalities. Rafts are slow and lumbering and piloted by oars. Canoes are gentlemen of noble lineage, controlled with a single-bladed paddle. Kayaks are quick, lean and unforgiving, but in practiced hands their two-bladed paddle can drive them to the limits of endurance. Kayaks dance.

Because of these inherent differences, and the type of water to which they're best suited, separate chapters on "Rafting," "Canoeing," and "Kayaking" follow in that order, each written by an expert in the use of his craft.

Whitewater boating techniques account for the core of each of these chapters, but also included is a wealth of information on choosing, buying and building whitewater equipment, boating safety and, for lack of a better term, some different views of a river.

"Armchair Exercises" is the final section of this book. In it, you'll find reviews of those books we feel make excellent companions to this one, as well as some that tell about rivers you'd like to know.

Ritual, ceremony, celebration, skill and sport . . . whitewater boating can be called all these things. Whatever term you choose, it will be an adventure you'll never forget. Once you know the "hows," you'll discover your own "whys" . . . and will surely return to whitewater again and again.

1 WHITEWATER
by Norman Strung

"The river knows it all. You learn from *it*."
—ARTA *River Guide's Manual*

The gutter of a dusty Brooklyn street is surely an odd place to begin a book on white-water floating, but in a way, that's where this all began.

I spent my childhood there, and one of the greatest of all delights on a hot summer day was the appearance of the water truck, a Department of Sanitation tanker, fitted with nozzles that sprayed the hot streets clean.

Most exciting was the run. I would follow the progress of the slow-moving truck, keeping pace with the cool drenching spray, and inhale the heady pavement-steam vapors that swirled around me. But there was still a point of interest after the truck was gone—the trickle of water that hugged the curb.

What magic it was, to see smooth pavement churn the trickle of water into corduroy rivulets. To witness the erratic paths of leaves and debris caught in the current; to watch a mini-dam build and block the "stream," seemingly of its own accord. And best of all, to launch a popsicle-stick raft at Bushwick, and follow its progress all the way down Chauncey Street to Evergreen Avenue!

Today, some thirty years later, I can't help but remember those summer days and, in so doing, make a comparison: the rain-gutter rivulet has grown to mighty torrents, the popsicle-stick raft has puffed up into balloony rubber, and I have grown to middle age, but it's the same thing that holds me rapt today: fascination with the form and natural progress of moving water. Life moves in cycles upon itself—expanding, enlarging and hopefully improving—but a circle is still a circle no matter its size or the territory it encompasses.

There are parallels to be drawn with water, for it too moves in a cycle.

THE MECHANICS OF A RIVER

Water has no beginning and no end, just form in one of three conditions: liquid, solid or gas. These conditions are, however, constantly in a state of flux. Water continually changes from one state to another.

Water evaporates from the oceans in response to the power of solar energy, and enters a gaseous state. Onshore breezes blow the moisture-laden air overland, and a combination of barometric pressure and temperature changes associated with land masses condense the moisture into tiny beads— clouds. When clouds become thick enough, the beads of moisture precipitate and the result is rain or snow.

Of the rain that falls on land, some is temporarily held prisoner by the soil and some is contained by vegetation. The major share of the moisture evaporates or is transpired back into the air by plants and trees. The excess moisture either becomes surface runoff or seeps down through the soil until it reaches an impervious layer—a substratum of rock, hard-packed clay or a similar substance through which water cannot filter. At higher elevations or in northern climates, the moisture is held in a solid state, ice or snow, until the warm rays of spring and summer can encourage it to slowly leak to the sea.

These three sources—snowpack, groundwater and runoff, all the result of rain—feed our streams.

The pattern in which most waterways are nursed is interesting in itself. A tiny trickle, sprouting from a spring, the foot of a glacier or the collected drops of a shower, joins a similar trickle at a Y junction. That thread of water joins yet another thread at a Y, and the thread becomes a rill. Several rills meet to become a brook. The brook joins others of its kind to become a stream, and the stream eventually joins a river. The pattern is called dendritic; should you ever view a typical drainage from the air you'll see a design evident throughout nature, from the root structure of trees, to the veins in their leaves, to the circulatory system in the human body.

As solar energy is the force that lifts water into the air through evaporation, gravity is the force that drives it through the pulsing arteries we call rivers; down the steep slopes of mountains, down deep-cleft valleys and across gentle plains, until its final return to the sea—the completion of the cycle.

As gravity propels water downslope, however, a second factor enters the picture—friction. Friction occurs in any flow of water, even a smooth pipe, and that friction or drag, when small, produces a property of water called laminar flow.

The principle of laminar flow is best understood by imagining several sheets of plywood, separated by layers of ball bearings. Assuming resistance to be a constant, moving the top layer of plywood would also move the underlayers of plywood, but each would move

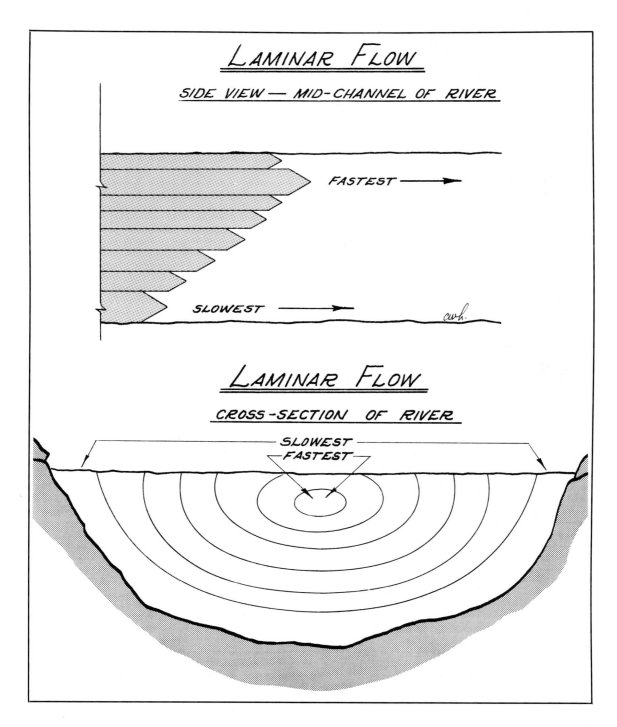

more slowly than the board above it. Tip the sheets downhill, and the effect would be even more pronounced: the lowest layer of plywood might move at a rate of a mile an hour. At that rate, however, it is also moving all the layers above it at a mile an hour. They too are responding to the pull of gravity, so as they begin to move independently the second sheet would actually be traveling at two miles an hour, the third sheet at three, and so forth.

Essentially, this is how smooth water flows in a straight stretch of river. Because of friction, the slowest water will be closest to the bottom, the fastest water will be on top. This isn't precisely the case; because of friction with the air, the fastest part of such a flow will be between 5 and 15 percent of the river's depth below the surface, and because of friction with the bottom, the deepest "laminate" barely moves at all; but the difference to the floater is so slight as to not rate concern.

Laminar flow is also related to depth. Riverbeds, even straight runs, are not square boxes; they have receding banks that gently dip to the deepest part, the main channel. Thus the rate of current close to the bank will be significantly slower than the current at midstream, because there are fewer layers of "plywood and ball bearings" there.

The rate of laminar flow is also limited. At four to five knots, turbulence begins to develop, interfering with the kind of regular shear planes illustrated by those sheets of plywood. This phenomenon is best understood if you now envision the laminates as sheets of air and the ball bearings as Ping-Pong balls. When a certain rate of speed is achieved, the Ping-Pong balls not only roll but begin to whirl about, agitating the smooth flow of water current, and thereby creating flow resistance as gravity propels the water downstream.

"Energy may be neither created nor destroyed" is a basic tenet of physics. The steeper the gradient, the greater the potential energy of moving water, but if it can't release that energy through greater speed, it must be released elsewhere. That power is spent in three ways. By a scouring action of the riverbed (the process we call erosion), by transportation of suspended particles (it takes energy to hold silt and gravel in suspension), and by surface agitation (whitewater).

This is but one series of characteristics of water on the move, and a patently manufactured one. Except for short runs, no riverbed will be symmetrical, nor will its channel run in a straight line, nor will the gradient be uniform. So complex are the laws governing water flow that to describe one accurately and thoroughly raises the possibility of losing sight of the system as a whole. A river is like your body: not just a heart, or a brain, or skin or bones, but all these things delicately balanced to work in perfect harmony. You can't understand the function of a heart without considering blood and nutrition. In turn, when discussing blood, you must take note of the cleansing action of the kidneys, and the cycle set up by the arteries and veins. So it is with our straight river. In a natural setting, water does more than run straight downhill.

Currents and Discontinuities

Water on the move creates reflex currents: currents that form in response or "reflex" to the overall downward flow of a river. Helical currents are one such response to laminar flow. They are a spiraling, coiled-spring flow that corkscrews downstream. Facing downriver, helical flow will be counterclockwise on the right side of our hypothetical straight, symmetrical river, and clockwise on the left side of the main current.

This second component of river current is the result of friction and drag set up by shoaling banks, combined with the impetus of the main current. The two factors create a circular, whirling, secondary current that goes down along an ill-defined shear line near the point of maximum flow. Helical flow follows the bottom of the river out toward the riverbank, then surfaces and spirals back into the main current at a downstream angle. This helical flow then pushes floating objects into the main current and holds them there. Even

4

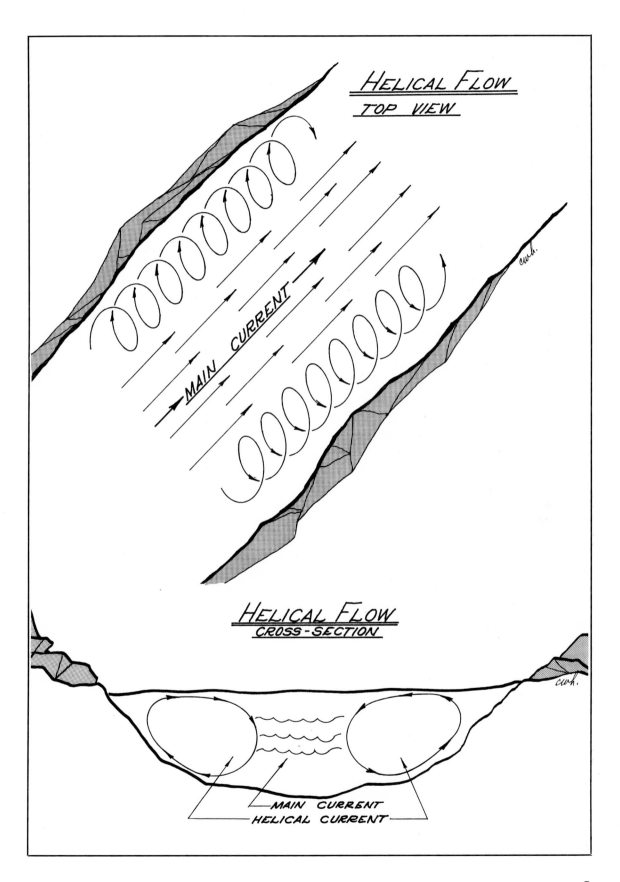

HELICAL FLOW
TOP VIEW

MAIN CURRENT

HELICAL FLOW
CROSS-SECTION

MAIN CURRENT
HELICAL CURRENT

in the tiniest trickle, a popsicle-stick raft placed at the quiet edge of the flow will be drawn inexorably into the strongest part of the current.

Laminar and helical flow, then, are the two currents that will always be present in a fast-flowing river (changes in current characteristics do occur when rivers are low-gradient or shallow, but they need not concern us here). With them in mind, let's begin to reshape our stream along more natural lines.

The "thalweg" of a river is a more definitive term than "main channel," though the two are closely related. The thalweg is the line of maximum river depth; this is usually the main channel too, but rain rises or spring runoff can change the direction of the greatest volume of water, so this term is more exact.

The thalweg, even in a straight stretch of river, will wander from bank to bank. As it does, turbulence erodes gentle curves into sharper curves, and meanders eventually develop.

When a river makes a sharp turn, the current becomes affected by centrifugal force, swinging wide into the outside bank. In addition, helical flow on the outside of the curve is diminished (smothered by the encroaching laminar flow might be more descriptive) and the corkscrew effect is increased on the inside of the curve. The surface water whirls hard in the direction of the outside curve. The faster the water, the stronger the push. The tendency is for floating objects to be forced into the outside bend, and indeed this is a place where you'll usually find a nightmare of tangled debris shoved up against the shore.

The powerful helical flow does more than push surface objects outward. As it swirls up from the bottom, it carries an overload of sediment. Because of the helical current's conflict with downriver flow, this sediment, as well as some of the particles carried in the river above the curve, is deposited at the apex of the bend. This sediment is usually dropped during high water, and when waters recede, a sand-and-gravel bar called a "point bar"

emerges. This point bar normally juts so far out into the stream that floaters are funneled into the swiftest part of the river in order to skirt the shoal tip of the bar.

When stream volume and velocity are both high, centrifugal force exerts still another influence on flow characteristics. The phenomenon is called "super-elevation," and it finds the river surface dishing up toward the outside bank, creating a situation a bit like a banked turn on a racetrack. It's a sobering illustration of the duality of whitewater; that dished inside curve is child's play to navigate, like a Coney Island slide. If you hit it right, you rise slightly as you come into the curve, then slip gently off the wave into the quiet pool waters below. But if you cross the current line, the power and force of the river on the outside of the curve are devastating. Anything caught there is either smashed and pinned against the outside bank or sucked under by the dominant inside helical flow.

Moving up yet another step on the whitewater scale, should the gradient be so great as to create macroturbulence, tackling this kind of turn is risky indeed. Excessive froth under a hull creates a situation roughly comparable to a hovercraft's—the machine that rides on a cushion of air. Gravity's effect on the boat is increased because the boat is floating on a combination of water droplets and air; you gain surprising speed. Yet control is severely limited because you find little resistance to oar or paddle in the air-shot water. The possibilities of a grinding crash into the outside bank are great; this stage of whitewater is for experts only, and can be impassable.

As the river comes out of a sharp bend, the currents are in a state of confusion. There is still the overall downstream movement, but the result of laminar flow shooting into a bank creates an overall helical effect immediately below the turn, which the river then tries to bring back into its natural scheme of flow. The result of these energies is usually a deep pool of gently swirling water that broadens into a shallow, wide apron of stream rubble, curving downstream.

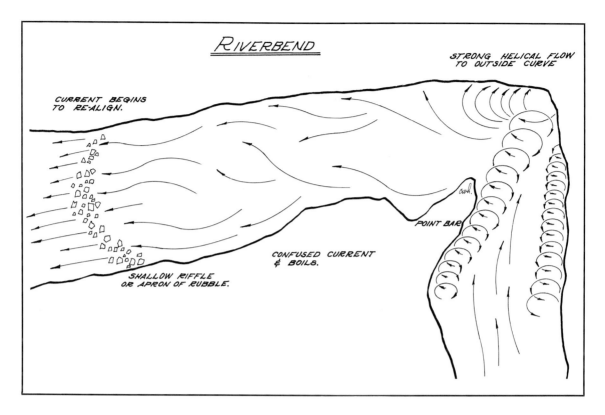

RIVERBEND

STRONG HELICAL FLOW TO OUTSIDE CURVE

CURRENT BEGINS TO RE-ALIGN.

SHALLOW RIFFLE OR APRON OF RUBBLE.

CONFUSED CURRENT & BOILS.

POINT BAR

This apron is commonly called a riffle, and it might be quite shallow with champagne-bubbly agitation evident. In a broad sense, riffles are the start of a river's food chain, for that highly oxygenated, sun-drenched water and the finely graded rubble of the bottom is home and breeding grounds for a vast variety of aquatic life. Insects, minnows and crustaceans all need those conditions for survival, and these smaller aquatic life forms feed larger predators in the pools below. Riffles are also the nursery for the young of predatory species. Most cold-water fish eggs need agitation and high oxygen levels to hatch.

Riffles are interesting too in that they occur in a pattern, usually spaced at regular intervals five to seven times the average width of the river. They remain in place virtually forever, but each high-water period moves rocks from one riffle to the next one downstream in a never-ending changing of the guard.

By the time water reaches the foot of the riffle or apron, it has gained positive direction, and helical and laminar flow characteristics begin to take over again.

As the river gathers itself up and moves through a typical bed, it will come into contact with a variety of obstacles. Most common are submerged boulders. Water, being a fluid, cannot resist stress, but must respond to it.

When water flows over an obstruction, its laminar characteristics create a separation or discontinuity of flow.

Viewed two-dimensionally, with the current moving from the right to the left, as if we split rock and river in half, the water close to the bottom on the upstream side of the obstruction would whirl counterclockwise, and the water on the downstream side would whirl clockwise. The flow patterns of these discontinuities resemble tiny water wheels driven by the impetus of the current.

In addition, the planes of laminar flow are compressed by increased speed as they pass over the top of the rock. There are some parallels to be drawn between water passing over a hump or bulge and air in the same situation. When air encounters this kind of foil, it accelerates as it passes over the rounded surfaces, and creates its own discontinuity, an area of low pressure. This is the "lift" of the airplane wing.

The acceleration of laminar planes of flow combined with the reflex effect (you could also view this as a kind of "vacuum" formed as water flows around an unmoving rock) creates an area of disturbed and confused currents immediately below the obstruction; this area is called a hydraulic.

"Hydraulic" is a general term. Just as "trees" can be elms, maples or lodgepole pines, and "clouds" can be nimbus, cumulus or cirrus, there are many kinds of hydraulics.

Surges Surges are a river's gentlest response to an obstruction. They generally occur when the water is quite deep and the current not too swift. The hydraulic that forms downstream of the obstruction pulses on and off and occasionally appears to be a large fish gently finning in the current. Surges present no real navigation problems, as the boulder that creates them will be far enough below the surface so you can float over the top without contact, but you should be aware of them. When you have to dip an oar or paddle at a critical point, you don't want interference with your stroke, and the boulder that creates a surge could be that close to the surface.

Sleepers As the depth of the water flowing over that underwater obstruction decreases, the surge becomes a sleeper. A sleeper has insufficient clearance to float a boat over its top. Depending on the size of the sleeper and the velocity of the water, failing to recognize one will result in penalties that range from a warning bump on the butt (or boat bottom) to a ripped raft, severe spinal injuries or a ruined canoe or kayak. In addition, with the larger sleepers, the water that's going over the top knifes through the water downstream. Rather than maintaining their surface orientation, the maximum-velocity planes of flow are forced underwater by sheer momentum. This characteristic, aided by the current discontinuity below, creates a powerful reflex current—a positive, strong, secondary current that swirls on a cross-maincurrent axis— and the surface waters behind the sleeper push *upstream*. Still another way to conceive of this action is by recalling that the hydraulic downstream of an obstacle creates a kind of vacuum. The upstream push of water is essentially the river filling that vacuum.

This form of hydraulic, technically known as a three-dimensional eddy, can be seen in action on any babbling brook, as it's the mini-sleepers that do most of the "babbling." On a grand scale, however, vertical eddies become

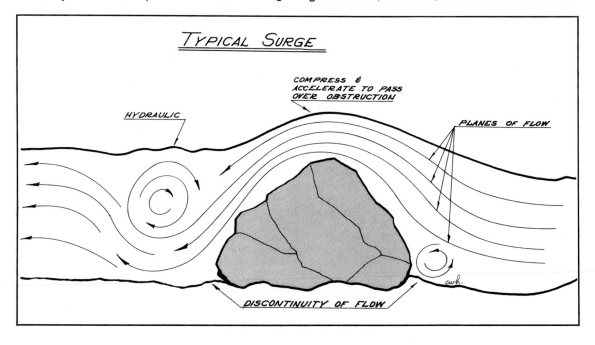

TYPICAL SURGE

COMPRESS & ACCELERATE TO PASS OVER OBSTRUCTION

HYDRAULIC

PLANES OF FLOW

DISCONTINUITY OF FLOW

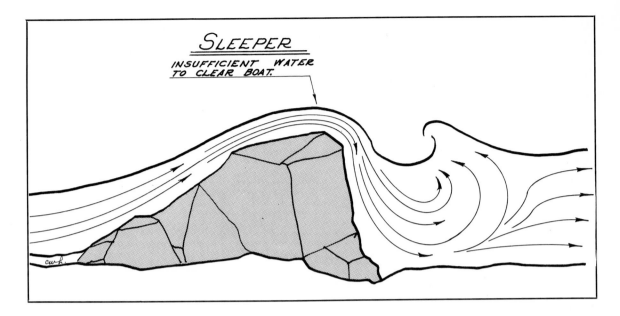

SLEEPER
INSUFFICIENT WATER TO CLEAR BOAT.

frightening traps known as suction holes—suckholes, for short.

Suckholes Suckholes, sometimes called "keepers" or "souse holes," are sleepers large enough to float over, but once you get caught in the eddy beneath them, you could be trapped there for days.

The force of water pouring over the sleeper and cleaving into the current below is more than sufficient to shove a jacketed swimmer along with it. You're pushed under, whirled to the surface downriver, then returned to the cascade by the upriver flow to be pushed under once again. Things too buoyant to go under are simply trapped there to drift around and around.

Suckholes are insidious too in that there's seldom an indication of their existence; there is no curling water, and not too much of a roar, just a good-sized bulge in the river to hint at what might wait below.

The "out" of suckholes involves three possibilities. The first one is that somewhere below the upriver flow lies water going in the same direction you want to go. You might be able to reach down and find it with oar or paddle, and force your way against the reflex current.

In big suckholes, however, that downstream flow will be too deep to reach. At the bottom of the worst suckholes, you see men wearing Chairman Mao outfits. The only way out of these suckholes is to try to get a blade into the water rushing by at the *side* of the eddy (along the shear line or eddy fence, which we'll talk about in a moment).

The third and best solution is to scout ahead, identify the location of suckholes and skirt them entirely.

Dribbling Falls Dribbling falls are another form of large sleeper. In this situation, there will be a substantial drop below a large, submerged boulder, with barely enough water shooting over the top to float you. An encounter with this type of sleeper usually finds you bumping bottom, which slows your speed. You end up dribbling rather than shooting over the top, and are likely to upset in the process. Like a suckhole, the best way to handle this situation is to avoid getting into it in the first place.

Breaking Holes The breaking hole is essentially the opposite of dribbling falls. Here a great deal of water is going over the top of a sleeper, without a steep enough drop to create a suckhole. The result is a wave of standing water below, much like an ocean breaker, except that this wave remains stationary. As in all forms of whitewater, the advisability of tackling a breaking hole is

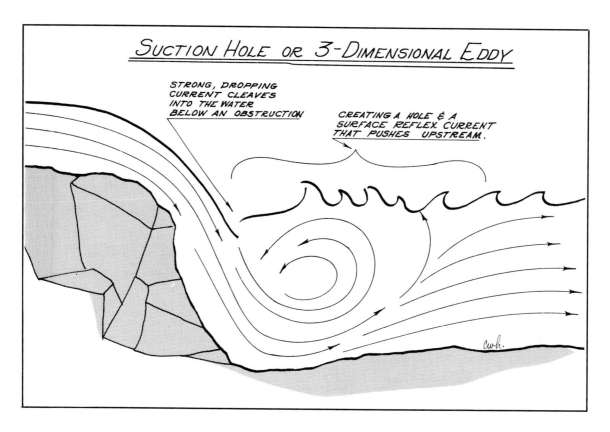

Suction Hole or 3-Dimensional Eddy

STRONG, DROPPING
CURRENT CLEAVES
INTO THE WATER
BELOW AN OBSTRUCTION

CREATING A HOLE & A
SURFACE REFLEX CURRENT
THAT PUSHES UPSTREAM.

purely a matter of the size of the thing relative to your boat and your ability. The standing wave behind a breaking hole can be anywhere from a foot to ten feet high. Although they lack the strong upriver flow of a suction hole, they too can be traps for a boat too small to climb up and over their crest.

Falls Waterfalls are the ultimate in the sleeper-and-suckhole phenomenon. Falls are the result of either of two geological situations: a plug that stretches across the entire river or a fault in the riverbed.

The plug may be a dam of tightly packed boulders or the rock formation known as a

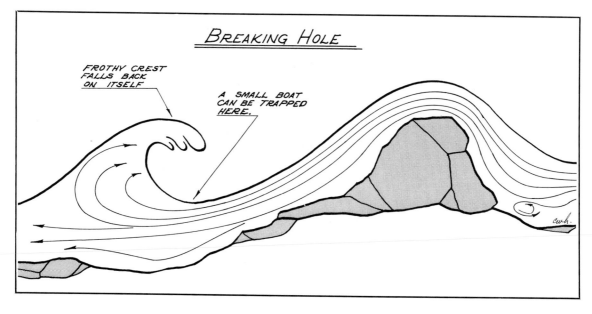

Breaking Hole

FROTHY CREST
FALLS BACK
ON ITSELF

A SMALL BOAT
CAN BE TRAPPED
HERE.

dike. Dikes are intrusions of hard rock between softer rock that have been up-ended by earth movements. Water action eats the soft rock away, leaving the hard rock jutting up as a stone wall. The plugged-river waterfall is usually identified by a deceptively placid pool above the cataract.

The faulted falls just suddenly drops away. This type of fall also has two causes. In read-justing and allowing for shifts in pressure, the earth occasionally shears its crust, like the forever-shifting ice of the polar cap. When such a shear crosses a riverbed, falls are formed.

Erosion lies at the bottom of the second class of faulted falls. They are the result of a hard layer of cap rock, with softer rock under-neath. At some point in the riverbed, the cap rock is eaten away, exposing the softer rock. The soft rock is scoured and eroded rapidly by the river, and it undercuts the hard rock. When the cut works back far enough, the cap rock lacks sufficient support, and it tumbles to the base of the falls. The undercutting goes on, with the falls working upriver, gaining height as they go. The most famous example of this variety of river action is Niagara.

There aren't many rivers with true falls—that is, a cataract of free-falling water. The work of the river quickly erodes them into a glorified suckhole (though river rats usually hang on to the ''falls'' label when identifying these places).

In true falls, however, the base of the drop

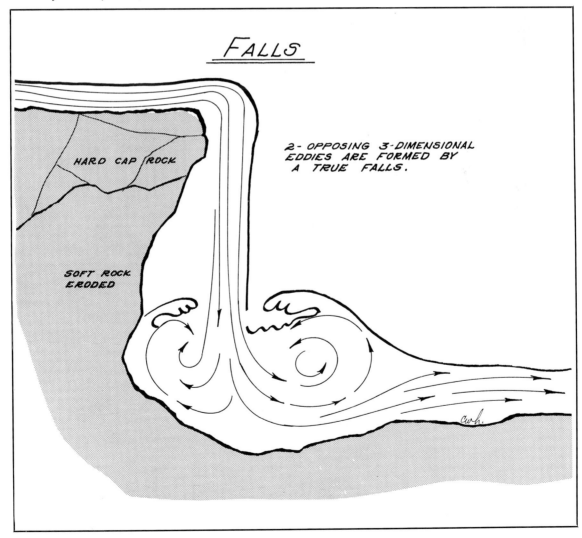

FALLS

HARD CAP ROCK

SOFT ROCK ERODED

2- OPPOSING 3-DIMENSIONAL EDDIES ARE FORMED BY A TRUE FALLS.

finds two suckholes or reflex currents forming, both of which whirl on a crosscurrent
axis into the falls, one behind and one in front
of the crashing water. When you're confronted with a two- or three-foot drop, that factor
isn't of tremendous consequence, but when
you talk about heights of six feet and above,
falls can be deathtraps.

This caveat is particularly true in terms of
man-made dams—not of the Grand Coulee
genre, but irrigation and diversion dams.
Their construction is such that the suckholes
that form below them are virtually inescapa-
ble. Another danger lies in the foam and froth
at the bottom of any falls. They could well
hide jagged boulders, or in the case of man-
made dams, concrete reinforcing bars.

Boils Downstream of the curling, reverse-
current suckhole below a falls or sleeper, the
water will assume a dome or mound shape.
This is the result of the planes of flow hitting
bottom, then being directed upward. When
they reach the surface, they part. The effect is
a flowerlike flow, with the water blooming in
every direction. This condition is called a boil.

Boils are noteworthy in two minor ways.
Once you're on their downstream side, you're
free of the suckhole, and boils are often
super-oxygenated—highly charged with air
bubbles. This takes much of the poop out of
an oar or paddle stroke.

Under conditions of extreme turbulence,
fountains form from the boil phenomenon. As
the term indicates, these are spires of water
directed upward by some sort of underwater
deflection of a wild, powerful current. Fountains tend to pulse on and off, and they often
have "sucks" near their perimeter. These
sucks are small, strong whirlpools that form
in response to the vacuum created when all
that water shoots skyward. Like fountains,
sucks pulse on and off too, so should your
boat be caught, hang with it and you'll eventually be released. You'll also probably have
been made a Christian: getting caught in one
gives you religion fast.

Three Dimensional Eddies Three-dimensional eddies are the type of hydraulic that

occurs downstream of an underwater
obstruction. When a boulder pokes its head
above water, the resulting hydraulic has only
two dimensions.

As water flows around each side of the
obstruction, the speed and power of the current super-elevates the water along the mainstream of descent to a point where it is significantly higher than the level of the water
directly behind the boulder. This creates a
hole, and water pushes upriver immediately
behind the boulder to fill it in.

The river flows in two distinct directions:
slowly upriver in the eddy and swiftly downstream in the main current. The dividing line
between these two flows is known as the eddy
line or eddy fence. It is not a knife-edged
divider, but rather a line of mini-whirlpools
spun off the upriver current by the power of
the downstream volume. The swirls revolve
on a vertical axis, out from the reflex current
to meet the major force.

Depending on their magnitude, two-
dimensional eddies can be a bane or a bless-
ing. House-sized boulders with the power of
the full river rushing around them create terrific super-elevation that's difficult to drop
down from. And the combined speed of the
two conflicting currents can be so great that
you can't row or paddle fast enough to cross
the eddy fence without being spun around like
a pinwheel. If the eddy occurs where the current isn't of bulldozer proportions, it can
make for a pleasant resting spot to gather
your strength and wits as the river rushes by.

Bank Eddies Two-dimensional eddies
occur in midstream, and throw up two fences,
one on each side, with water entering the
depression more or less equally from both
sides, with the greatest volume of flow going
up the middle of the backwater. Bank eddies
occur in response to some sort of projection
jutting out from the bank. They develop a
circular flow, clockwise on the right bank,
counterclockwise on the left.

The ultimate bank eddy, with very strong
circular motion, becomes a whirlpool.

Centrifugal force super-elevates the outer

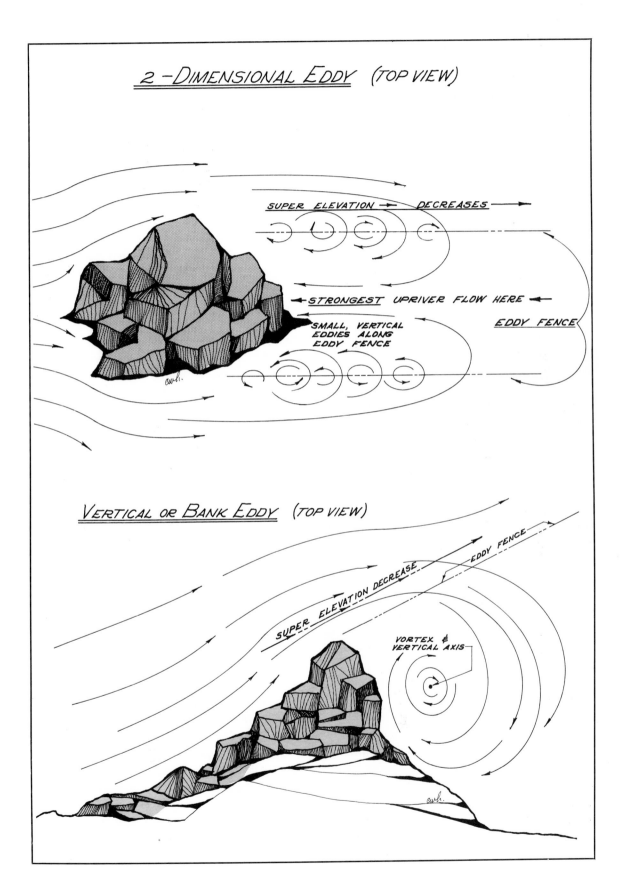

2 - DIMENSIONAL EDDY (TOP VIEW)

SUPER ELEVATION → DECREASES →

← STRONGEST UPRIVER FLOW HERE ←

EDDY FENCE

SMALL, VERTICAL EDDIES ALONG EDDY FENCE

VERTICAL OR BANK EDDY (TOP VIEW)

SUPER ELEVATION DECREASE

EDDY FENCE

VORTEX & VERTICAL AXIS

reaches of the whirling water and a vortex develops like the drain in a bathtub. Don't spend too many sleepless nights worrying about whirlpools, though; they're very rare save on huge rivers.

Rollers Rollers are another difficulty encountered when you run a fast river. They are large, cresting waves, and they're caused by a variety of situations.

The wave below a breaking hole is one type of roller.

Velocity waves occur on straight stretches of a fast-dropping river, and are caused by the drag of shoal banks. They can be large, but they're usually regular, and avoidable.

Tail Waves Tail waves are large, regular waves that develop when fast-moving water hits the flat bottom of a slow-moving pool. Planes of accelerated flow bounce off the bottom almost like ricocheting bullets. When the "ricochet" hits the surface, gravity pulls it down. The effect is a series of cresting waves that decrease in severity as you enter the calmer water of the pool.

Bank Rollers Bank rollers take the same crested, licking form as tail waves, but their cause is different. They occur when the riverbed turns so sharply that the water can't make the bend. It slams into the outside bank and super-elevates to a point where the water falls back on itself. Large bank rollers, five feet high and up, can turn even a balloony, clinging raft on its back like a turtle.

Three terms define the height or severity of rollers. A "washboard" is a series of swells that undulate gently: a safe roller-coaster ride. "Standing water" indicates rollers are cresting; here flow velocities and bottom contours are such that the tops of the swells begin to fall back on themselves. "Haystacks" or "roosters" are the real Frankensteins. They look like haystacks, with water coming down from every direction; giant bulges of froth that seem to seethe with anger. They can be insurmountable: the pull of gravity can overcome the drift of the river, and your boat will backslide rather than climb the wave. A frightening treadmill. If you get over the top, the push on

your stern could become so great that you'll broach—turn sideways to the current. Both mistakes could trap you in a deep trough as securely as in a suckhole, or bury you under tons of water, or both.

The troughs between rollers deserve some forethought too. I've occasionally found them hiding sharp rocks at shallow levels which resulted in bad bumps and ripped raft bottoms. I've noted this situation most in the case of velocity waves.

Chutes Chute (or "tongue") is a term that refers to a swift, often narrow passage between river obstructions. For example, the damming effect of two large boulders would create a chute between them. Because of the amount of water tumbling down a chute, it usually provides the most logical route to take. But chutes are no guarantee of smooth sailing. Their nature accelerates the flow of water, and that power has probably done some work below. The end of a chute usually holds a suckhole, a bank roller or, at best, a set of heavy tail waves. Unpleasant surprises aren't necessarily part of running a river. If there's one point I feel licensed to belabor, it's this: *scout ahead.*

Logjams Logjams and drift piles—logs, brush and other debris of high water lodged along or across the current—constitute one of the greatest dangers on a river. They are deathtraps in that they are stationary, while the river flows through them.

If your craft should be swept up against a log, it will be pinned in place by the force of the current versus the resistance of the jam. Should you tip a gunwale, your craft will be swept under. The same consequences are likely if *you* go overboard. You can be carried under even with a preserver on, and there's a good chance a twig or branch or sharp stub will snag your clothing and hold you there. You will drown.

Give any knot of debris on the river a more than wide berth.

Just any old river rock, in the middle of a swift current, deserves similar respect. Perhaps even more respect than a logjam, a suckhole or a ten-foot haystack, because they seem so innocuous. But realizing the power of moving water, imagine hitting that rock dead amidships, and in an attitude at right angles to the current. Everyone's first reaction is to lean away from the collision. Weight shifts in your boat, and the upstream gunwale tips under. The craft is now pinned against the rock by the force of the water, and I do mean pinned. I have seen fiberglass canoes snapped in half this way. And aluminum canoes pulled apart by a block and tackle in an attempt to get them off. And a fully inflated raft, with the bottom split end to end to reduce the pressure, left with a note tacked onshore stating that the owner planned to return when fall and extreme low water rolled around. The same river can be a coy mistress, a cruel deceiver and a mean master, depending on how you treat it. Maintain an awareness of its potential and an abiding respect for its power whenever you're riding its bucking back.

Judging a Safe Passage

When assessing any whitewater passage, there are several yardsticks to measure difficulty. The steeper the gradient of the riverbed, the more violent will be the water. Velocity is created by the pull of gravity; the greater that pull, the greater speed the water will develop in turn, creating turbulence. When the drop is steep enough, the river will become impassable.

Always pay attention to signs that might indicate a fast drop ahead. Learn what the tops of trees and bushes look like as opposed to lower branches. As you're moving along, you might be looking at a young fir tree downstream, or the tip of a mature tree. If it's a mature tree, there's a big drop ahead.

Distrust placid pools. They are usually created by some sort of plug ahead. Pay attention too to very narrow canyons and passages looming up, as these usually mean accelerating water. Always look before you leap. Pick out the best passage through whitewater from the cool reason of the shore, not when

you suddenly find yourself confronted with a nightmare of rapids.

Tree roots tell a tale too. If you can see them along the bank, where water has eroded into the shore, you're probably dealing with the low-water stage of the river. On the other hand, if the roots are submerged, the river is bank-full and at high water. Turbidity is another giveaway. If the river is carrying sediment and debris and looks brown and dirty, you're dealing with some sort of river rise, and an attendant increase in the power and potential of the water.

You also must learn to read water, to interpret what's happening on the surface as a signal of what lies ahead.

Reading these signals on the river and along the bank isn't particularly difficult to learn, but it does require a conscious shift from human inclination.

We are possessed of binocular vision, with close-set eyes fixed deep in our head. This is the eyesight of the predator—the fox, the eagle and the lion—as opposed to prey species like rabbits, deer and cattle. These latter animals have eyes set on the sides of their heads, and those eyes protrude slightly, affording them a tremendous periphery of vision. They very nearly can "see out of the back of their heads," and probably view the world with a totality beyond human conception.

To read water, however, you've got to train yourself to look at the river in total, as a deer or duck might. A good way to initiate this ability is to look at things at night. When it's very dark, the only way to perceive dimly lit objects is to direct your vision slightly away from their precise location. The object will then appear rather clearly, not at a point of focus but at its edge. If you try to look directly at the thing it will disappear, or blink in and out of view. To identify it, you must learn to study its features without looking at it directly. This isn't difficult to do, but it does require practice.

This too is the way to read water. You focus on the point you deem best for passage, but at the same time you must be aware of minute subtleties on the periphery of the picture you see. The speed of bubbles and scud and their direction constitute one important indicator. Drifting down on a sleeper, a perceptive eye would notice very few bubbles passing over the rock. They'd tend to stack up on the upstream side, then cleave left or right in response to the greater volume of water that's skirting the obstruction, rather than going over it.

When the floating is easy, these same bubbles will indicate deep channels and tell you where the river is going so you can avoid grounding out on a bar. Open your eyes and look at the *whole* river and you'll see definite lateral motion, a sorting out of scud in response to water volume. The place where the most scud is being directed is the most powerful part of the river.

Current swirls, boils, eddy fences and the conformation of the bank of the river will also tell stories of what lies ahead.

In the process of cleaving, water will stack up in front of a rock in a slight bulge. There will be a noticeable slowdown of the current there, and probably a warning in the form of a small hydraulic, the result of upstream discontinuity.

Watch too for the splashing tops of big rollers. On a big, long pool, they might appear to be just a dancing ripple way down at the end. But given sufficient drop—and the likelihood of it in that location—you might be watching the tip of the iceberg—a thrashing giant hidden by the gradient of the river.

There is also a direct mathematical relationship between volume and gradient that can give you clues to the severity of whitewater it can churn up. A drop of 40 feet per mile will churn up extremely heavy water on a river carrying 15,000 cubic feet of water per second. On a stream of 4,000 cubic feet of water per second, it takes a drop of 100 feet to the mile to create similar conditions.

To look at this another, slightly less complicated way, if you measured a riffly little brook with all its little suckholes, haystacks and eddies, you'd find its drop quite steep.

But because the brook isn't carrying much volume, the turbulence is confined to small stuff.

Now enlarge that brook, maintaining the same gradient, as if it were blown up in a cosmic photo enlarger. Standing water grows to house-size dimensions, and suckholes drop off into cavernous pits. This is exactly what happens when large-volume rivers fall at a steep gradient.

Following that analogy, one of the best lessons in learning to judge and interpret the river is provided not by a man-sized boat but by a raft made of popsicle sticks.

One day last summer I hiked high into the mountains behind my cabin on a warm, dry day, and as I descended to the valley floor, I crossed a small irrigation ditch carved into the hillside by some settler ages ago. Water is still pure enough to drink in most mountainous sections of Montana, so I squatted on my haunches and scooped several handfuls of clear, icy water into my mouth. Standing then, enjoying the sweetness of the water and the sensuous pleasure of a thirst being slaked, I happened to glance down into the water, and found myself in an airplane.

Two years previously, I floated the Middle Fork of the Salmon. The time was August, and the river was unusually low—so low that a typical launch at Dagger Falls would have involved a great deal of scraping and grinding on bars and through narrow passages before we hit the deeper water downstream.

We had a large party and heavy rafts, so we elected to fly into Indian Creek, a tiny landing strip where we felt the water would be better. We took off early in the morning with a full load.

The plane took forever to get off the ground; the air around Stanley is thin and unusual speed is needed before you get your lift. Then we were aloft, climbing high over glittering alpine lakes to meet with the thermals—rising gusts of air that buffeted the single-engine Piper at each ridgetop.

Suddenly the mountains fell away and we were over the canyon of the Middle Fork, a deep gash carved in unyielding granite. Far below was the thin pencil line of a primitive airport; getting down to it required a combination of tight circles and fluttering like paper; the canyon walls were that close. As the pilot laid the plane on its side, I was momentarily disoriented, looking out the starboard window at what should be sky, but was canyon; centrifugal force balanced out gravity. For a second, I had the sensation of flight.

And below me wound the Middle Fork; point bars and chutes, meanders and pools were framed by the window. It seemed close enough to touch; a tiny model of that mighty river. And there it was again in that little irrigation ditch; all rivers, with riffles and bars, and thalwegs on the outside bend of each turn. You find in running water Blake's "eternity in a grain of sand."

Launch a stick or a small model boat in any brook, and watch what it does. Learn to anticipate and read the direction of the water to a point where you can accurately predict the boat will end up *there*. Note too the surges as water passes over small rocks, and the suckholes and eddies behind larger rocks, and what they do to floating objects. Perceive the pattern of water flow that results in meanders, and the oil-slick whirling that indicates deep pools.

Another pastime that will teach you a great deal about water and rivers is fishing. A good fisherman knows how to find quiet water, for that is where the trout will lie. And quiet water is not always obvious; some of the best fishing will be under rather swift-appearing currents, quiet places created by the reflex effect.

Realize too that we've examined a river's flow characteristics and resulting turbulence with plenty of time for reflection and careful analysis. In practice, these things usually occur with machine-gun rapidity, and in a nonsequential tangle of happenings. When you take that step beyond the popsicle stick, it's a big one indeed, so even though you think you know how rivers work, tackle a tame one first, something that's a safe testing ground for your theories.

Float smooth water several times before engaging any turbulence, and as you drift along, think about what you're seeing and how that view might change with the addition of a few extra knots of current. Learn to identify point bars, and navigate the bend below

Moving water, from the tiniest trickle to the mightiest river, has much in common. Note the point bar, the riffles, the deep channel on the outside of the bend. Rill or river? It's the Middle Fork of Idaho's Salmon from 2,000 feet. *Photo by N. Strung*

as if it were a bank roller. Slip into and out of an eddy, taking care to make a smooth transition, and try avoiding imaginary obstacles in the river. Above all, get to know your oars or paddles, and how they work, as if they were your own hands.

When you're sure you're competent enough to handle more difficult passages, work up the grade of whitewater difficulty slowly.

WHITEWATER RATING*

Nearly every whitewater river in this country is mapped, and the rapids on many of them are rated. In this system a number is assigned to indicate difficulty of passage—the higher the number, the tougher the water.

There are two systems of rating rapids. The first, created by Les Jones of Bountiful, Utah, is used mainly by raftsmen. It is a one-to-ten scale. Ten is defined as the "limit of runnability": a rapid will capsize one of every two boats which try it. And by boats Jones means the craft which are best suited to that stage of water and that river, be they pontoon, kayak or inner tube. Anything above a ten receives a "U," for unrunnable.

Jones's system has found wide currency, mostly because of his accurate and most curious river maps (one of them has a poem running along it and another has the not uncharacteristic notation: "8-19-57 Les Jones saw crow here."). They are among the few profile maps now available (they show the gradient of the river as a slanting line and are thus of inestimable use on an unknown river) and make use of this rating system. But it has found no favor with kayakers, who have their own international system. It uses Roman numerals from I to VI; presumably you can get away with plain numbers 1 to 6 but it is less classy. One can make a rough conversion between the two by equating Jones's "U" rating with VI on the kayak scale, and then

assigning two of Jones's numbers to each number on the kayak scale. But the Jones system has few definitions and an excess of numbers, while the kayaking system is rather strictly defined.

I. Very easy. Little gradient, wide and unobstructed channels, riffles and tiny, avoidable waves.

II. Easy water. Low ledges and rapids of moderate difficulty with wide passages. Regular (not breaking violently) waves to about two feet in height.

III. Water of medium difficulty. Lots of waves, irregular and reaching perhaps three feet. Clear but small channels, beset by rocks and diversified eddies. Scouting is advised, especially on the first run, though experts can probably sight-read their way through.

IV. Expert water. The rapids are long with violent and irregular waves to five feet. There are dangerous rocks and suckholes, with a difficult but mandatory reconnaissance for the first run. Lots of turns and drops in the river. This is serious water.

V. Almost continuous violent rapids spattered with dangerous rocks and more dangerous holes, waves over five feet and irregular, with high flow and large gradient. Reconnaissance is mandatory but dangerous. This, even to experts, is frightening water.

VI. Here we have a difference of opinion. It is said that Europeans accord this rating only to rapids which have not been successfully run, and many of the most extraordinary and sensible kayakers I have met concur. At the other extreme are blithe neophytes who have been boating all of three months and have already run dozens of Class VI rapids. The official definition is that this is water of Class V carried to the outer limits of navigability, passable only by a team of experts at favorable water levels, using every possible safety precaution. A Class VI rapid is a nightmare; hallucinatory water. There is danger, not just of losing a few boats, but of dying.

There are difficulties with the rating scale; it hasn't much relationship to big rivers—say, rivers whose average flow is over 8,000 to

*Here, Earl's obvious mathematical genius holds sway. Frankly, I've always been confused by numbers.

18

10,000 second-feet (cubic feet per second). How do you deal with the Grand Canyon running at about 20,000 second-feet? There are no bends to speak of; there is no maneuvering worth the name for kayakers, who are accustomed to threading the needle; there are violent eddies and whirlpools but highways lead past them; there are a few holes big enough to roll pontoons but you have to fight to reach them. So many commercial parties are on the river that you need only wait half a day to have a radio out for a chopper if you have trouble. There is really nothing to it except the immense size of everything. What to rate it? I don't know. I suppose there should be a scale which rates big water separately. Grand Canyon requires a beginner's ability to maneuver, but only very stable intermediates and experts come through the rapids upright. I wouldn't be happy entering the canyon without a team of experts, yet water which requires a team of experts is far more complicated according to the ratings.

Or to shift the question up yet another notch, 1974 in Idaho was a preternatural water year. The lower section of Hell's Canyon reached about 180,000 second-feet; the Main Salmon crested at about 138,000; the Middle Fork must have reached close to 50,-000. This meant vertical rises of 20 to 40 feet. Those who ran these rivers near the crest stages all agreed on a few things: it was technically easy; there was little left to avoid except driftwood. What was left was so big it ate up (on the Main Salmon) not just pontoon rafts, but 42-by-20-foot motor rigs. Eddy fences were terrifying. And the final thing they all agreed upon was fear; few of them could recall being in more immediate danger of dying, not just in a rapid, but for days on end. It may have been technically easy, but it was not easy water, it was deadly water. And in fact some folks did drown, although they were with professional outfits. How to rate it? I don't know. Only a team of experts should try it, yet it does not seem to have been what is normally called Class V water.

It should be pointed out that a river rating,

whether Class I or V, holds only for the stage run. Most of those who give you ratings will indicate an approximate stage for the rating, and will try to give you an idea of how the river will change as the water rises and falls. With abnormally low water a pleasant Class III may turn into an unpleasant day's hike. With abnormally high water it may turn into a furious Class V. But this works both ways: Salmon Falls, a sedate Class III at the normal low flows (8,000 second-feet or less) that kayaks run on, vanishes entirely, leaving not a wave behind, above about 30,000. Horn Creek Rapid in Grand Canyon, a terror below 8,000 second-feet, is said to have vanished utterly on 92,000. So you cannot be sure; the only probability is that abrupt and isolated rapids are more likely to disappear than are bad drops with rapids above and below them. Count a rating good only for the stage offered you.

The question must arise, how do you know how much water there is? The USGS Stream Flow Division maintains gauging stations across the United States; call and ask. Now, since their figures assume a stable and recently surveyed bed profile, and riverbeds are almost never stable, their figure will not be perfect. But it is the standard of reference and will be far more accurate than even the seasoned eye of an old boatman. If there is a dam nearby, the operators will know how much water they are conceding you. It is most important that a floater develop an eye for second-feet; he will need it to put a leash on his wild stories, and more, others will come to depend on him. The only way to do this is to guess hundreds of times on all sizes of rivers, and check each guess with a gauge. Without this self-checking there can be trouble.

On some rivers it may be necessary to establish a folklore type of gauge. Marker Rock on the Middle Fork comes to mind; it is a roughly pyramidal gray rock forty or fifty yards downstream from the boat ramp some ten to thirty feet out from shore, depending on the stage. Water two and a half feet below the top is low or very low; water six inches or more over the top begins to be scary. More than a foot over the top and the professionals don't run. If there is no gauge for your runs, you will have to create them, and get firmly in mind what a run at each gradation means. For in the flat water above a canyon, a rise of only a foot can mean a rise of two or even three down in the rapids, enough to make a mild run impassable.

Let me offer a few guidelines about rapids rating and flow. I am assuming (it must be stressed) an evenly distributed gradient with no segments of flat water running for days through soft rocks, and the appearance of abrupt outcroppings of hard rocks which push the average up. A *steady* drop of 10 feet per mile should produce water classed as expert with flows over 35,000 to 40,000 second-feet. Grand Canyon averages 9.7 and the Main Salmon 11. A drop of 20 feet per mile (Split Mountain Canyon on the Green) produces Class IV at stages of perhaps 12,000 to 15,000. A drop of 30 feet per mile (the Middle Fork of the Salmon averages, depending upon your authority, 27 or 35) produces expert water above 7,000 or 8,000 second-feet. Forty feet per mile produces expert water above perhaps 4,000. Expert water is produced by a gradient of 50 feet per mile on flows above about 2,000 second-feet. Anyone contemplating running a gradient over 60 feet per mile at any stage is an expert and needs no guidance of mine.

The Arighis' book *Wildwater Touring* contains a table, on page 10, which summarizes these matters in more detail. A close comparison will reveal that they require much lower flows or gradients than I do for a given rating. Their ratings, I think, are well adapted to beginning boaters; I hope more advanced ones will see merit in my suggestions, which tally with considerable experience. I should also point out again that I have projected my ratings on the basis of relatively even gradient. The Middle Fork, for instance, should be an expert river only at quite high flows. But that average drop of 27 or 35 feet per mile conceals the extremely steep declivity of the first eight miles and the last twenty by blending them with about three days of relatively easy flat water in the

middle. So it is a river which requires expert skills for two days and wastes them for the middle three. The gentle drop of Grand Canyon (9.7 feet per mile) has lurking within the number whole long, flat, restful days in the soft Bright Angel Shale and Redwall Limestone, as well as the constant roaring drops of the fluted and obdurate Vishnu Schist. Cataract Canyon's 16 feet per mile hide Big Drop, where the declivity runs over 40 feet per mile and the water, especially at stages over 35,000 second-feet, grows very heavy, heavy enough, if the tale be true, to have exploded and sunk a pontoon with sponsons.

So contour maps are extremely important. More important still is a guide who knows, on the river you choose, what that cluster of contour lines crossing the river at a given point will mean when you get there.

RATING VARIABLES
The Season

There are yet other variables to consider when dealing with whitewater. Heavy rains, spring runoff and August drought all have an effect on a river's difficulty and condition.

It is not necessarily true that low water automatically makes for the safest, easiest passage. Very often, low water creates suckholes where there was once a surge, and dribbling falls where there was an easy chute in the spring. Conversely, high water can turn a low-water fun-run obstacle course of boulders into a nightmare of haystacks and suckholes. Because of volume, high water is always when the river is at its most powerful—and potentially dangerous.

For the most part, ephemeral (running only after a rain) and intermittent (running only part of the year) streams and rivers are of marginal interest to the river rat. They're too undependable about enough water to float on. Perennial rivers, those with running water all year long, may be floatable only at certain times.

Rivers carry their most water under two conditions: spring runoff and a rain rise.

Spring runoff occurs everywhere, but it is most pronounced in mountainous areas that hold a lot of snowpack. The rise in water is the result of the stored moisture of an entire winter melting and running downslope in a period of a few weeks.

The increase in stream flow at this time can be quite spectacular; northern rivers will carry ten times or more of their normal load, and desert perennials like the Colorado will carry up to two hundred times their summer volume (estimated flow at Lee's Ferry during one spring rise: from 950 cubic feet of water per second to *300,000* cubic feet of water per second!). Consequently, some streams that are virtually unfloatable at other times of the year flow bank-full and wild during runoff.

It's a wise rule of thumb that high water is a bad time to take on rivers that can be floated the year round; they're too violent, and the water is icy cold. There is a danger in that cold water that transcends mere discomfort, a condition known as hypothermia.

Hypothermia

A downward spiral of heat loss from the body's central core results in *hypothermia*. In earlier times, this situation was loosely defined as "exposure," but more is known about the process today; hence the more definitive term.

Simply stated, exterior conditions take more heat away from your body than it can produce, and your temperature drops. In extreme cases, you can't reverse that spiral, and your temperature continues to drop until unconsciousness and finally death ensue.

Cold air temperatures, wind, and dampness, along with body fatigue, go into producing this phenomenon. It's further aided by lack of energy. In nearly every case of hypothermia, a meal or two was skipped immediately before its occurrence. You can cut your chances of an encounter with hypothermia by eating well and regularly, but all the other contributing factors are there if you tackle high water during spring runoff.*

Swamping is the greatest danger because immersion in icy water—35° F—can cause death in as little as fifteen minutes. But for a boater who's tired and damp, running in air temperatures of 40 to 50 degrees can be dangerous.

The first sign of danger is uncontrollable shivering—your body's attempt to produce more heat. This is followed by poor coordination and faulty judgment. Further heat loss produces muscle stiffening, irrational behavior and, finally, unconsciousness.

At the first appearance of any of these signs, the victim should be sheltered from the wind and put into dry clothes. Provide outside heat from a fire and wrap him in blankets or a sleeping bag that's well insulated from the ground. In the worst cases, since his own body can't generate heat, someone should strip and climb in with him. The opposite sex will warm a person fastest, but whatever the source, heat must be supplied immediately.

If the victim is conscious, give him hot drinks and candy, but not alcohol. An unconscious victim should be sandwiched between two companions and his body massaged until he becomes conscious enough to down hot food. The important thing to remember is that warmth must be provided from some *outside* source until the spiral is reversed.

Whenever hypothermia is a possible consequence of floating, take special precautions to avoid its occurrence. The use of a wet suit is a good start; at least wear wool (wool is the one fabric that will remain warm when wet). In addition, bring along dry clothes, a sleeping bag and hot drinks. Everyone in your group should know the danger signs and be able to treat a victim.

The safest precaution, however, is to stay off the river until water and weather warm up.

Rain Rises

Rain rises are common in the Southwest. A hard rain will raise river levels in the mountains, but because of entrapping vegetation and root work, the water flows downslope slowly, gradually feeding the river. In desert or semi-arid country, the hardpan soil absorbs

---

*Sam Curtis, survival expert, contributed his knowledge to this discussion of hypothermia.

water slowly and there are few grasses to hold the water back. There, the results of a rain enter watercourses in a rush.

A rain rise in dry country is always a spectacular thing to watch, with the river growing before your eyes. It changes color too, often becoming so loaded with sediment that ripples and swirls become a pastiche of reds and browns, resembling a solid more than a fluid.

As is sometimes the case with spring runoff, a rain rise may be the only time a river can be run, but the wisdom in doing so is debatable. High water of any kind not only means a river is at its most powerful, it is also a time when the water will push along the most debris, rolling rocks that range in size from cobbles to boulders, and sweeping branches, logs and whole trees along with it. Worse yet, these potential battering rams are often camouflaged from view by the roily water.

LAWS AND THE FLOATER

Many states where floating is popular have passed rather intricate laws and regulations governing what floaters may or may not do. Generally, these laws are in direct proportion to the notoriety of a river and the number of people who run it.

The following is a listing of requirements currently enforced in one state or another. It is by no means definitive for all rivers, but it should give you an idea of what might be expected of you. Check with local authorities for specific regulations.

Equipment A floater must have, and may have to wear, a life jacket. It may have to be of a certain type, and Coast Guard-approved. He or the party may have to carry: signal mirrors, maps, signal panels, a radio, first-aid kit, bailing devices, spare paddles, patch kits, stoves, ax, shovel and bucket, and a guide.

He may have to demonstrate competence to get a permit which assigns him dates and camps; every regulation on it is to be followed. He may not be permitted to run because of incompetence, inadequate equipment, direct order of an officer, fire or flood.

He may not have to get a permit but may still have to register with a federal or state government agency, giving his plans.

He cannot litter or discharge untreated sewage without a permit into or within fifty feet of the waters of any stream. He cannot run his boat under the influence of alcohol or any narcotic drug, and he may not be able to run his boat in a heedless or reckless manner, endangering himself or others.

Licensing and Registration He may, if he gets any sort of pay for a trip or all expenses are not equally paid, have to have a professional boatman's or guide's license, issued by a state or the Coast Guard, good only for certain waters, upon the taking of a test and the payment of a fee ranging from $3 to $150. This license he must show upon request, always to officers and sometimes to passengers. His boat may have to be licensed and registered and a fee paid for the registration. He may have to paint his registration number in a certain position on the bow in letters of a certain size and color. He may be required to carry $100,000 worth of liability insurance on his boat.

THE ULTIMATE RULE

Reading and understanding a river is complex business, but all the whitewater savvy and wisdom of the preceding pages can be summed up in one easy-to-remember homily:

Never Float Alone . . . Never Float Unknown.

Always plan your floats to include at least one other boat, and make it your business to know just what is coming up downstream. The "unknown" also has to do with your ability. If a stretch of water appears to be beyond your knowledge of boat handling, go around it, not through it.

You can never "beat" a river, you can never "tame" it. You can only get good at working with it. And acknowledging its moods, some gentle, some incredibly violent, is one of the many condescensions required for safe whitewater navigation.

2RAFTING
by Norman Strung

Rafts conform to the contours of whitewater, making them virtually untippable. (Main Salmon River, Idaho.) *Photo by Earl Perry*

Stability, capacity, company and a relative margin of safety are the qualities that make a rubber raft my ideal for floating.

The flexible nature of all that inflated rubber finds a raft clinging and conforming to the contours of whitewater like a soaked sheet of newspaper. Rafts are nearly untippable, and that kind of stability, aside from the obvious safety factor, lends itself to another reason I float, almost as important as the thrill. "Wild" water usually means wilderness as well, and the fishing is tops because of its inaccessibility. Rafts make for a better fishing platform than either kayaks or canoes.

Camping goes hand in glove with floating and fishing, and in this department, rafts come out on top too. The lift of those big air-filled tubes can support tremendous weight (the standard six-man import is rated at a capacity of 1,200 pounds), yet they still maintain the buoyancy needed to climb up and over angry crests. This means that you can comfortably carry enough camping gear for several days on the river, as well as passengers. If you ever want to sample whitewater adventure at its finest, try a three- or four-day fish-and-float through a true wilderness.

Another source of pleasure you'll find in a raft's capacity comes by way of your passengers. In a raft, only one man, the oarsman, needs to worry about navigation. Everyone else can sit back and enjoy the ride.

In short, rafts are good-time craft on the river, like red balloons and blimps on puffy-clouded summer days, but I don't mean to imply you can turn yours loose and let the air, the rubber and the river do the rest. Rafts and rafting have their peculiar requirements, quite different from either kayaks or canoes. To sum them up in one word, I'd call rafting a matter of cooperation with the river, while canoeing and kayaking are more aggressive.

The river determines raft size; your craft must be large enough for a safe float, yet small enough to squeeze through the river's narrowest chutes, with room for oarwork. The need for portage should also be a consideration when choosing size. (Selway River, Idaho.) *Photo by Roy Cromer*

CHOOSING A RAFT

The size of the raft you choose is but one small example of how the rafter must learn to work with the forces of moving water.

Your raft's dimensions should be more or less directly proportional to the amount of water a river carries. For example, 25- to 40-footers are favored on big water like the Colorado. The most-used raft size on the Middle Fork of the Salmon falls between 16 and 20 feet. On smaller rivers, like Montana's Beartraps of the Madison, or the Middle Fork of the Flathead, rafts from 11 to 15 feet are preferred.

Rafts need to be sized to the river for several reasons. Most important is the matter of passage. Invariably, when you have a river that wears whitewater, there will be one or several runs that churn through a narrow

chute. The chute might be a deep-cut cleft in rock, or a tight squeeze between two boulders, but not only must your boat be narrow enough to squeeze through, it must be narrow enough to give you room for oarwork on the way. On both the Flathead and the Beartraps, there are several tight squeezes that would pinch an 18-footer too close. Ditto on the Middle Fork of the Salmon if you tried to take a raft much larger than 20 feet.

There's also the matter of weight and bulk. Smaller rivers are the ones where you're most likely to encounter impassable conditions: big falls, unnavigable curves and logjams that span the entire current. A small raft means easy portaging around the jackpot. Larger rafts (a Hypalon 18-footer weighs in the neighborhood of 325 pounds) can be unmanageable.

Maneuverability is another determining

factor in the dimensions of the raft you choose for running a particular river. Steep-gradient small water usually comes attached to a steeplechase of boulders, sleepers and small falls (commonly called a rock garden). You need light weight and snap to your oars if you're going to thread those needles. On the other side of the coin, big rivers conjure up immense rapids, but they lie far apart, with long stretches of placid pools between. This gives the man at the oars or outboard plenty of time to move a big blob of inflated rubber into precise positioning for the safest run down through the stacks. Another yardstick to consider—with narrow passages and maneuverability part of the equation—is to choose a craft roughly three times as long as the crest- to-trough height of a river's worst curls. If that elusive average is four feet, a 12-foot raft should be ample. If it's six feet, choose an 18-footer. Ten-foot curls indicate a 30-foot behemoth, and so on.

It might be worth going back to the parallels between a tiny babbling brook and a mighty froth of river. In many ways, suiting a raft to a river is merely an exercise in proportions.

A particularly misleading rating you might run into when assessing the size of a raft is its people capacity.

Inflatable craft were originally developed as survival craft for pilots downed at sea. Under the true survival conditions, with sharks finning nearby, you'd be amazed at how many airmen can cram themselves into a 12-footer. But you'll be taking a dangerous chance if you try to do the same and float anything over Class II water.

When sizing up a raft, take the people capacity and divide by two. A five-man raft fits two adults and a little gear, a six-man raft is roomy enough for three adults or two with plenty of camping equipment and a twelve-man raft will comfortably hold six people, or four adults and camping gear.

Weight capacity is another misleading number when you're dealing with whitewater. A 12-footer loaded with the maximum 1,200

pounds is safe enough on a millpond, but it handles like a bathtub with that kind of load in rough water. Maneuverability is severely limited, and the craft will be too heavy to rise out of deep troughs. Cut the posted weight at least by a third, taking everything—gear, platform, passengers—into account. If you'll encounter water of Class III or above, cut that maximum weight in half.

Design Types

There's been a proliferation of rafts in the past ten years, partly because of the popularity of floating and partly because boat owners have come to realize a stowable raft makes a good dinghy or tender on a small motorboat. But just because a boat classifies as an "inflatable" does not necessarily mean it's suited to whitewater work.

Toys are on one end of the scale. Inflatable boats are currently being made for kids, ponds and wading pools. They're fine in that milieu, but foolish on any water this side of a sluggish stream. They're rather easy to identify by size and construction. None of these craft are being produced larger than the six-man class, and they're made of unbacked plastic/vinyl, stuff just a little stouter than the average clear plastic garbage bag. Never float in any raft made of unbacked material; they tear like tissue paper at the slightest provocation.

"Outboard inflatables" are at the other end of the scale. They're expensive, with some of the better ones being priced above $1,000. They make excellent dinghies because they possess a surprising degree of rigidity. This is usually accomplished through the use of plywood floorboard inserts that have the effect of firming up the raft to a point where heavy outboards can be attached and the boat will plane. This sort of rigidity is undesirable in a river raft because the craft then loses it's caterpillar-like ability to cling and conform to curling water. When a raft is firmed up to this point, it can capsize easily.

Inflatables that fit between these two extremes deserve consideration as river boats, with several design and construction features taken into account.

Rafts are frequently dubbed "rubber," and there might be a few products still being turned out that are indeed rubber. But it is a less than desirable material because sunlight initiates a reaction whereby the rubber is destroyed and made porous by ozone. Rubber rafts seldom last a season.

The backing or bonding material used in the construction of the craft needs identification too. Whatever compound is used to make a tube airtight, it needs extra reinforcement to keep it from popping like a balloon. In years past, the material bonded to the "rubber" was usually some form of cotton drill. This natural fiber disintegrates when exposed to moisture and fungi, so it was possible—and common—to pump up a sound-looking raft that came apart when put under the stress of a hard pull on the oars or a minor skirmish with a rock.

Synthetics are the best materials for rafts today, and those that have proven themselves able under pressure include neoprene-impregnated nylon and nylon bonded between two layers of Hypalon, a neoprene-like substance manufactured by Du Pont.

Aside from construction materials, there's also a weight problem to consider. The heavier the weight of the raft material, the stronger and more durable the raft will be; there's just more neoprene and nylon holding it together. But there are sensible limits. A 15-foot raft, safely loaded, won't carry the same cargo weight, and consequently possess the same kinetic energy, as a 30-foot raft fully loaded. When the larger raft inadvertently collides with a rock, there might be several tons to stop, versus perhaps a thousand pounds in the 15-footer. Strength equivalent to that engineered into the big raft just isn't needed in the smaller one, so lighter material can be used when constructing these smaller rafts. By way of a yardstick, I'd say no raft designed for whitewater work should be made of anything lighter than 24-ounce nylon/neoprene, and no raft need be stouter than 48-ounce

material, with the possible exception of floors.

I do feel it prudent to have a floor of heavier material than is built into the tubes. It's the floor that takes the real beating, as much from the abrasion of sand and pebbles on your feet as scrapes with sleepers. I've had so many problems with ripped floors that whenever I buy a raft with one I deem too thin, I add an extra in the form of additional neoprene/nylon, or the cut-free floor from the craft's predecessor, if it is still in good condition.

The number of flotation chambers a raft has is a sign of quality and a measure of safety. Most imports have only two separate air-filled tubes, port and starboard, which both serve as gunwales and provide buoyancy. Puncture one, and you've lost half your raft and all means of control. Puncture both, and the boat sinks.

A far better arrangement is compartmented flotation chambers, at least four air tubes independent of each other. If one gets popped on a snag, you still maintain some degree of buoyancy and overall firmness, which in turn will give you enough control to get the crippled craft to shore for repairs.

The overall shapes and contours a good whitewater raft can take are many, and the desirability of individual features—or the lack of same—is impossible to nail down since they're all children of boatmen's opinions.

Like them, *this* boatman has some opinions of his own, so it's best to list the most popular options you can buy in a raft, and add my own personal observation where applicable.

Tube Dimensions (the diameter of the air-filled tube that's keeping you afloat, at its smallest part). If you're tackling water over Class III, use nothing smaller than 17 inches; Class I to Class III water, nothing smaller than 12 inches.

Bow Type Bows and sterns perform much the same function in a raft: slapping water down and rising above huge curls. If you can buy the same features fore and aft, this is wise. Bow types include a pointed bow, a

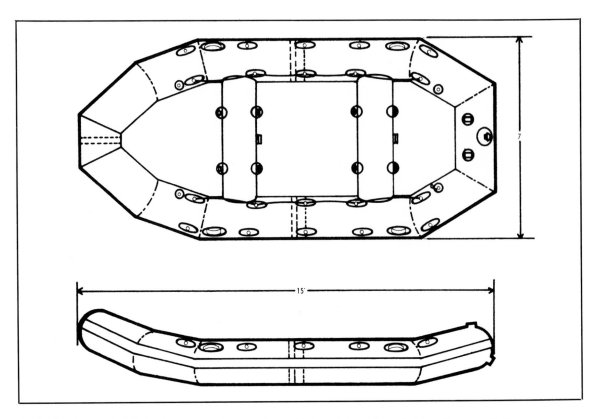

Rockering fore and aft helps keep spray down and gear high and dry. *Avon Rubber Company Ltd.*

tapered pram-type bow and a rounded bow. I care least for the pointed bow, since I've had them wedge between rocks while long-lining, and I see no benefit to having them on the boat. Pram-type or rounded bows and sterns are both acceptable to me, though I want them blown, rockered or both.

Blowing & Rockering Blowing and rockering are both ways to get your bow and/or stern up higher than your side tubes. A blown bow is achieved by adding more material at the end of the tube, creating a balloony effect out front. A rockered bow tips up, like a pram. Both features tend to slap down sloppy spray, and make climbing up and over standing water a lot easier than would be the case in a flat-bottomed even-diameter craft. A blown or rockered stern also means you can carry more gear there.

Air Chambers Flotation chambers are constructed either as individual compartments within a tube, or as several tubes stacked on top of or beside each other, sponson-style.

I favor the parallel tubes that run the full length of the boat, since the loss of one of these won't affect the integrity of the craft so much as losing a whole section of a firming gunwale. Unfortunately, sponson flotation chambers are not a common option in the smaller craft.

Thwarts Inflatable thwarts are nothing more than blown-up rubber seats that stretch between your gunwales. They help to firm up a raft, give you a little extra flotation and provide a comfortable seat for passengers, but they do interfere with free location of gear.

Tie-down Points These can be D- or O-shaped metal rings imbedded in a ball of cast rubber and then firmly joined to the boat, or on less expensive models, grommets in an apron that skirts the raft's perimeter. Whatever the tie-down's nature, there can't be too many of them, and you'll probably want to add more as you begin to establish your own techniques of platform location and patterns of

The Green River model raft sports rockering fore and aft and inflated thwarts. Length 17 feet, beam 8 feet, tube diameter 18 inches. It has six air chambers, weighs 260 pounds, and costs between $1,000 and $1,500, depending on fabric weight and extras. *Photo by Inflatable Boats Unlimited*

The Snake model raft is a durable design that helps keep spray out with its sponson-type upper airlocks. This raft sports ten chambers, is 18 feet long with an 8-foot beam and has a tube diameter of 18 inches. The Snake weighs 325 pounds and costs between $1,000 and $1,500, depending on fabric weight and extras. *Photo by Inflatable Boats Unlimited*

Avon's River Runner class of inflatables is growing in popularity. These rafts have a reputation for toughness and long life. The Mark II Professional, pictured here, is 15 feet with a 7-foot beam and 18-inch buoyancy tubes. The raft is rockered fore and aft, weighs 130 pounds and has six air chambers. Price is around $1,100.   *Photo by Avon Rubber Company Ltd.*

The Japanese or Taiwanese import is the most popular raft for beginners, primarily because of its $100 price. This raft, made by World Famous Sales, has two airlocks and weighs 90 pounds.
Photo by N. Strung

gear stowage. A safety feature that fits into this tie-down category is a series of D rings somewhere along the gunwales through which a rope can be rigged to give passengers a handhold in heavy water. The need for something for everyone to latch on to when crests start licking the sky might not be all that apparent, but I've seen a two-hundred-pound man batted overboard by a surprise curl as if cuffed by some invisible monstrous paw.

One place not to have ropes on a whitewater raft is anywhere near or below the raft's outboard perimeter. In this location they easily catch and hang up on sharp rocks and snags, a lesson I learned the hard way on my first trip down a strong river.

It was some fifteen years ago, and Eli Spannagel, now a Montana rancher, and I did everything wrong. But on the plus side, I learned a great deal, literally by mistake.

It was an unusually warm day in April. A strong spring sun graced a deep-blue sky, there was no wind, and the thermometer hovered near the 70-degree mark. When you get a break like that from the normally cold and clammy Montana spring, you make the most of it, and Eli and I planned to celebrate the rites by floating the Yellowstone and catching a limit of trout.

The Yellowstone above Livingston, Montana, couldn't be called whitewater. There's a run or two that might approach a Class II rating, but even this stuff is avoidable, so adventure wasn't our object, just a fish fry. We launched our raft at a bridge near Pine Creek, after making arrangements to be picked up downstream.

The first half of the trip was uneventful. We concentrated on fishing, not rowing, and the five-man raft careened off rocks and brushed by tangles of snags as we cast to likely holes. The day was beautiful: cool in the shade, but a warm glory as we slipped from shadow to sunlight and felt the promise of summer beat down on our backs.

It was a gentle conspiracy: the warmth, the birdsong and the Doppler effect of musical riffles as we approached, then passed them by. Even the fish cooperated; we were taking browns and rainbow up to three pounds. Lulled, we turned our back on the river, and got a hard slap on the wrist for not paying more attention.

It happened so quickly that we still had our rods in our hands as we were being washed overboard. The raft swung wide to the outside bank on a long, lazy curve and brushed by a jetty of rock riprap built to discourage riverbank erosion. The river was silent and deep at that point, but very swift and powerful. The rope around our raft's perimeter caught on a jagged edge of rock near a small curl. Eli leaned over to disengage us, tipped a slightly soft gunwale under and the raft was filled in an instant.

With the added weight of water, the river had no trouble flowing over as well as under the raft, scouring our tackle boxes and fish overboard, and very nearly us too. We were so unstable as the swift current swirled around us that we couldn't get to our knees or feet; we could only hold on, hoping that we didn't go overboard. The water was bitterly cold.

Then, just as quickly as it happened, the river relented, shifting its power to a huge boil that burped up next to us. Pressure was suddenly taken off the raft. Eli found his balance and some slack in the rope, and we were free to row ashore, where we shivered uncontrollably while our clothes dried on a rock.

The next time I floated a raft, I made sure there were no entangling lines overboard, and my future relations with rivers were similarly altered. From that point on I made it my business to know exactly where the current would carry me on a free drift, and both things taken into consideration, I haven't been in that particular bind since.

Your First Raft

There are some parallels to be drawn between the raft types and options outlined and Ferrari sports cars, Leonard fly rods and Purdy shotguns. These craft and features are the tops, with prices to match their quality.

Odds say most of the readers of this book will be rank amateurs or, at the outside, novices, so these recommendations are on a par with telling someone who has expressed mild interest in racing, fishing or hunting that the "right" car cost $20,000, the "right" rod costs $300 and the "right" gun costs $3,000 with a two-year waiting list on the purchase.

These are undeniably the "right" rafts in terms of safety, reliability and performance. But though my experience has convinced me they're "right," I also recognize the absurdity of expecting a casual or beginning floater to start with the best. In realistic terms, you'll probably tackle your first whitewater in the least expensive raft you can find, and this will probably mean a Japanese or Taiwanese import, of many possible designs.

If this is your choice, beware of several things: Borrowed or secondhand rafts can spell immediate trouble. Look for signs of checking along creases. Ascertain they're neoprene/nylon, not rubber/cotton (this applies to new purchases too). Inflate them and leave them full for two days before you float, for signs of leakage.

On new rafts, check the weight of construction material. On all rafts to be used in water over Class III, look for 17-inch tubes. Choose a raft with a reinforced or heavier-than-the-tubes floor. Check for strong, well-bonded tie-downs, and when inflated, there should be no pinches in the walls or floor. The raft should be full-sized, without any material constraint.

There is nothing inherently unsafe about these cheaper rafts if you choose and use them wisely. They are the craft I first used, I've rowed them through monumental water, and in certain situations I continue to use them. But pursuing our analogy, while an expert driver could wheel a Vega, and an expert boatman pilot the import, I'd rather have a sports car under me coming into a tight turn at a hundred miles per hour, and a rockered, 17-inch-tube Hypalon raft when I'm looking down on heavy rapids.

By way of manufacturers and products I

can personally recommend, World Famous Sales (WFS) makes an 11½-foot import that I saw misguided through a rock garden I thought would tear it from stem to stern. It made it, but my raft didn't with *very* careful piloting and one disastrous mistake. The interesting thing is I had a WFS raft too. But an older model. This was before I knew about things like 17-inch tubes and neoprene/nylon construction. My experience adds fuel to the check-before-you-float fire. I currently carry my own WFS 11½-footer in my rafting stable and have been most happy with its performance, though I wish the floor were a bit stouter. Prices on this raft are suited to the beginning river rat—around $100—and they're delightfully light for portaging.

Avon makes a virtually indestructible product. A good friend of mine has had one of these rafts for eleven years, doing duty as a yacht tender (in salt water) under the captainship of pre-teenage kids, and his only damage has been explainable (and understandable) pinhole punctures. Further, I know others who have used these craft in whitewater situations, and they don't break up, no matter how you misjudge or mispilot into abrasive rocks. That these rafts are tough is a foregone conclusion, but the makers are historically into the yacht-tender, high-speed outboard market. Consequently, most of their models lack some whitewater refinements and considerations. For example, the Avon Redcrest (9′3″), Redseal (10′3″) and Redshank (12′3″) have tube diameters of 13, 13 and 15 inches, respectively. That's too little height for serious water. But Avon has made a pitch for the American whitewater market (Avon is a British firm, and Britain has few steep-pitch rivers) with their River Boats. Their 13-footer has tubes of 17 inches and is rockered fore. Their 15-footer has 18-inch tubes and is rockered fore and aft. I haven't had the opportunity to try out their River Boats personally, but looking at their design, and knowing something about the company, I can't help but conclude that this is a fine whitewater craft. Like all good things, they don't come cheap. The 15-footer

Outboard power is usually used only on large commercial rafts plying huge rivers. (Hermit Rapids, Grand Canyon.) *Photo by Roy Cromer*

currently costs 1,100 bucks.

If you are versed enough in whitewater to have your own ideas about design and special boats for individual rivers, look into Inflatable Boats Unlimited, P.O. Box "0," Kanab, Utah, 84741. This company supplies commercial and private floaters with inflatables that suit their particular notion of what it takes to handle their favorite river. Inflatable Boats have fully nine designs of rafts in their catalogue, and if one of theirs doesn't suit you, they'll build one to your specifications. Their material is of military quality, and they can also supply the fittings you might need to alter your raft to your needs. This includes starting from river level and building your own raft. Their list includes: rowing frames, tubes, patching and floor material, pumps, D rings, valves and patching (or bonding) cement. They offer complete rafts from $3,498 (37 feet without floor) to a 12-foot, 16-inch-tube Rio Grande model, with a reinforced floor, for $549.

POWER, PADDLES AND OARS

Muscle and motors are both used to push a raft along, though the word "push" or "propel" is imprecise. Control is what oars or an outboard provide the boatman—the means to position his craft according to the dictates of the water that lies ahead. In most cases, once that positioning is achieved, the river does the rest.

Outboard power is common only on the largest rafts plying big rivers, the 20-foot-and-up giants used as commercial touring craft for large parties. There is a place for an outboard on smaller rafts, but it is truly for propulsion—a fast way to get through long, placid stretches of water. When whitewater with the need for tricky maneuvering looms up on midrange and smaller rivers, an outboard is unreliable power because of the probability of rocks and shoals. The middle of churning rapids is not the place to shear a pin or crack a prop.

Jet outboard power is one possibility on smaller rafts, since there is no prop to shear or break. But jet systems are inefficient in that they cut usable horsepower by as much as half, and this in turn means you need an unusually large motor for this system to work.

Paddles and oars provide the control for most amateur whitewater work today, and paddles are the less preferred of the two. Like jet versus prop, there is no comparison between the purchase and power of a locked oar and that of a hand-held paddle. Another negative aspect of paddle power is the need for precise coordination among the paddlers. When a suckhole shows its humped warning twenty yards downriver, you're going to have to go either to the left or to the right. Even an experienced team of paddlers takes a little while to get that move together, and beginners might never get it organized in time. Contrast this with one man and two powerful oars. The time required for response is shaved to nothing, while power and control are doubled. The paddle approach to whitewater work also involves extensive forward-ferrying—moving faster than the current to maintain steerage and control. This finds the raft rocketing along at quite a clip, and affords very little time for executive decisions about crossing eddy fences and the advisability of going around rather than through a set of rearing tail waves. Obviously, I'm not at all impressed with paddle power, and feel anyone is taking a risk by going this route down any rapids above Class II.

Oars are the most reliable means of control for the rafter, and the way they're mounted falls into two categories: fore-and-aft and port-and-starboard.

Sweeps "Sweep boats" employ the fore-and-aft technique. To understand this method of control, imagine an oarlock centered on the bow of a raft and one centered on the stern. Extremely large oars are used, with shafts up to 14 feet long. The oar blade angles slightly away from the shaft, the full "oar" resembling a Paul Bunyan-sized hockey stick.

The boat goes down the river bow first, the boatman standing amidships and facing downstream. The raft is pumped into position by rowing it sidewards. Sweeps are intriguing things to watch, moving from one side of the river to the other with the smooth grace of an expert skier, but with them a back ferry—essentially a braking maneuver—is impossible. You move with the speed of the river, which, again, doesn't leave you a lot of time to assess what lies ahead or to decide what to do about it.

Sweeps are generally best for larger rafts, those so big that it would be nearly impossible for one man rowing conventionally to move them quickly and accurately on an all-day float. And in fact that's where you usually see them used: on big rafts plying waters where motor power is prohibited.

Platform Rafts The "platform" or frame technique is the most practical form of propulsion and control for rafts 20 feet and under, and consequently it's the most popular with free-lance river runners.

Oars are locked into some sort of frame or platform that, in turn, is lashed tightly to the raft. The boatman faces downstream and the raft quarters the current. A backstroke is the primary stroke on a platform raft. Quartered to the current, this stroke finds your craft scooting across the river—a maneuver to gain position. Parallel to the current, a backstroke (or back ferry) slows down the raft's momentum, affording time for analysis of a safe passage or for the bow of the boat to rise and meet a big curl. Drop your oars inches below the surface and stand fast, and the boat moves with the speed of the river. Push forward, you accelerate. Drop your oars deep and the slower laminates of water near the bottom will in turn slow your progress.

The maneuverability inherent in a platform raft carries an element of safety, but nearly as significant is a kind of artistic side to it all. Rowing down a wild river under exquisite control is a mating of your knowledge and ability with the power and beauty of natural force. Darting into an eddy or gracefully skirting an angry crest involves a combination of

Sweep boats have oars mounted fore and aft. The oars look like mutant hockey sticks, and the boatman stands to row. (Middle Fork of the Salmon, Idaho.) *Photo by N. Strung*

swordplay, bullfight and dance.

It is as if there were three definable relationships between a boat and a river: When you are in full control, which is a pleasure; when the river is in full control, which is a terror; and when you are on an equal footing, moving and working together. This is the art.

I can't help but recall a repulsive platitude from a grade-B flick I once sat through. "You and the river are one" was the line. But there are times you'll feel that way in a raft, and those singular moments of perfect balance are always the best of any trip.

Rafting Platforms

Most mass-produced rafts come with oarlocks bound to the gunwales, and their implication is that you sit on the floor or on an inflated cushion and use them to row. This is a workable situation for Class II water and below, but when you move up the scale of difficulty, the man on the oars soon finds out that the bottom of a rubber raft is a clumsy

spot for rowing and offers a limited view downriver.

If you get off the floor and up high, you'll be far more comfortable, in a position to exert more positive pressure on the oars, and you'll get a much better look at what's coming up downstream. The simplest way to do this is to lay a board across the top of the raft and sit on it, but this kind of temporary make-do isn't the best. The gunwales will flex against the board, and after a lot of this abrasive wear, the raft will probably develop pinhole leaks. Because the board isn't firmly anchored to the raft, you and it can get pitched overboard in bouncy water. Under extreme strain, those oarlocks are a problem too.

A very strong stroke will collapse a raft. Because a raft is flexible, when you lean hard on the oars that are locked into the raft's factory-built gunwales, much of the pressure you're exerting never reaches the water but is lost in the energy-sapping give of the material. If you really put your back into a stroke, the

35

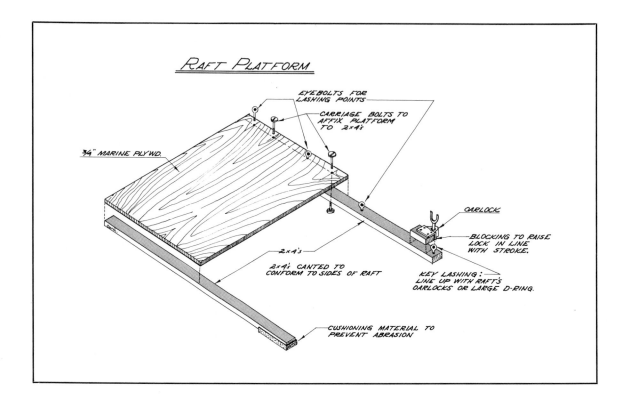

RAFT PLATFORM

EYEBOLTS FOR LASHING POINTS

CARRIAGE BOLTS TO AFFIX PLATFORM TO 2×4's

¾" MARINE PLYWD.

OARLOCK

BLOCKING TO RAISE LOCK IN LINE WITH STROKE.

2×4's

2×4's CANTED TO CONFORM TO SIDES OF RAFT

KEY LASHING: LINE UP WITH RAFT'S OARLOCKS OR LARGE D-RING.

CUSHIONING MATERIAL TO PREVENT ABRASION

raft will buckle and collapse in the middle, using up nearly all the energy that should be transferred to the water to move the boat.

For these reasons and a few more that I'll explain as I go along, floating any water above Class II points toward the installation of a rowing platform.

The function of the platform can be best understood by imagining a rigid frame bonded to a portion of the raft. Oarlocks are affixed to this frame.

This arrangement does several jobs at once. Most important, it provides a near-rock-solid link between the oars and the rubber boat. There is no give between the oars, lock and horseshoe frame, and very little give between the frame and the top of the raft once the device is lashed tightly in place. This means energy is transferred from you to the oar to the boat with negligible loss; the raft moves faster, and is more responsive.

Just as important, you have sacrificed a bare minimum of the raft's ability to conform to the twists and turns of moving water. Much of the tube area is still free to bend and turn

any way it wants, and the bottom is free to flex as well.

Rowing platforms can be bought from raft suppliers or they can be a home-workshop project. The easiest one to build is the horseshoe platform, and it is the one I favor for 10- to 14-foot rafts. This platform affords the additional benefits of gear stowage above the wet bottom of the raft, and discourages water from pouring over the stern when you're down in a trough.

The Horseshoe The horseshoe platform is essentially a piece of plywood that spans the stern of the raft and is bolted into two 2×4's that rest on each gunwale. It's impossible to provide measurements for this job because they'll be determined by the dimensions of your raft. Instead, I'll key construction to raft features.

Materials include: Two 2×4's, ¾-inch marine plywood, eight to twelve 2½-inch carriage bolts, a dozen screw-type eyebolts, oarlocks and some sort of cushioning material—an old carpet, fishing waders or a defunct raft.

36

Cut the 2x4's so they reach from the stern-most point of the raft to the raft's built-in oarlocks when laid on top of the gunwales. This will fall somewhere between one-third and one-half the distance between the bow and stern of the craft. If your raft has no factory-supplied oarlocks, cut the 2x4's so they fit within this general area, making sure they end at some point of strong attachment—a large 0 or D ring or grommet.

Cut the marine plywood so it conforms to the stern half of the 2x4 frame. This should create a nearly square deck, approximately one-fourth the size of your raft, which fits flush to the 2x4's and spans the stern from gunwale to gunwale. Line up 2x4's and plywood for a perfect fit, and bolt the plywood to the 2x4's, screwing the nuts from the top of the platform super-tight, so the bolt heads are drawn up and countersunk in the 2x4's.

A cushion between the platform and the raft comes next. You must line all points of wood-and-raft contact with soft but sturdy material. Keep the lining in place with rubber-based contact adhesive. You can use tacks on the side of the 2x4's to hold this cushion in place, but don't use them on any surface that will rest against the raft.

The eyebolt-type wood screws make for the lashing points. With the platform in place, locate the tie-downs on your raft. These could be grommeted holes in a raft apron, 0 rings, D rings—any sturdy place you can latch on to without damaging the raft. The raft's original oarlocks, if present, make particularly good tie-down points; that's why the 2x4's should reach them.

The method of lashing that will have the least give is a zigzag pattern, so strive for this effect in your arrangement, staggering eyebolt against tie-down. If you plan to camp or carry a lot of extra gear, add a few eyebolts toward the center of the platform, making sure they don't interfere with your seat. It is there, across the stern of the raft and behind the oarsman, that gear you wish to keep relatively dry is carried, and the eyebolts will be needed for lashing it down.

Determining the position of the oarlocks comes next. Sit straight, squarely in the middle of the raft-mounted platform, and extend your clenched hands out in front of you. The location of the oarlocks should fall in line with your fists. You might also want to block the locks up higher; I raised mine four inches to get the pull of the oars in better line with my shoulders.

Another possible addition to a wooden platform on larger rafts is a foot brace. This is nothing more than another 2x4 that spans the forward end of the rafting platform, providing you with a place to put your feet when you lean into a hard backstroke.

A foot brace increases the power you can throw to your oars, it gives your passengers something to hold on to, and it strengthens the integrity of the platform. But it makes for tight quarters on smaller rafts. They're not really needed on small rafts, since there isn't all that much bulk to move around.

The Pipe Platform The wooden rowing platform is advantageous because it can be built in a home workshop with minimal tools in about an hour. But it does have limits in that it's not adaptable to the larger rafts. When you move up beyond 14 feet, the rafts are too big and flexible, and the torque they exert might eventually pop the platform, leaving you sitting on a pile of splinters.

On a larger raft, consider a pipe platform. This type of platform can be built along the horseshoe principle, or it can be a square brace that is lashed to the center of the raft. The latter design is the most popular on larger rafts, since it puts the oarlocks closer amidships, and this is the place from which a boat is easiest to control.

Of the types of pipe braces I've seen, the best have two pipes to a side, laid parallel along each gunwale. This allows the brace to conform to the round top of the airlocks. A brace stretches from gunwale to gunwale on the forward and rear ends of the platform, and a seat is fitted to the stern end so the oarsman faces downstream. The forward brace also functions as a foot brace.

A typical and well-thought-out pipe brace. Note oarlocks up high for a stroke in line with the boatman's back, and parallel braces conforming to the gunwales. Decking is in an interesting spot too; lashed gear would be boxed in and secure. *Photo by Avon Rubber Company Ltd.*

Unique U-shaped foot bracing for extra power and control on a large, heavy raft. Note the many positions of leverage it affords. (Note the sweep boat, with spray shields, in the background.) *Photo by N. Strung*

The pipes are either welded or bolted together. Welds are superior since they do away with a lot of sharp edges on bolt heads, threads and nuts, and have greater rigidity, but a welded brace can't be broken down and packed in an airplane for a fly-in float.

Still another construction technique is to use heavy-duty aluminum conduit over close-fitting hardwood or top-grade spruce dowels. Bolts hold it together, and can be cinched down tight enough to bury the heads in the soft aluminum. As in the wooden platform, all frame-to-raft points of contact should be lined with a buffer.

Foot braces can be improved if you're a welder or know someone who is. In their simplest form, these braces are in line with your seat. When you pull on the oars, your legs and back don't line up perfectly with the direction of the stroke, and you lose some power.

You can raise your seat a bit (this will also require raising your oarlocks) to get in better line, or you can manufacture a U brace, first conceived by John Doar of River Adventures West. This brace resembles an upside-down version of the Greek letter omega, and it gets your feet down close to the floor of the raft. A second brace runs from the center of the U up to the stern crossbrace or equipment deck, and a long seat is bolted to this brace. With this arrangement, you can put your posterior anywere, and even slide with your stroke like a rower in a scull.

EQUIPMENT

Spray Shields

Shields are another specialty item that will keep your raft and its occupants dry. They're made of light tubular framing that conforms to the contours of the boat. Once the framing is lashed firmly in place, canvas is stretched across it. When you enter standing waves, any sloppy water or flying spray is cast back on itself.

Seats

Seats for passengers are a matter of safety as well as comfort. In rapids, sitting on the edge of the raft is out—or your passengers might be. Kneeling or sitting on the bottom of the raft holds the potential of a collision with a sleeper and a rip or a bad bruise and perhaps even a bad spinal injury.

The most practical alternative to being bounced or bumped is either an inflatable cushion or an inner tube. This provides a buffer for you and the raft. But both items are bouncy things, and you tend to become unseated at the first hard slap. Worse yet, you never seem to be able to get back into the right cushion position until the water slicks out. This usually finds passengers grabbling at cushions under them while they flail the air above them for balance, missing the best part of a good run.

To counter this ungainly situation, I glue tie-downs for cushions in the bottom of the raft. The easiest way to do this is with some contact cement and webbed belting. Cement a strip of belting to each side of the cushion and cement matching belting to the floor of the raft. All you need add is a few clasps and you can anchor the seat in place.

Oarlocks

If I were asked to pick the most important part of any raft, my answer wouldn't require a second's hesitation: the oarlocks. They are the point of union between you and the boat; the fulcrum of power; the determining factor in any safe passage.

Oarlocks are composed of two parts, the lock and the horn. The lock is a female receptacle into which fits the revolving horn. The lock, in turn, is affixed to the rafting brace.

Any lock to be used on a raft should have a short enough receptacle so the horn shaft passes completely through it, with a half inch or so of shaft exposed beneath. This is so you can pin it. More about that in a moment.

There are three types of horns in current whitewater use: the buckhorn, the locked horn and the 0 horn.

Buckhorn Locks The buckhorn cradles the oar in a U-shaped frame, and the oar is in turn pinned in place by a shaft that passes through the top of the U and the center of the oar shaft. This type of horn is the least desirable. The shaft is weakened by the drilled hole, and weakened in a critical area. This is the precise spot where the most pressure develops on the oar shaft as you row.

Bolt Locks The locked horn collars the oar firmly in place by way of a bolted clamp. This keeps the shaft strong, but holds the oar blade at a constant right angle to the water, affording no opportunity to feather the oar. In a tight passage, the only way to ship an oar locked in this horn is to sweep it full forward or backward. That kind of room isn't always available.

0 Horns The 0-type horn fully encircles the shaft of the oar. There is no lock or pinning hole, so you're free to draw the oars inward. This can be a plus on narrow passages in that you can pull in your shafts and row cross-armed, in a short arc. Not the most powerful stroke to be sure, but you have more control than with no oars at all.

In addition, because you don't hold your oar in the same position for every stroke, 0 horns don't work and worry on one small part of the oar shaft. Strains are distributed. I've never seen an oar break in an 0 horn; I've seen pinned buckhorns snap.

If in a lapse of good judgment you turn loose of your downstream oar, the 0 horn is less likely to jam you up. If the oar blade catches on bottom or on a rock, the shaft will slide up through the horn. A pinned buckhorn will jar the boat badly, breaking the oarblade or shaft, or it may hang you up.

One logical objection to the 0 horn I've heard is that because it doesn't hold the blade at a constant right angle to the water, you're never sure you're getting maximum dig with the blade. But you'll find that when you do enough rowing, you can judge maximum dig by feel the second you dip the oar.

0 horns do present one other problem that must be compensated for: because they don't pin your oar in place, the shaft will slide downhill, and into the water, should you turn the oar loose. This is an embarrassing and potentially dangerous situation; there is nothing that will make you feel quite so dumb as drifting helplessly with one oar in hand and the one in the water gradually outdistancing you—and they do it every time.

Oar Collars

Collaring the oar will prevent this. To do this, find an old fan belt. Slip on the lock and cut the belt so it goes once around the shaft of the oar. Tack it to the shaft a foot to a foot and a half below the oar grip. Wrap black plastic tape liberally around the belt and tack heads, and you've got a collared oar that won't slip out of the lock.

Herter's, Inc., Mitchell, South Dakota, sells oarlocks, horns and ready-made leather collars for oars. These leather collars don't do a better job than fan belts, but they look awful professional.

Pinning Horns

The next step in the unity of muscle flex in moving a boat is pinning the horns. The male horn shaft should have a quarter-inch hole in the bottom of it. Most of them come from the factory this way. If not, you can easily drill one with a high-speed bit.

With the horn in place, slip a stout cotter pin through the hole and expand the tip. Carefully assess the tolerance between male shaft and female receptacle. If there's any chance the cotter pin can be bent and drawn up through the lock, ring the shaft above the cotter pin with a close-fitting washer. The tremendous pressures exerted on horn and lock under certain conditions will pop even a big cotter pin with incredible ease. This once happened to me.

Bill Browning (a photographer from Helena, Montana), Sam Curtis and I were floating the Beartrap of the Madison. Bill was shooting the wilder action from shore for an article we were doing together, and had several thousand dollars' worth of camera equipment. Although he kept it in a waterproof case, it still gave me the willies. When Bill and his gear were aboard, we plied the pressure waves very carefully.

A growing thundercloud blocked out the sun halfway through the trip, making for flat light that undid Bill's sense of drama, so we decided to float on through and shoot the rest of the pictures another day.

We were halfway through a crazy section of river known as the meat grinder—a jumble of boulders, small falls and suckholes—when it happened. I knew one particularly tricky passage occurred just below a huge, house-sized boulder. The water above the boulder was deceptively passive, and it was rough to tell which narrow route was the best—the swift flow on the right of the rock or the shallow-appearing tumble of rapids on the left. I chose the right run, and groaned when I saw better what we were into.

The water accelerated greatly as it funneled into that chute, so narrow that I wondered if the boat would fit. On the downside of the rock, it went over a falls—spewed over is a better word—with a velocity and roar that reminded me of a giant faucet. I put my back hard on the oars, trying to beat the river and ease in front of the rock to the other passage. The odd angle of the oars and the pull of muscles I never knew I had drew a quarter-inch cotter pin up through the oarlock like the cleaning brush on a shotgun. The horn popped free and I was left with only one oar.

In retrospect, it was a very telling experience. Time seemed to slow down. Sam and Bill were immediately aware of the problem and the best solution to it. "Can you get the shaft back in the lock?" I asked Sam, who was sitting closest to the lock.

He didn't jab, fumble or jerk, but worked with cool precision, trying once, twice, very deliberately to reinsert the shaft. But now the cotter pin prevented re-entry, and it was too twisted and too strong to remove by hand. "No, I don't think we can do this," Sam replied.

I glanced up at the chute now looming closer and heard Bill say, "At least we know that nobody in this boat panics."

I still chuckle over that cool observation today.

Then suddenly we saw our chance. A slight shift in the current brought us nearly within reach of the left shore. I hit my good oar hard and the bow whirled close enough for Bill to reach the shore. He scrambled overboard with the painter in his hand.

After making repairs, we decided to run the chute—with Bill and his battery of cameras ashore. Our luck changed for the better; the sun came out briefly through a slot in the clouds as we shoved off, and Bill ended up with some of the best shots of the day.

Oars

Oars are the final link in the chain of propulsion and should be selected as carefully as any of the other pieces of equipment that keep you in control. For serious whitewater work, ash or oak oars are the only way to go. Pine and even fine-grained airplane spruce—if you can find it—just aren't as tough or dependable as straight-grained hardwood.

Select only oars with grain that runs the length of the shaft. Grain is essentially a side view of the tree's annual rings, and no grain should come to a V along the shaft. Wood will separate and splinter at this point, and it's a sign that the shaft is inherently weak. Another sign of weakness is knots. Don't buy a shaft with any blemish larger than a pencil eraser and these should not be too numerous.

Oar blades should likewise be straight-grained and knotless with no signs of splitting. In addition, you should cap them.

Blade Caps The cap can be tin or copper. Copper works best because it will conform to the blade's contours more easily. Tack the material along both sides of the tip of the blade, extending it three inches up from the end. Capping is wise because the blade of the oar is bound to be bounced off a few rocks, and you'll use it as a push pole. The cap prevents the blade from splitting in the wake of this hard use and will extend the life of the oar threefold.

Oar Length The length of the oar to buy is a bit trickier to outline than the quality of it. A very long oar—12 to 16 feet—has the potential to move a boat most quickly because of the broad arc of its sweep. However, not many people have the muscles to drive an oar of that size, or to control it in heavy crosscurrents.

Realize too that an oar works on the lever principle, the lock being the fulcrum of the lever. So an 8-foot oar locked a foot below the handle is harder to pull than a 10-foot oar locked three feet below the handle.

Still another consideration: too long oars can create problems when you have to navigate tight, boulder-strewn water.

A few rules of thumb then: Buy an oar that's long enough to make your muscles work, but that you can control under all conditions. Balance the length of that oar against the floating conditions you expect to encounter, and against the length of your boat. It would be foolish—though easy rowing—to try to control an 19-foot raft with a 6-foot oar. Generally, an oar that's half the length of your boat is the place to start: a 6-foot oar for a 12-foot boat, a 9-foot oar for an 18-footer and so forth.

If you can't find top-grade oars locally, try South Branch Lumber Company, Howland, Maine, 04448. They sell fine ash oars for between 38 and 58 cents per foot, depending on quality and length. Shipping is extra.

Life Vests

Life preservers must be with you, and they should be on your back in any water that's more turbulent than a millstream. After you see your first man overboard, you'll know why that caveat must be in force for anyone on the waves. Even in Class II water, the undertow and conflicting currents will toss a floater like a rag doll and will plainly try to pull him down. In heavier water, a jacketed man will go completely under, but the buoyancy of his jacket will pop him back up within seconds. It might also be worth pointing out that anyone considering tackling Class IV water and beyond should have confidence in his ability to swim, and should have no fear of water (healthy respect is, however, recommended).

There are two types of life preservers suitable for whitewater work. Both are jacket types that are worn on the torso and cinched in place.

Mae West The Mae West is unquestionably the best. This preserver is basically a long tube of light canvas filled with sealed plastic tubes of kapok or a similar soft floatant. The tube stretches from your beltline, up your chest, around behind your neck and down to the opposite beltline. A webbed waist belt holds the bottom of the preserver in place.

The reason I rate this preserver as best is twofold. The cushioning floatant around the back of your neck safeguards against a sharp rap from a rock should you be tossed backwards. In addition, the design of this preserver will force even an unconscious person to lie on his back, with the back-of-the-neck flotation holding his head out of the water.

As with all things in heaven and earth, however, the Mae West isn't perfect. When you're at the oars, you'll find that its puffy bulk restrains your movements a bit and the cloth behind your neck will chafe skin in the course of a full day on the river. This isn't quite so true with passengers, though; they don't do the twisting, turning and pulling that the man at the oars must do.

Vest Preservers If you find the Mae West binding, the best second choice is the vest preserver. This preserver looks very much like a dress vest. The two front panels and the back of the garment are filled with a soft, high-floatant material that feels a little like foam rubber. They are quite comfortable, they don't interfere with movement, but they don't hold your head out of water, and they don't offer it any protection.

Whichever preserver you settle on, be sure the label says "Coast Guard Approved." And be aware of the preserver's net flotation capabilities. The "net flotation" of your preserver should come to 20 percent of your body weight: 40 pounds net flotation for a 200-pound man, for example.

Wet Suits One other type of "preserver" used on the river is the wet suit. A wet suit is a pants-and-jacket suit made of neoprene foam between one-fourth and three-eighths inches thick; it is designed to keep a diver warm in very cold water. Water seeps between the suit and your skin (hence the term "wet suit") and is trapped there by the tight-fitting garment. The many bubbles in the neoprene act as insulation, and once your body temperature raises the temperature of the cold water next to your skin, you stay quite comfortable, even though the water you're diving in or floating on might be 40 degrees.

Floaters use wet suits when running a river in cold weather. Because of the trapped air in the neoprene, wet suits are extremely buoyant; an average-sized diver wearing a wet suit needs approximately 20 pounds of lead around his waist to get below the surface. But wet suits present some dangers because of that buoyancy. A man overboard floats like an ant that's fallen into a puddle—very high and very flat. It's difficult to control your direction, and you tend to float face down. This combination is an open invitation to a collision with a rock. Wearing a Mae West will counter the face-down danger, but it's truly bulky for rowing, and you won't get much more control should you go overboard. Full wet suits, though necessary if you'll be floating when it's cold, are tricky in fast water. Be conscious of their dangers when you don one.

Body Protection

The need for hard hats when you're rafting is debatable. Surely, they provide an extra margin of safety, but so would never going near whitewater in the first place. There is a point in life where concern for personal safety begins to shade into sterility. A Mae West is good sense; a hard hat is getting a little sterile. I must say, however, that I have asked people to wear hard hats while negotiating particularly rough passages—particularly young adults who were light in weight. It is easy for a lightweight to be tossed six to ten feet in the air by the right flex of the raft and slap of the river. Add a sharp rock in the right place, and you could have a real tragedy on your hands.

Motorcycle-type crash helmets make good hard hats, and so do "hockey" helmets. They're light and form-fitting, and they have holes in them to reduce water resistance and allow fast drainage.

One piece of often overlooked "safety" equipment is shoes. I always insist that all passengers wear them and that they remain on everyone's feet until it's sack time or the float is over. The sand that feels so great underfoot could well hold pointed twigs, jagged rocks and perhaps even broken glass or sharp tin. The boulders common to steep-gradient whitewater will be sharp too. All these edges add up to the likelihood of a foot injury, and being so hobbled is dangerous in itself when you're running a river.

Tennis shoes are the standard, but you can go one better: fishermen's wading shoes. These are strong, ankle-high boots of reinforced canvas with a composition-and-felt sole. The felt bottom grips slippery rocks lik glue, and the reinforced uppers and thick composition sole soften sharp jabs and the hurt of jamming your feet between rocks when long-lining or jumping ashore. These shoes dry just about as fast as sneakers, too. One mail-order source I know of is the Orvis Company, Manchester, Vermont, 05254.

If you're attached to the notion of tennis shoes, at least carpet their soles. Use indoor/outdoor carpeting, available as scrap from any flooring store. Buff the sole well with a wire brush, and glue the carpet "up" side down with contact adhesive. This will at least give you a good, solid grip on slippery underwater rocks.

SUPPORT AND REPAIR EQUIPMENT

Support equipment for rafting revolves around the question "What might happen?" and a list of what I normally bring implies the answers.

Repair Kits My repair kit contains a square yard of patching cloth. This can be obtained from raft manufacturers or can be taken from an old raft or pair of fishing waders. Inside that square of material, I wrap a pint can of contact cement. Its brand name is Barge and it has proven to be my best friend on the river. It is used to glue shoes together, so if you can't find it anywhere else, try a cobbler (if you can find one of *them* these days).

I also include a large carpet needle and 100 feet of waxed thread. This thread should be at least 12-pound test. You can use carpet thread that has been drawn through beeswax or paraffin, or dental floss as a substitute.

Tools A few hand tools will help you avoid hang-ups. Always bring at least a pair of pliers, a small adjustable crescent wrench and a screwdriver. These tools will be needed should you snug air valves down too tightly, if the leathers on your pump go on the fritz, if platform bolts loosen, or should any number of "ifs" go haywire.

Pumps I also like to bring two hand or foot pumps (one is a must). These should be capable of producing large volumes of air rather than high pressure. A bicycle-type pump will prove unsatisfactory; instead, buy a short-stroke pump with a large escape aperture and a barrel diameter at least as thick as your wrist.

Oarlocks Bring extra oarlocks and baling wire or cotter keys. Oarlocks can shear under the strain of a hard pull on the oars.

Extra Oars Bring one extra oar for a day float, and two if you'll be on the river overnight.

Ropes Rope is another necessity; no matter the kind of water you're covering, you'll always find a use for all the rope you have. I carry a minimum of fifty feet of ⅜-inch polyethylene over and above the lines I'll need for lashing, camping and portaging around rapids.

Bailing Devices A large-capacity bailing can rounds out my support equipment. As soon as water comes in, it must be bailed out, the quicker the better. The most practical bailing can is a plastic bleach bottle, cut like a scoop. It will shape itself to fit the bottom contours of the raft and won't tear the materi-al with sharp, jagged edges. It's a good idea to bring two bailing cans, as they're often bounced or washed overboard. Water fights are something else to think about. They're sure to be part of any float involving more than one raft, and a two-can boat is gallons ahead of the party with one.

SAFETY

In 1970, eleven people died in rafting mishaps during a two-week period on the Middle Fork of the Salmon River in Idaho. Eight people have died on Georgia's Chattooga River since the release of the film *Deliverance*. The Beartraps of Montana's Madison has claimed an average of one life a year for the last ten years.

Still, rafting is not inherently "unsafe." The potential for danger is certainly there, but recognizing that potential and taking pains to avoid it is as important to whitewater work as learning to navigate. With that in mind, let's again look at those statistics.

In 1970, the Salmon River drainage experienced a spring runoff that broke all records. Not only was the runoff monumental in terms of volume, but it came late, stretching well into the period when the waters normally recede. The people who perished during those violent times had no business being on the river under those conditions; most of them were novice or intermediate rafters, and their boats were far too small for the gigantic water conditions that developed. They didn't realize what they'd be up against, and they paid a dear price for their ignorance.

Prudence is an important asset when you're dealing with a river.

The incidents on the Chattooga are even more unfathomable in the incredible ignorance—and to some extent arrogance—that led to lives being lost.

The whitewater sections of *Deliverance* were a composite. To make the river seem virtually impassable, clips were shot of the wildest sections of several rivers: the Tallulah, the Coosawattee and the Chattahoochee, along with the most violent runs of the Chattooga. The director just couldn't find a river wild enough, so he created one. I didn't realize this when I saw the movie, and was more than impressed with what I saw. "That," I can remember saying to Sam Curtis, "is a river like no other I've seen. I'd never make the run."

With only those clips to give them an idea of what they'd be up against, people have since tackled the Chattooga in canoes, aluminum johnboats, inner tubes and *styrofoam coolers*—many of them without life jackets! Of the eight people who have died on the Chattooga to date, seven of them had no lifejackets. The eighth did, but he only had it draped over his shoulders and lost it upon going overboard.

The incidents on the Beartraps provide still another warning. In 1972, two boys launched a six-foot raft at the end of the access road. They had no life jackets and no experience. They tipped the raft within sight of their launch and drowned. The place where the mishap occurred could barely rate as Class II water.

Ten years ago, two men tried to run the Beartraps in a fiberglass canoe. What is so puzzling to me is why they continued; not a mile from the launch is a very difficult passage, even for an expert canoeist. Three miles from the launch there's a set of tail waves that surely must have swamped them, but they went on and tried to shoot the Kitchen Sink.

This is the most difficult piece of whitewater on the river. The run begins by two steep cliffs, one a sheer rock wall. At this point, the Madison River, which averages seventy-five yards across, is necked down to thirty or thirty-five feet. The bed of the river drops off on a steep gradient, and the water accelerates so fast and is so smooth you can hear it suck as it shoots by your feet. The surface of the water is oil-slick calm as it gathers velocity; then it breaks into the first roller, a curl about six feet from crest to trough. It's heavy water period, but the real Frankenstein lies just beyond. At a point slightly ahead of where the next mon-

strous curl would form, and in perfect line with the center of its probable crest, is a sharp boulder jutting just above water. It's the shape of an upside-down V. The boulder allows a lot of water to go around it, but there isn't enough to float a raft over the top of the rock. There is also a big buildup of water in front of the rock, which acts like a dam in the swift current. This water is channeled left at nearly a 90-degree angle to tumble over a four- to five-foot falls. At the bottom of the falls is a beastly suckhole: a dished-out pock in the river that keeps sliding back on itself—a real trap.

Nobody knows exactly what happened, just that two men drowned there. I would imagine that the canoe was caught crosswise on the boulder, snapped in half, and the two men were trapped in the suckhole. For several years the bow of the canoe, about two feet of it, was wedged between some bankside boulders downstream, and then it was taken back by the river. Still today, as I'm floating along below that point, I occasionally see some small pieces of fiberglass in the deep, clear holes, none of which are bigger than a 45-rpm record. They're sobering reminders of what a river can do if you treat it lightly.

The sad thing about all these tragedies is that they were eminently avoidable. In fifteen years of floating, I've never been witness to an injury worse than a cut or bruise, by following the "never float unknown, never float alone" rule.

Whenever tackling a potentially dangerous river, always have at least two rafts for the trip, and more than that is even better. Not only will this provide a means of rescue if something should happen to your boat, but it makes the trip more fun. You take a run under the watchful eyes of the passengers in your buddy boat, then they make theirs under your scrutiny. You'll learn a lot by watching others' mistakes, and have some laughs in the bargain.

"Floating unknown" means going down a river blind—not having any idea of what's coming up around the next bend or of the rating of the water you might encounter.

Part of the planning of any float should be tracking down complete information about the river you'll be running: the names and locations of different rapids and their difficulty of passage. Most popular whitewater rivers flow through public lands administered by either the U.S. Forest Service, the U.S. Park Service or the Bureau of Land Management. All three of these agencies are headquartered in Washington, D.C., and each has descriptive brochures about and occasionally maps of those rivers that come under their aegis.

Additional information can be gleaned from whitewater associations and clubs. Several of these groups have put together booklet-sized guides to individual rivers, which can be purchased for a dollar or so.

Word of mouth is another important source of information. Talk to people who have floated the river before; they can give you important clues not only about the rough rapids but also about the best time of year to float. Don't forget, low water can be just as dangerous as high water. This sort of "in" information comes only by talking to people who have experienced what you're about to.

The rule about unknown, however, also comes into play when you're on the river you've studied so carefully. Before you make a run through the rapids, pull ashore and study them carefully for the easiest passage. Carefully plot the point where you'll make your entry, the chutes that look the safest, and conjecture too about what you'll do if you get into trouble. And don't forget that you've got the option to portage or long-line your raft around the rapids if they look too tough. There's no shame in good sense.

Life jackets are more than important; they are just what their name implies: life. Wear them when on any sort of whitewater—even bare slips of six-inch curls.

All rafting parties should carry at least one first-aid kit and know how to use it. When packing the kit, don't forget to pay special attention to the sun and its potential for damage to skin and eyes.

NAVIGATION

Whitewater navigation is as simple—and as infinitely complex—as the commonality of patterns evident in all waters from the trickle in a rain gutter to the torrents of our mightiest rivers. Control under all conditions is a matter of learning to identify and follow the path of least resistance. To play the river as a mayfly does a hard wind; dancing from the slow lie behind a rock, out into a raging current, and back behind another safe breakwater. It requires courting the river, not overcoming it.

It is difficult to say which is more important to a safe passage in heavy water, control or reading the river correctly. You need both, but let's take a look at control first—most specifically, oarsmanship.

Learning to Row

Oars are your wires to the river, a connecting link of communication between you and moving water. Once you learn how to listen to them, they will tell you secrets about navigation, warn you of what lies ahead and become your silent partner as you slip along.

Before you tackle any river above a Class I rating, you should know how to row, and I mean an understanding that borders on reaction. You shouldn't have to think "if I pull on my right oar, the front of the boat will swing right," or "if I push on my right oar and pull on the left the boat will spin abruptly to the left"; you should know these basics without having to think, as you know walking, braking a car or perhaps turning on skis.

If you lack this ability, begin the learning procedure in quiet water, preferably on a lake, so you can carefully analyze each stroke and its effect without the compounding confusion of moving water. The best boat for this sort of practice is a light aluminum johnboat. These craft are flat-bottomed and boxy like a raft, but more responsive.

Start by concentrating on two things: keeping your oar blade at a right angle to the surface of the water at all times, and rowing in a straight line. Both exercises are more difficult than might at first seem the case. The oars will twist in your hand, altering your course, and normal human muscle structure will find one side of your body stronger than the other. Like the lost hunter walking without a compass, you'll find yourself tending to row in a wide circle.

Along with rowing in a straight line, also concentrate on making the most of each stroke, an accomplishment indicated by the entry and exit of the blade in the water. An efficient stroke will enter cleanly and leave the same way, with only a quiet swirl in its wake. Any sort of splash, slurp or sucking sound is a waste of energy and power.

Pull is a component of efficient motion; it should always be equal on each oar unless, in a particular situation, you want it to be otherwise.

Getting the feel of the oar is another important skill in running the river. Without looking at the blade's position, you must be able to tell by feel how efficient your stroke is, and be capable of changing the blade position to a point of greater or lesser resistance.

This skill is necessary because of the conflicting currents in a river. As water tumbles along, it swirls, turns, circles and curls back on itself. When this is happening underwater, the ability to read a river on top means nothing; you've got to feel it. Crossing an eddy fence is a good example. One side of the fence will be the fast-moving mainstream. The other side will be flowing upstream or nearly stagnant. To maintain your raft's orientation, one oar must move much more rapidly than the other and your sensitivity to the bite your blade is getting will tell you how fast. Bubble-charged water is another situation where this sensitivity comes into play. You'll feel the lack of resistance telegraphed to your hands.

Turning a boat by oar is most quickly learned if you'll envision the raft as being part of a draftsman's compass, free to scribe a circle. Pull on a left oar, and the boat will revolve around the compass point, swinging counterclockwise. Push on the left oar, and the boat will turn in the opposite direction.

In practice, you'll discover that the abruptness of your turn is determined by what your inside oar is doing. If you'll pull on your inside oar half as hard as on your outside oar, the raft will scribe a wide circle. Feather the inside oar so it's not working at all, and the circle will tighten up. If you drag the inside oar so that it puts up water resistance, the tip of its blade will be close to the center of the circle the "compass" will scribe, and if you push on the inside oar while continuing to pull on the outside, the boat will "turn on a dime," spinning on a point amidships.

Being able to slow your pace is a vital component of control too. Because the water on top of a river will characteristically flow faster than the water on the bottom, you can slow your rate of drift by dropping your oars deep and holding on tight. Practice this in calm water by rowing forward hard and fast, then dropping your oars and leaning against the pull they'll exert. This is the most difficult stroke to learn and surely the most taxing on your muscles. The "forward ferry" is used to accelerate, and puts quite a strain on your stomach.

Feathering is a technique seldom needed in calm water, but it can be important in whitewater.

How it's done is best understood by imagining an airplane propeller or an electric-fan blade—devices that move air (or water) by a series of slanted blades.

An oar blade is feathered by dropping it deep, then tilting it. If you bring it up sharply, the blade acts a little like a prop, driving the boat forward or backward depending on the direction of tilt. Feathering affords a degree of control without the need for a long, sweeping stroke. It is useful for maneuvering in close quarters.

A blade can be fully feathered to advantage under some conditions, too. This is a matter of twisting the blade in line with the surface so it cuts through, rather than sets up resistance to, the water. By using this trick, it's possible to row without ever lifting your blade from the water. The full feather is brought to bear when you swing too close to an overhanging branch, a leaning rock or a jutting snag.

Another way to deal with the problems that arise when you are too close to a cliff or snag for a normal stroke is to ship your oars. This finds your shafts drawn inward to shorten the arc of your stroke.

While these rowing variations are weak sisters to the powerful back ferry, their little extra push will often get you out of serious trouble, so they're worth practicing—and remembering.

Working with the River

Once you reach the point where a boat responds perfectly to your will, you're ready to tackle the more sophisticated stuff of whitewater control. Don't start on the toughest river around; pick something rated between Class II and Class III and try out your wings (or tubes) with a buddy boat along.

Ferry Position The key to running any sort of water lies in what is called ferry position. Ferry position means the position of your boat in relation to the river, or more specifically, the main current.

The principal ferry position finds the boat quartering the current, with the bow and the boatman facing downstream. In a perfectly straight river, an imaginary keel on your raft, if extended in a line, would intersect the main current at a 45-degree angle. If your stern is facing the bank on your right, this is called "ferry right"; if it faces your left, your position is "ferry left."

Ferry position sets the scene for three components of control. First, because you're looking downstream, you're in a position to see what bend, twist or rock in the river is coming up next. Second, you're rowing against the helical current, holding in slower water than the mainstream. This provides extra time to place your boat in just the right slot for a smooth passage. Third and most important, "ferrying" allows you to move across-current without sacrificing your view or slowed pace. Remember, whitewater rafting is little more than getting your boat in the right place, then letting the river do the rest.

Returning to our straight stretch of river, its underwater characteristics would find the bed angling down from either bank to meet at the thalweg—the deepest part of the river.

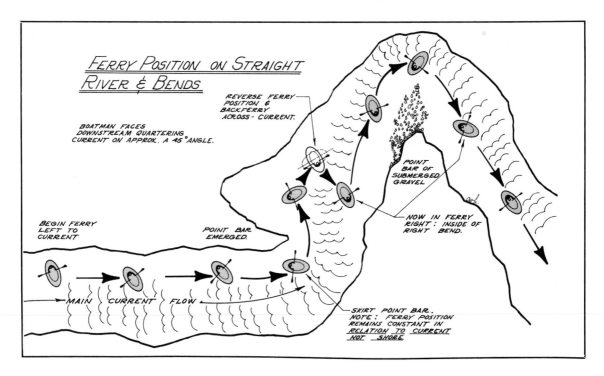

FERRY POSITION ON STRAIGHT RIVER & BENDS

BOATMAN FACES DOWNSTREAM QUARTERING CURRENT ON APPROX. A 45° ANGLE.

REVERSE FERRY POSITION & BACKFERRY ACROSS-CURRENT.

POINT BAR OF SUBMERGED GRAVEL

NOW IN FERRY RIGHT: INSIDE OF RIGHT BEND.

BEGIN FERRY LEFT TO CURRENT

POINT BAR EMERGED.

MAIN CURRENT FLOW

SKIRT POINT BAR. NOTE: FERRY POSITION REMAINS CONSTANT IN RELATION TO CURRENT NOT SHORE.

The surface of the water would find rollers cresting above the thalweg, and a helical current corkscrewing downstream and out from the bank to either side of the rollers.

An uncontrolled boat would be drawn into the rollers by the helical current, yet if you hug the bank too closely, you'll barely move along and it will be too shallow to dig with your oars. The right position here is is midway between shore and the rollers, ferry right to the curl if you're on the right side of the current, ferry left if you're on the left side of the current.

In this particular situation, you won't have to row much at all; just an occasional pull is needed to maintain your orientation and overcome the gentle reflex current. You could float from now until the river ran dry in this ferry position so long as the current ran straight and true, but rivers never run straight, so let's add meanders to the picture.

Taking a Curve: Let's say the river takes a curve to the left. Because water tries to flow in a straight line, the main channel will shoot into the right or outside bank as the bed begins to curve. This is a place to avoid. If you cross the current line, the corkscrew effect of spiraling water will push your raft hard into the right shore, the place where the heaviest water will occur.

From a ferry-left position you're in perfect shape for this bend. However, you'll have to take a few other peculiarities of moving water into consideration as you drift around the curve.

The inward spiral of the water will draw you away from the inside and toward the swiftest part of the current. You must overcome this secondary reflex current. It isn't much work, the pull is gentle, but its presence and direction are tough to predict unless you know how to read the water.

This inward drift will occur at an approximate 45-degree angle to the main current, and that current won't precisely parallel the shore. You must maintain your ferry position in relation to this current, not the shore. This will find you in a ferry-left position anywhere between 45 and 90 degrees to the shore as you drift around the curve.

From this ferry position, let's throw another curve into the river, this one swinging to the right. "Always take a curve on the inside" is a standard rule in floating. To get on this inside, you ferry right by spinning the boat 90 degrees, then row across-current. You're now in the correct ferry and location for this curve.

The Pivot Climbing up the scale of difficulty, the next bend in the river swings sharply left. You ferry left, cross the current line, and discover there's a sleeper just below the point bar, and that it has set up tail waves and bank rollers below.

If it's a small sleeper, the easiest way to handle this obstacle is to pivot around it. As you approach the sleeper in ferry-left position, a back ferry with your left oar just as the blade nears the rock will swing the raft around the obstacle as if the tip of the oar were the point of a compass. You can shorten the arc of the pivot if you'll forward-ferry on your right oar at the same time.

As a rule, this maneuver is useful only in low-class water, and as a means to dodge small rocks. When you come out of the pivot, you're in an improper ferry position: right to a current where you should be left. If there are heavy rollers downstream or super-elevation along the eddy fence downstream of the obstruction, the safest route is usually to slip behind it.

The Sideslip When a protruding boulder or shallow sleeper (no suckhole below, just an eddy) occurs on an inside curve, the super-elevated water flowing by it dishes down, like a slide, to meet the eddy. You can use this slide to sideslip off the main current and into the slow, protected water.

Given your sharp left bend and your ferry-left position on the inside of the curve, all you'll have to do is cut close to the rock, then back-ferry hard. You'll slide down off the dished back of the current and hit the eddy fence behind the rock. On a straight stretch of river, that super-elevation could take the form of a near-wall of water—a liquid cliff that

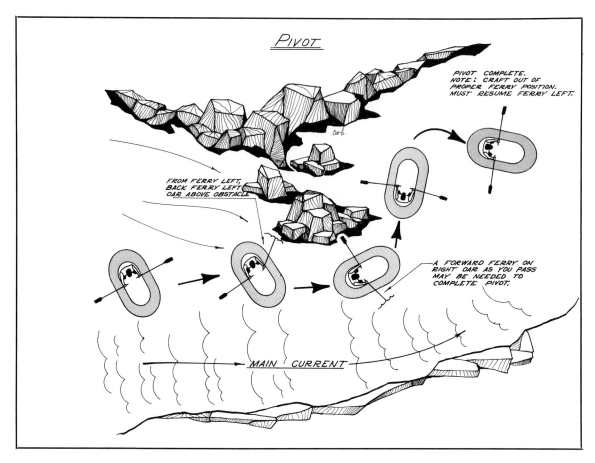

PIVOT

PIVOT COMPLETE.
NOTE: CRAFT OUT OF
PROPER FERRY POSITION.
MUST RESUME FERRY LEFT.

FROM FERRY LEFT,
BACK FERRY LEFT.
OAR ABOVE OBSTACLE

A FORWARD FERRY ON
RIGHT OAR AS YOU PASS
MAY BE NEEDED TO
COMPLETE PIVOT.

MAIN CURRENT

could upset the boat if you tried to slide across it immediately below the rock. When this is the case, don't try to cross the eddy fence until you're far enough below the elevated water to achieve a smooth transition.

Crossing the Eddy Fence Crossing the eddy fence takes a little doing too. Water on one side of the shear line is moving fast downstream. Behind the rock there will be a slow upstream flow.

If you cross the line under free drift, the boat will spin like a pinwheel. Another important rule of whitewater work: *You must maintain correct ferry position at all times.*

In this situation—crossing an eddy fence from the right—the ferry-left position is the correct attitude. To keep the boat from spinning, you'll have to back-ferry rapidly on your right oar. Depending on the severity of the upriver current filling behind the eddy, your left oar requirements might be light back-ferry, stand fast or light forward-ferry. The

important thing is to maintain your raft's orientation as you cross the eddy fence, and to accomplish this, the need for expert oar handling can't be emphasized enough.

Using Discontinuities Current discontinuities are common in any swift water, and they're not always obvious. The only way to keep your raft in position and under control is through an ability to work your oars independently of each other, including tricks like feathering and knowing where to find the best bite.

Water flows at different speeds, and sometimes even in different directions, at different depths in the river. In a normal, unobstructed flow, the fastest water will be inches from the surface, the slowest water will be near the bed.

It follows, then, that a back ferry will be more effective the deeper you dig your blade. It's purely a matter of the blade finding the most resistance down there.

50

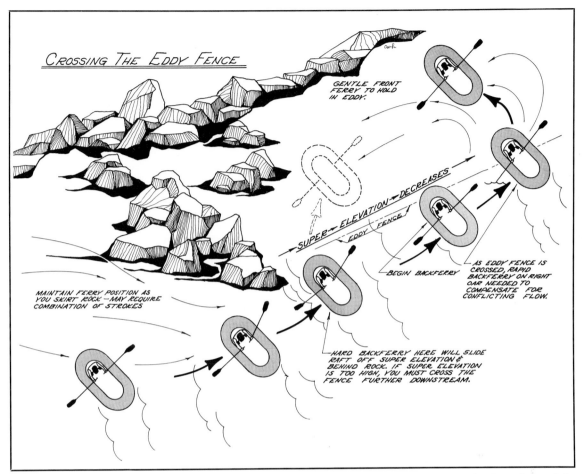

CROSSING THE EDDY FENCE

GENTLE FRONT FERRY TO HOLD IN EDDY.

SUPER ELEVATION DECREASES

EDDY FENCE

BEGIN BACKFERRY

AS EDDY FENCE IS CROSSED, RAPID BACKFERRY ON RIGHT OAR NEEDED TO COMPENSATE FOR CONFLICTING FLOW.

MAINTAIN FERRY POSITION AS YOU SKIRT ROCK — MAY REQUIRE COMBINATION OF STROKES

HARD BACKFERRY HERE WILL SLIDE RAFT OFF SUPER ELEVATION & BEHIND ROCK. IF SUPER ELEVATION IS TOO HIGH, YOU MUST CROSS THE FENCE FURTHER DOWNSTREAM.

Conversely, a forward ferry will be most effective if you keep your blade inches under the surface. By keeping the blade just below the point where it would suck air, you'll get the greatest power for a downstream stroke.

The same rules apply to turning. Digging deep with an oar will turn you most efficiently, if you're pulling back. Running shallow will spin you fastest on a forward stroke.

When the river flows around obstructions, you seldom get into dangerous conditions. It can be a lot of work rowing down a boulder-pocked course, but you always have quiet eddies for a rest.

When water goes over the top of obstructions, however, things get a lot more interesting—and dangerous.

Heavy Hydraulics Big sleepers, breaking holes, falls and suckholes are the next category of whitewater problems. The first thing to consider is that they might not be floatable.

This is one place to stop, look and carefully consider if you should portage or long-line. Look too for a gentler route than right over the top. Often, the very edge of a falls will have a safer run: a series of surges, small sleepers and chutes that will stair-step you down. If so, take that route. Suction holes can often be skirted by flirting around the edge.

If such a route doesn't exist, consider the length of your raft in relation to the drop and the water conditions below. I would call it courting disaster to shoot any drop that's greater than half the length of your raft, and I'd call it wise to reduce that fraction to a third: 4-foot falls for a 12-foot raft.

Look too at the reverse-current suckhole below. There will be a boil downstream of the confused froth where the water divides direction. Below the center of the boil, water will flow downriver. You're asking for trouble if the bow of your raft doesn't reach the center of that boil once you hit bottom and straighten out.

If your appraisal is positive, see now if there is a sufficient volume of water coming down from above to shoot you forward and clear of the cascades, rather than dribbling you over. If it too checks out, get ready to go. But first hear two short stories.

Walt Hodges, Steve Freidah and I were floating the Beartraps at medium-high water in a 12-footer. We came around a stretch of river pockmarked with rocks, out of ferry position and disoriented. Steve was at the oars, and none of us spotted a great boulder, barely under the surface, around which the current split into two swift runs. Thinking the center to be the deepest part of the current, we took that route, and dribbled over a five-foot falls. The boat came close to tipping in the process, but we kept its balance and made the descent. Unfortunately, our forward speed was so slow that our stern didn't get out from under the falls, and hundreds of gallons of water per second came cascading down on our heads. The boat filled immediately, and was trapped in the suckhole behind the rock. We went in, we went out, we went in, we went out, the power of the water scouring us around in the raft. Walt was nearly washed overboard twice, and I broke my favorite fishing rod before we busted loose of the trap.

On a trip down the Middle Fork of Idaho's Salmon River, we made camp above a three-and-a-half-foot falls. It was an exciting place to swim, and all that evening was spent shooting the little falls on air mattresses. Perhaps familiarity bred contempt. Whatever, when we took our boats over it the next morning, the last boat made a poor approach, and the water went over the stern tubes and caught and held the raft. Three people and a great deal of gear were washed overboard, the rest jumped because they couldn't take the beating, and it eventually took all twenty people in the party, pulling on ropes, to break that raft free of the suckhole. The raft, incidentally, was an 18-footer!

In short, falling water isn't to be fiddled with.

To take on falls, you must first line up so the axis (or imaginary keel) of your boat is at a right angle to the falls. As you go over, then down, you'll need the lift of your bow to keep the raft from burrowing under and filling with water. Enter into this position via a hard back ferry. For all practical purposes, the flow of a river will be evenly distributed across a falls, so the right- or left-ferry position to the main current is unworkable. You're in the main current.

Once you're hovering over the slot you deem to provide the best passage, drop your oars and anchor your feet for a mighty forward ferry. At this point, the faster you can get the raft moving downstream, the better your chances of making the passage. A lot of forward momentum is needed to carry you over the crest without dribbling and, when you hit bottom, past the suckhole effect and into the boil.

As you go over, there's not much you can do but hold on and hope. Remember to anticipate a mighty flip that will try to catapult you forward. This occurs as the front half of the raft breaks downward, then your end joins it.

The second your end lands at the foot of the falls, dig your oars in deep and forward-ferry hard. Depending on just how big the falls are, you'll find a downstream current somewhere beneath the surface. Remember that the water on top will be moving into the falls.

Keep rowing hard until you cross the boil and the river is fully reoriented to downstream flow. The one thing you must avoid is getting a gunwale trapped under the falls. Once you're downstream of the boil, assume a right or left ferry depending on your relationship to the current and breathe easy . . . you've made it.

Chutes There will likely be tail waves, suckholes or bank rollers below a narrow, strong chute. These are the problem children, not the chute itself. Since a chute, like a falls, involves no helical current, correct ferry position is parallel to the flow and in the center of

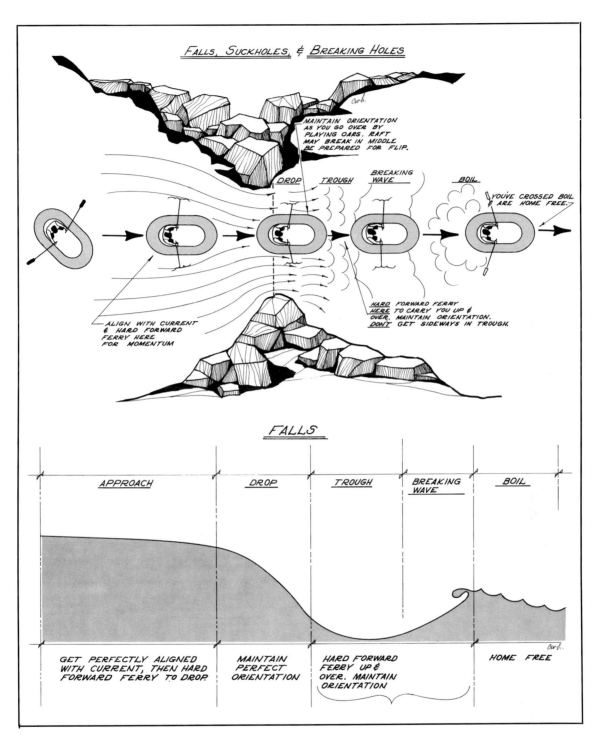

Falls, Suckholes, & Breaking Holes

MAINTAIN ORIENTATION
AS YOU GO OVER BY
PLAYING OARS. RAFT
MAY BREAK IN MIDDLE
BE PREPARED FOR FLIP.

DROP   TROUGH   BREAKING WAVE   BOIL

YOU'VE CROSSED BOIL
& ARE HOME FREE.

ALIGN WITH CURRENT
& HARD FORWARD
FERRY HERE
FOR MOMENTUM

HARD FORWARD FERRY
HERE TO CARRY YOU UP &
OVER. MAINTAIN ORIENTATION.
DON'T GET SIDEWAYS IN TROUGH.

FALLS

APPROACH	DROP	TROUGH	BREAKING WAVE	BOIL

GET PERFECTLY ALIGNED
WITH CURRENT, THEN HARD
FORWARD FERRY TO DROP.

MAINTAIN
PERFECT
ORIENTATION

HARD FORWARD
FERRY UP &
OVER. MAINTAIN
ORIENTATION

HOME FREE

the chute (unless there's something below to dictate a different approach).

A gentle back ferry to slow you and keep you oriented is good insurance going down a chute, but it's not mandatory.

Eventually, you'll be in a position to see what's coming up below. Let's posit it's a series of four-foot-plus breaking tail waves.

The problem with large curls of this type is that too-small boats can't get over their backs. There's an analogy to be made between a raft and a sled on a greased conveyor belt; even though the belt is going up, the sled will slide back. Like the sled, a too-small raft will continue to slide into the trough of really big standing water.

You need a raft so large that the water in back of you will help push you up and over the wave in front of you. If you feel you're in a raft of sufficient size, position yourself by back-ferrying until you're poised in a spot that lines up with the full height of the wave.

Go down the chute with one thing in mind: keeping the raft parallel to the current, so you can take the tail waves bow-on. It will be a much smoother and drier ride if you back-ferry a bit as the raft rises to meet the top of the waves, *so long as they're not too big!* Once you hit the top, stand fast or forward-ferry to get down off the back of the wave. You must maintain steerage as you're sliding down off a wave. If you don't, you're in danger of broaching (being pushed side-to to the next roller). When you reach the bottom of the trough, begin back-ferrying again to meet the next crest if there is one (and there probably will be).

Keep the boat straight as long as you're in the set of rollers and be prepared for a lot of bucking. This is another place where a great deal of flipping and flexing will take place.

Avoid taking water on. The more you ship aboard, the easier it will be for more water to slough in and the more difficult it will be for you to control the boat. A full boat in cresting rollers is an experience you won't soon forget. A dry raft dances above angry water. A swamped raft plows through it. At the mercy of the current, you're thrown rudely about, slapped and smashed by the water. It's a sobering lesson in the power of a river.

Bank Rollers Big bank rollers require skirting, since going through the middle of them might turn you turtle. To get around this towering water, you've got to make use of that sled-on-a-greased-conveyor-belt principle, and keep backsliding until the overall downstream flow of the river carries you on by. This isn't quite as easy as it might seem, as the speed and momentum of a free-floating raft could well be enough to carry the boat up into the licking crest.

As you approach the roller, a hard back ferry is prescribed. If you can slow your downriver progress to a snail's pace, that's just right. Allow the raft to rise up the front of the wave slowly, and hold it there. You will note a slow, lateral drift carrying you around the crest. It's worth mentioning that this maneuver done correctly has an artistic tension about it; you and your boat are poised head to head with towering, crashing water. It seems to take days but in fact takes only a few seconds. Then, slowly, you part. It's really a ballet, not a battle.

As you pass the crest and slide around the back of the wave, you'll probably be confronted with a set of tail or reflex waves immediately downriver. Quickly orient your ferry posi-

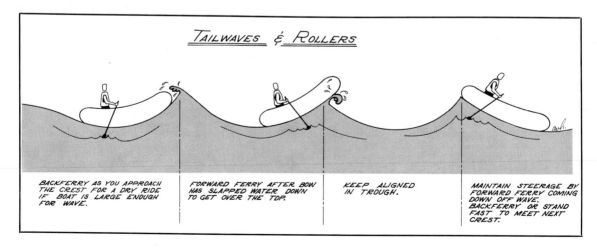

TAILWAVES & ROLLERS

BACKFERRY AS YOU APPROACH THE CREST FOR A DRY RIDE IF BOAT IS LARGE ENOUGH FOR WAVE.

FORWARD FERRY AFTER BOW HAS SLAPPED WATER DOWN TO GET OVER THE TOP.

KEEP ALIGNED IN TROUGH.

MAINTAIN STEERAGE BY FORWARD FERRY COMING DOWN OFF WAVE. BACKFERRY OR STAND FAST TO MEET NEXT CREST.

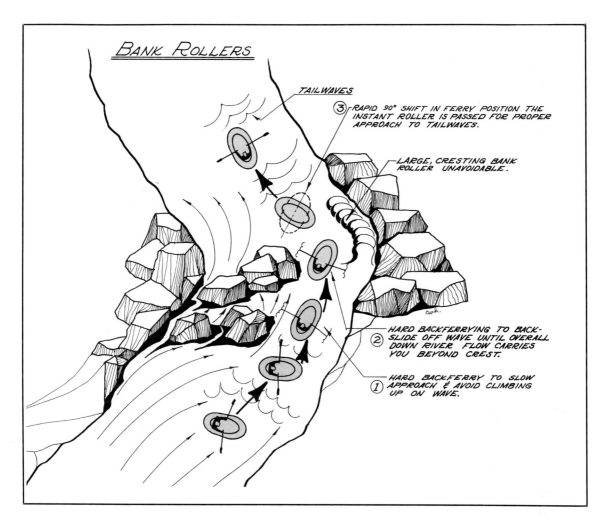

BANK ROLLERS

TAILWAVES

③ RAPID 90° SHIFT IN FERRY POSITION THE INSTANT ROLLER IS PASSED FOR PROPER APPROACH TO TAILWAVES.

LARGE, CRESTING BANK ROLLER UNAVOIDABLE.

② HARD BACKFERRYING TO BACK-SLIDE OFF WAVE UNTIL OVERALL DOWN RIVER FLOW CARRIES YOU BEYOND CREST.

① HARD BACKFERRY TO SLOW APPROACH & AVOID CLIMBING UP ON WAVE.

tion to take them bow-on, as when going through a chute. Which brings me to my next point.

From Theory to Practice

I would say that none of these aforementioned conditions of whitewater, given the right-sized boat, proper equipment and a little savvy on the part of the boatman, are any trouble at all to navigate, *if* you have the time to prepare for them. Time to get into position for a perfect entry into a chute, time to change ferry positions and cross a swift current to get on the inside of a curve, and time to line up with the crest of a shootable falls.

The problem is that often you don't have that time. As a river runs from pool to pool, it carves a whole steeplechase of rocks, chutes, falls and bends that occur staccato. You

come off a wave slightly disoriented, and you miss achieving a perfect ferry position for a sharp bend. That mistake then costs you more position, and like Walt, Steve and I did, you go over an unannounced falls, or smash through the middle of haystacks you should have skirted. This is why length of rapids as well as severity of the water is taken into consideration when rating their difficulty, and it's something for you to consider whenever assessing your ability to run them.

When you feel competent to undertake these heavier-class rapids (Class IV to Class V—if you try Class VI you either know a lot more than I do or are too foolhardy to heed advice anyway), the time has come to consider breaking a few rules . . . sort of.

I have discussed that all-important matter of ferry position in terms of either quartering or paralleling the current. In very bad water, when you're a very good raftsman, it sometimes pays to hold at right angles to the current flow. The purpose and advantage to all this is solely the increased speed at which it allows you to scoot across-current. In a rock garden or fireworks of heaving, crashing water, this cross-current mobility might provide the way to pick out a smoother, though twisted, path through the gentler hydraulics behind major obstacles—the boil behind a suckhole, the eddy behind a dribbling falls or the calm, slow water up against a shallow shore, for example. When vile water is coming up fast and furious, the more normal quarter-ferry position, since you're rowing both up-current and across-current, might be too slow to position you for this kind of slalom, and it's always wiser to go around heavy water rather than through it.

Realize, however, that you still never take heavy rapids side-to if you can help it. At the last, vapor-thin instant, you'll always see such seeming bravado capped by a violent jab at the oars that realigns the boat into a more conventional ferry position before the trough is entered or the haystack directly confronted.

RAFTING MISHAPS

Spills, swamps, people overboard and pinned boats are the piper's dues when you don't pay attention to the river's lively tune. They can have tragic consequences or provide fodder for a lot of laughs once the raft is wrenched free or the man is back aboard. What makes the difference is the same thing that makes a good boatman: learning to work with the river.

Man Overboard A man overboard will probably achieve that state of unwanted grace in bad rapids. If you're the one in the water, don't fight it or even try to swim until you float to calm, well-oriented water. Trying to overcome conflicting currents will wear you out, and you probably won't have any idea where shore is anyway.

Once you reach calm water, swim with the current, quartering toward shore in a downstream direction.

Unless you can pop right back aboard your raft, get clear of it fast. It could squeeze you against a rock, or you could get hit in the head with an oar. Go downstream face first, with legs and arms extended in front of you to ward off possible collisions with a rock. You might pass under the crests of big rollers but don't panic; you'll bob up again on the other side. If you're caught in a suction hole and dragged under, try to swim downstream the minute you pop back up to the surface. If you can't reach the downstream side of the boil, swim to the side of the hole and try for the current there.

If you're the man at the oars and someone goes over, be very careful of your oar blades. Don't try to row until you know exactly where your passenger is. Oars can inflict deep gashes, even knock a man unconscious, should they connect with his head on that fast, above-water arc. Remember too that the man in the water will need help getting aboard, if it is advisable. The best handle to reach for is the scruff of the preserver around the back of his neck.

If everyone gets thrown or washed out of a raft in bad water, stay behind the craft. Don't get pinned between it and a rock. You'd be better off to make for shore and let the raft take care of itself. You'll find it a mile or two downriver at the most. If you are ever pinned to a rock by a raft, the only way out is to go down, pushing up against the entrapping tubes until you slip free.

Swamping A swamped raft is usually the result when you take on a heavy curl—or several of them—sideways. This can also come from getting drawn under falls, being caught in a suction hole or tearing the bottom.

A full boat per se doesn't hurt a thing, but it is potentially very dangerous. Weight is the problem. When a raft fills with water, the water becomes part of the "cargo" of the raft, increasing its weight by hundreds to thousands of pounds. Roll a tennis ball down an incline and you can stop it with your hand. Roll a bowling ball down the same incline and it could well go through a brick wall. This is essentially what happens to the raft; the river is the incline, and the raft no longer has the light weight of a tennis ball. On a sharp bend in the river, it will lumber across-current and into the opposite bank, defying any control. It won't bounce off a rock, but will coarsely brush by it. If there's a sharp edge on the rock, or a snag on the opposite riverbank, the momentum of the raft will tear the material end to end. If you hit a solid wall, the airlocks could well rupture like water-filled balloons. Last, but not least of the worries associated with water-filled rafts: they're easily pinned by the river, a subject we'll discuss in a moment.

Rule number one about water in a raft, then, is get it out. You'll avoid potential grief if you impress this on your passengers, and have them keep the bottom free of any accumulation whatsoever. You'd be amazed at the ballasting effect two bailing cans of water in the bottom of your raft will have.

Should you take on a great deal of water, your only out is to get to shore or some backwater where the water can be bailed out. If you take the water on a curl, tell your passengers to be very careful about sitting or stepping on the floor of the raft. You've got tremendous weight that makes you float lower in the water, and mammoth potential energy. I've seen very bad bruises to the spine when someone sat in the bottom of a full raft and was bumped hard by an underwater rock. From the raft's point of view, this is one of the major causes of a bottom being ripped out.

Falls or suckholes are even worse because the reverse current can keep you there forever. You go in and out, around and around, getting a fresh dousing of new water on each pass.

Should you get caught in this unfortunate merry-go-round and can't row your way out, get all movable weight downstream of the hole, drop your oar blades deep and hold on. You might make five to ten more passes, but chances are quite good that the underwater

currents working against your oar blade will eventually swirl you free. Remember, it's the water on top that's going backwards. Several feet under the surface, the river is still flowing downstream. If you can't find an "out" by digging deep, pull to the edge of the suckhole and try to get out by crossing the eddy fence.

If you feel it's impossible to get the raft out by oar power, you've got to get a rope from the raft to shore. By this time your buddy raft should be on the scene; tie a rope to your painter and cast it shoreward.

Once you get a line to shore, if the passengers can safely get out of the hole, it's best that all but one leave the raft. They'll be needed to pull on shore, and they'll lighten the load on the raft. In pulling the raft free, you'd be wise to take a dally around a tree or rock to take up and hold the slack you gain. The raft will exert a steady, determined pull to get back into that hole until it reaches the top of the boil where the waters divide direction.

Once it does reach that point, the man on the dally must take in any slack that develops. Don't forget, that raft weighs a great deal, and once it gets moving, it could drag everyone on shore along with it. It must be snubbed up to something very strong and solid.

It is conceivable that you won't have enough people in your party to pop the raft free. The pull will simply be greater than your combined effort. In this case, the only alternative is to cut the bottom of the raft. A three-foot-long slice will allow some of the water to drain out, the airlocks will float the raft up, and it will be light enough to wrench out of the hole.

Pinning on a Rock A pinned raft is probably the ultimate hassle you'll run into on a river. It happens when you hit a big midstream rock at right angles to the current and amidships, or when you wander across the current line on a bend and find yourself on the outside of the curve. Your raft is then held in place by the push of the current. This isn't a disaster if your troubles don't go beyond this point. Immediately, get all passengers on the downstream or obstacle side of the raft.

At first glance, this appears to be a man marooned on a rock. Look closely: there's a fully inflated 18-foot raft buried under the upstream swell.

The same raft on top, and about to be pulled free—after the bottom has been cut out. Note the difference in the progress of the sun. This was a two-hour undertaking.

A classic can-up in an innocent-looking suckhole. The approach is good but . . .

. . . the carry-through isn't, and the raft broaches. The suction effect takes over, the raft fills and unlashed gear begins to go (note the buddy boat in the background).   *Photos by N. Strung*

The buddy boat wisely skirts the hole as passengers look on in wide-eyed wonder. Swamped raft begins to be scoured and passengers are having trouble staying in. Note the boatman trying to move gear. The right move, but a little late. *Photo by N. Strung*

The last resort: a long-line to shore as a few diehard passengers hang tough. It took twelve on the rope to pop the raft free. *Photo by N. Strung*

Next, *very* carefully, shift all weight to one downstream corner of the craft. If this extra resistance to the current doesn't drift you loose, try prying with oars. Another ploy— *if it looks safe*—is to get into the water and lift/push the unweighted end of the raft upriver and out.

All these tricks are designed to create more resistance to the river on one side of the raft than on the other. When you exceed the balance the current has established, the raft will spin free.

This is not the case when the raft becomes pinned: when water gets over the upstream gunwale and literally wraps the raft around the obstruction. When this happens, you'll learn yet another sobering lesson in the power of a river.

I was in a buddy boat when just this thing happened to another raft. We were on Montana's Flathead when the boat below us went up on a rock in *Bonnie and Clyde* slow

motion. It slowly flexed, bottom down, and people were washed out like chaff in a breeze. Two oak oars lashed to the side of the raft bent like spring steel, undulating and vibrating in response to the current. Then they snapped with a bang like a rifle shot, their ends splintered like crude brooms.

Gear was next; first the little items that were foolishly wedged here and there rather than lashed down floated away—a camera bag, someone's lunch, a six-pack of pop. Then the lashings themselves submitted to the unrelenting persuasion of the river. Black bags, ammo cases and the platform strung out from the stern of the raft like a necklace of odd seashells. It was a memorable jackpot.

Not only is getting pinned on a rock a destructive mess, it's the toughest of all situations to extricate the raft from. Should an airlock break, there's a good chance you'll never get the raft off the rock; the per-square-inch pressure that's being applied by the river to the fabric of the raft adds up to a herculean total. By way of an educational experience, try dipping the gunwale of even a small raft underwater sometime. The strength of three men, pushing in exactly the same spot, will just about do it. Now consider that the river is holding around half the inflated raft in its grip . . . and that's just a little pinch when compared to the water's full potential.

There are two shots you've got at getting the raft free. The first and easier is to try to pull it over. Although parts of airlocks might be submerged, they're still trying to push upward—the river is just pushing down harder. If you can get a rope on the upper gunwale and pull it hard upriver, you might be able to tip the raft upside down and overcome the balance that is keeping the raft under. If the raft is going to come, it will, and quite suddenly, flipping over, shooting upward and snapping back into raft-like shape in a shower of spray. When this happens, it's perfectly permissible to feel a sense of triumph and relief.

If it doesn't come after a few sincere tugs, you might as well save your energy for the next step, which is cutting the bottom of the raft. This is tricky business because it usually must be done by a man underwater, and to get underwater, he must cast off his life jacket. Life ropes are a must.

When working with a life rope underwater, never tie it securely to your body, and never use any kind of slipknot that is self-tightening. A bowline knot, with the loop snugged in the crook of your arm, is one safe option.

A second danger lies in the fact that the man will have a knife in his hand and will be buffeted about by currents. The wisest way to go about this task is to make several dry runs without a knife to get the feel of the current, to get the feel of where you'll cut and to work out safety signals with your rope men.

When it's time to cut, make the incision near whichever end is pinned the worst. Cut the bottom close to the submerged gunwale, but not so close that you won't have enough of an edge to make a stout repair. A cut two or three feet long should do the trick, though if the raft still refuses to pull over, you'll have to lengthen it.

The raft will probably have to be tugged loose from a shore position. Try to pull it in such a way that the river helps at the task. Make sure the rope is latched on to a strong tie-down point. The rowing brace will be the strongest, though the location of the raft might preclude this as a practical point. D rings rate as a weak point of attachment.

If you still can't get the raft off, wait for lower water and return when it occurs (lowest water is generally mid-August to mid-September). You might also notify the authorities (Forest Service, landowner, etc.) that the raft belongs to you and that you intend to come back for it.

RAFT REPAIR AND CARE

With the exception of air valves, rafts have no moving parts. They float on water, and except for an occasional brush with a rock or a beach, their tough skin experiences little abrasion. In short, it's impossible for a raft to "wear out"—at least in the conventional sense.

They can have a rather short life span, but their demise will be not so much from use as from weathering and improper storage.

You can very nearly see the life being leached out of a raft's supple skin on a scorching August day; light and heat are assaulting the craft from every direction. The problem isn't too acute when you're under way, since water is constantly slapping aboard, cooling the skin, while waves are flexing it. But a day spent at rest under a strong sun is damaging. Try to keep your raft in the shade whenever practical.

Over-inflation is another destructive situation, and it can be caused by the sun. When you pump a raft up to the proper pressure (one to three pounds per square inch, depending on construction), the air inside the craft will be relatively cool. Leave the raft in the sun, and the air warms and expands, stretching seams and locks. This is a particularly thorny problem, for if you let air out of the raft while it's hot to get it back down to the proper pressure, the reverse will happen as soon as you get on the river. Splash and spray will cool the skin and the air inside, and it will contract to a point below optimum, leaving you with a mushy, hard-to-control raft that's prone to snag on a crease if given the opportunity. Frankly, I'm at a loss to remedy this problem. I just try and live with it and make a lot of adjustments.

Water can damage your raft over a long period of time, and the most overlooked source of that water is your air pump. Most rafts transpire air in small amounts and you have to keep readjusting pressure from the cool morning to the hot afternoon. If you leave your pump in the bottom of the raft, the water that always accumulates there will find its way into the compression chamber, and will be transferred to the inside of the raft as you pump it up.

The interior of a raft's airlock can assimilate small amounts of water, absorbing it as humidity that escapes when you deflate the raft. But there is a point where the trapped air will no longer accept more moisture—the dew point—and if it is reached, moisture will remain inside the locks after the raft is deflated. This moisture will not dry out if you merely expose the raft to the sun; the raft must be pumped up, the air warmed by the sun, then the raft must be deflated, and the process continues until the inside of the locks are dry. If you don't do this, your raft will eventually be damaged. The best cure is prevention: either dry your pump out before using it or store it in a place where it can't get wet.

When storing a raft between floats, put it away dry. Let it lie in a breeze until there are no more wet spots. Check carefully along the crease between the gunwale and the raft bottom for stones and sand, then roll it up loosely. If you have room, store it partially inflated.

Be very careful about creases. They are unavoidable in certain spots, but checking

and cracks will always appear first along a prominent crease.

You'll prolong the life of your raft if you rub it down liberally with talcum powder before you retire it for long periods of storage. Talcum powder helps inside the tubes, too. You can spoon it in, with the valves unscrewed and the raft partially deflated. Reinflate the raft, close the valves, and shake the raft vigorously.

Keep the raft in a cool, dry place; an unheated basement is excellent. You're also miles ahead if you'll suspend the raft from a ceiling beam rather than storing it in reach of rats and mice.

Repairing Damage

Raft repair will be a subject confronting you someday. As a beginner, I had a rather rude awakening on my first midstream repair job. While I did exhibit enough sense to bring a repair kit, it was one of those tire-and-rubber-wader things with postage-stamp-size patches, and the tear in my raft was better than a foot long!

I did get the job done, but only after unbending a fishhook for a needle, unwinding a few feet of fishing line for cross-stitching, then cementing a crazy quilt of patches across the tear. Since then I bring more substantial equipment.

For any sort of repair, the area around the patch must be clean and dry. Lighter fluid and carbon tetrachloride are excellent cleaning agents. After cleaning, the contact area should be abraded. You should use coarse emery cloth for this, but I've found a rough, clean river rock works in an emergency. Rub the area hard until any shine the material has is gone and the surface is rough and pebbly. Do the same with your patch.

The next step depends on the nature of the repair. If It's a tiny rip in the bottom—less than three inches long—you won't have to reinforce it. A rip longer than that, however, will have to be stitched up. The stitching isn't so much for strength as for an even mating of the ripped material; a properly applied patch is fifty times stronger than sewing thread. Make your stitches about an inch apart, and knot each stitch so it has independent strength (the lock stitch is best).

Cut two patches that span the rip three inches on all sides, and spread contact cement liberally on one side of the raft bottom and one side of a patch. When the cement dries to a point where it's tacky, line the patch up perfectly, then let it drop into place, rolling any bubbles out with your hand as you go. Next, repeat this cementing procedure on the opposite side of the raft bottom, pressing both pieces against each other. There is far more strain on a raft bottom than on a raft air-lock, so all this reinforcement is necessary. Once the patches are in place, your repair is made.

A large rip in the airlock needs stitching, but opposing patches are impossible. Deflate the punctured lock if the rip hasn't done it already, and apply to the outside of the skin a patch that spans each side of the rip by three inches.

A slow leak is usually the result of checking or creasing. This is better tended to at home. You can find the leak (probably an extensive pinholed area) by going over the inflated raft with a strong solution of soap and water. The leaks will make bubbles.

When you identify the area, wash the soap off completely and prepare the section as for a patch. Contact cement or aluminized paint can be painted on to seal the holes. Better yet is neoprene cement, used to hold wet suits together. You can buy this at sporting-goods stores that cater to skin divers. Pinhole leaks are a sign of age, so consider buying a new raft.

PACKING A RAFT

Keeping Gear Dry

Whether you plan to go camping on your float or just to make a day of it, there will surely be some items you'll want to keep dry— camera equipment, lunch, your pump and perhaps a change of clothes.

The simplest and cheapest way to keep water off your dry goods is to store things in plastic bags. Find the toughest plastic you can, twist the top tightly and seal it, then slide that bag, twisted end first, into a second bag. Twist this and seal it.

Chances are this will keep the contents dry so long as you lash the package up high, out of the bottom of the raft. Note, I said "chances." If you swamp, it'll leak, and any plastic rips easily, so I'd never keep water-damageable equipment inside plastic—a fine camera, for instance.

Camera Protection Most manufacturers make waterproof protective cases for their cameras. The camera must be removed from the case to take a picture, restricting the pho-tographer to relatively dry conditions, but at least with this sort of protection you won't have to worry about where your camera is every time you take a wave.

Waterproof housings—sealed cases through which pictures can be shot—are also available, though these units often cost as much as the camera.

Nikon makes a 35-mm Nikonis model with a fixed 35-mm lens (creating a moderate wide-angle effect). This camera is fully water-proof and may be used as is, under or above water.

Positive protection for other gear exists in the form of black bags and ammo cases.

Black Bags "Black bags" were invented for Navy frogmen, who had to keep equip-ment dry for long periods of time underwater. They come in several different sizes and shapes, ranging in dimensions from a pocket-book-sized package up to a bag the size of a backpack. The container part of the bag is stiff, thick black rubber. It is rectangular, with reinforced corners. The top of the bag has a long, tube-like apron of cloth-backed rubber bonded to the stiff bag. There is also a strong black rubber flap attached to the back of the rectangular bag.

After gear is packed inside, the tube-like apron seals at the top a little like a modern plastic zipper bag. The apron is then rolled up tightly, and the flap is cinched over it with webbed belting. The larger black bags also have webbed shoulder straps for easy portaging.

That they keep gear dry was proven several years ago when a friend's boat got caught in a suckhole. A lot of gear was washed out, including a black bag that was lost. Other raftsmen found it floating in a backwater a week later and returned it. Its contents were bone dry.

Black bags aren't easy to find these days. They're surplus items, so one place to start looking is an Army-Navy surplus store—if you can find one of *them* that still deals in honest-to-God war surplus. I located one of the several I own in a small sporting-goods store in the Midwest, of all places. The owner didn't know what the bag was for and said it had been lying around for years, so it's worth casual inquiry in any logical place, no matter how vague the connection with rafting.

As of the writing of this book, Base Camp, 121 West San Francisco Street, Santa Fe, New Mexico, had small black bags in stock (8″x8″x12″) for $12.00 each, and they listed "other waterproof containers for river running at somewhat lower prices," though I can't say exactly what they were.

Ammo Cases Ammo cases are the other waterproof packing cases that receive my stamp of approval. Like black bags, these are surplus items, originally used to keep ammunition dry.

They're made of steel and have a rubber sealer on their top lip. The lid of the case swings on a piano hinge, and the latch is a lever-type affair that forces the lid tightly down over the lip. Water cannot get into these boxes, and they're virtually undamageable. They come in sizes from approximately that of a lunch box up to that of a portable TV.

I tend to lean toward ammo cases as the better packing medium because they're easy to lash down (just tie on to their handles) and because you can get into them with a snap of that latch, without any unlashing. But they are heavy and bulky to carry, so if I know I'll be doing a lot of portaging, I'll use black bags.

This is yet another area where a rowing brace becomes essential. It functions as something solid and substantial to lash gear to. Without that firm anchor, boxes and bags will be tossed about, very possibly injuring someone. If you're using a pipe frame, you'll have to use black bags for packing, since your cargo will be in the bottom of the raft, and a hard, heavy, steel box on the floor is an open invitation to a rip. A brace with a deck will accommodate ammo cases, and quite ideally.

Stowing and Lashing

To carry cargo in the bottom of the raft (beneath a pipe brace), string your black bags underneath the pipe upon which the oarsman sits. It's the most out-of-the-way place. If there is more gear than will fit there, use the forward brace for a tie-down, but make sure the location of the bags doesn't interfere with footwork. Distribute weight evenly, and lash each item with its own separate knot. This will prevent a large shift in the placement of your cargo, and should the bags go overboard, they won't string out like pearls.

To pack a platform, keep the profile low so there's no tendency to be top-heavy, and make sure your placement of gear doesn't interfere with your oarwork. My favorite packing arrangement is to make a little hill across the stern with the tallest box in the middle. This acts as a spray shield to ward off heavy water from the stern quarter.

Distribute weight evenly, and make sure your gear isn't so heavy that it buries your rear tubes. If your stern draws more water than one third the diameter of your tubes, you'll have trouble back-ferrying. Realize too that you can keep gear under the platform as well as on top of it, though the stuff stowed there must be soft, like black bags. Don't pack this space too tightly either. The bottom must be free to rise. If gear stowed underneath the platform is so tight that it gets caught between the bottom of the raft and the bottom of the platform, you're asking for a bad tear on the first sleeper you encounter.

Lash each item individually, and cinch down the gear on the platform tightly so it can't shift. If you think you'll need certain items while under way, don't forget to leave one box or bag accessible without undoing all your lashings, and stow your immediate needs in that. Flip-top ammo cases are perfect for goods that must stay dry. For wettable gear like ropes, repair kits, sunglasses, suntan oil, hats, etc., I lash a backpack to the top of the mound of gear. Its many pockets are like a filing cabinet!

RIVER CAMPING AND TOURING

Some people are of the persuasion to climb a mountain "because it's there," to hunt for a deer whose horns will rate high on some human-contrived scale or even to float whitewater for some imaginary badge of wilderness accomplishment.

I'm not of that persuasion. In my system of values, these things are important only when they're part of a grander scheme, a glorious whole, like packing up that mountain to camp and fish a lake at its top, or hunting a deer with stealth, knowledge, love, and for a finer purpose—meat for food, hide for clothing and then perhaps his horns and hooves for decoration. In this same vein, rafting a river is always more memorable when it involves more than going downstream.

There is no better way to do a river than to combine your float with a camping trip. You get to know a river from all sides—ashore, afloat, as it gently swirls by during the black night, and fresh with dew and the first rays of sunlight in the early morning.

Since it isn't the intent of this book to be a camping manual, you should be familiar with camping basics—fire lays and safety, campfire cooking, sleeping equipment, shelter and so forth—before trying an overnighter. Beyond these skills that are common to virtually every campsite, there are some specific requirements for raft camping that make it an art unto itself.

What to Bring

Equipment will prove most satisfactory and practical if you choose it along the spare lines of the backpacker. Not only is this gear light and compact, it's well integrated, with many pieces of equipment doing several jobs (metal dining plates that double as fry pans, or stuff bags that can be filled with your clothes and used for a pillow, for example). This lightness counts when you have to portage and when you pack your craft. The amount of weight you can carry is not limitless. There's also a sense of organization inherent in backpacking gear, a quality of "a place for everything and everything in its place." This is essential on any water, up to and including the ocean. "Shipshape" is the definitive term.

It is absolutely essential that you make waterproof provisions for at least one set of clothing, your sleeping bag and your food (black bags or ammo cases). If you run into cool, wet weather, that change to dry clothes in the evening will be the high point of the day. And you need plenty of food and a comfortable, warm night's sleep to be ready for tomorrow. You will find rowing all day to be energy-sapping work—and a sure cure for insomnia, I might add.

Pack a maximum amount of food. If you're used to three meals a day, plan for that. Don't count on catching fish or picking berries for a meal. Nature is a notoriously fickle provider in a pinch. If the fishing is good, and the berry patch brimming with fruit, count it as a bonus and enjoy.

Make careful inquiry as to the quality of the water. Although you'll see billions of gallons of the stuff, it might not be safe to drink. Diarrhea is a miserable companion on a camping trip. Don't overlook the possibility of feeder streams being pure. If so, you'll have to know their location and make plans to camp by them. Aside from carrying your own water (which is a bother, to put it mildly), you can also boil river water to purify it, or use purification tablets, if safe natural water isn't available.

Camping

The campsite will be most pleasant if you locate it in a backwater of some sort. Landing and loading will be easier than in a swift current, and you'll have a quiet place to swim, wash clothes, wade or whatever. The bottom there will also likely be sandy or of a finely graded gravel, another plus when you have to walk in the water.

When picking a backwater campsite, make sure you're not camping next to a swamp; the bugs will be intolerable. A site that catches the breeze will discourage insects.

There is no finer feeling underfoot (and to your body) than fine river sand. If you can find it high on a bar and thoroughly dry, that's the place to pitch your tent, and the safest location to build your fire.

You might consider bringing along sand spikes (wide, tapered spikes) for tent pegs. When you build your fire, don't line the pit with wet river rocks; they're likely to explode.

Pull your craft well up onshore and tie them to something solid that won't float away should the river rise during the night. Along these same lines, be aware of the chance for sudden and rapid river rises when you're floating downstream of a dam. Always camp above the high-water mark on these rivers, and anchor your boat there.

Planning the Float

Planning should be meticulous for a float camping trip. Buy topographical maps of the area you'll be covering and ferret out any additional information that might be available. Obtain any necessary permits.

Know well the conditions you'll encounter on the float, and pick the places you'll camp each night, plan how long you'll be on the river each day, and tell someone when you'll be out. A particularly comforting piece of knowledge to have under your belt is the location and direction of the nearest trail to the river— just in case you end up walking out.

Being on the river for several days dictates a near fastidious approach when matters of

common sense arise. Double-check the advisability of taking on what appear to be bad rapids. Losing it all forty miles in is a very different matter from dumping halfway through a day-long float. Always travel with a buddy boat or two, or three, and keep all your gear tightly lashed.

By implication it might appear that I'm accentuating the negative, but that's not really the case. I've been in my share of jackpots, on, in and under the water, and if I've learned any lesson from my mistakes it's this: When you're on the river, if you're prepared for the worst, the best will emerge quite naturally— and be abundant.

FISHING

Like camping, the art of angling is too broad a subject to cover here, but there are some observations of benefit to the raftsman.

Tackle

Equipment can't be of tackle-shop proportions. A medium-weight "trail rod" amounts to the most practical fishing rod. This class of rod breaks down into four to six ferruled sections, and an eminently stowable package 15 to 24 inches long. This is an important advantage in that the easy-packing rod can be kept out of the way, safe from breakage and the danger of becoming entangled with passengers when you're navigating rapids.

Trail rods are available as spinning rods, fly rods, or spin/fly combinations. If you're an all-around fisherman, it's this latter type I'd recommend because of the latitude it affords.

A six- to eight-ounce spinning reel amounts to the midrange class that will best handle the sport fish (trout and smallmouth bass) most likely to inhabit wilderness rivers. Six-pound test is a good all-around monofilament line, though you could buy a second spool for your reel and carry one spool of eight-pound test and one of four-pound test if you really want to be professional.

Two- to three-ounce fly reels will match up nicely to that medium trail rod. As with the spinning reel, consider carrying two spools of fly line: one of a double-taper floating line for fish that are breaking water to feed, the other a weight-forward sinking line for when they're feeding on the bottom (this will be the case about 80 percent of the time).

Lures come in a vast array, but you can pare your needs and their numbers down to a practical level by realizing that fish may occasionally strike from anger, but most of the time they think they're getting a minnow meal. Therefore, stick with those lures that imitate natural-looking minnows: silver-, gold- or copper-colored spoons, spinners and plugs. When it comes to size, large fish will take a small lure, but small fish won't swipe at a big lure. You'll be tempting the broadest base of resident fish if you keep your lures small; I'd say ⅜ ounce at the largest, for the typical river filled with typical fish (you'll have to make exceptions for species like steelhead, sturgeon, catfish and northern pike, but given the "average" river, they're atypical).

Fly patterns exhibit a diversity on a par with spinning lures, though they can be approached with equivalent pragmatics. The lion's share of a river fish's diet consists of the nymphal stages of aquatic insects (nymphs) or minnows. Flies imitative of either food source will catch the most fish under normal conditions. The "woolly worm" pattern, in an assortment of natural colors, can be mistaken by a fish for two dozen aquatic or terrestrial insects. It's a great fish catcher for this reason, and easy to make yourself if you'd like to get into fly tying. The muddler minnow is another catchall pattern that imitates many species of small fish and grasshoppers. As with lures, I favor small flies because they'll tempt the greatest number of fish.

Other equipment you might consider for floating includes a fishing vest and small landing net. A fishing vest is essentially a multi-pocketed tackle box that you wear on your back instead of carrying around in your hand. The net will be handy when you hook a fish from the floating raft and want to get him in the boat without breaking the line or tearing the hook loose. If you'll fish only from shore, you can forget the net and just beach the fish.

Technique

Fishing technique on fast-moving rivers revolves around two facts of fish life: they must eat and they must rest. This means they'll be in one of two places: at the foot of riffles or behind a rock.

While this assertion is a little oversimplified, it is, in fact, the case. When fish are on feed, they will be attracted to the most food-rich place in a river, and that is always the foot of a fast, shallow, bubbly riffle. It is there that aquatic insects find the high oxygen content and gentle waters (next to the bottom) they need to survive. It is there that bait and sport species of fish lay their eggs and where minnows thrive.

Conditioned to this presence of food, larger fish are attracted to these riffles when whatever force it is that controls fish behavior says "eat."

Realize, however, that even larger fish are easily frightened, so they instinctively seek protection as well as food. Because of this secondary behavior characteristic, you'll never find them in the shallow riffle itself, where they're easily preyed upon by eagles, bears or otters. Rather, they'll be in the deep, dark water right at the foot of the riffle. Following this line of thought, they'll be more likely to feed freely if that foot of the riffle is in a shadow. Or if they're protected by the half light of dusk or dawn.

When fish aren't feeding, they're resting. If they were to rest in midstream, they'd spend all their lives swimming against the stiff current and use up more energy than they could consume. So they find calm water to rest in: the hydraulics behind rocks resting on the river bottom, the vertical eddies behind protruding banks or the two-dimensional eddies behind midstream rocks. While they might not be actively feeding from these "lies," by dragging a meal right in front of their noses you might well elicit a response.

When they're on feed, fish the riffles.

When they're off feed, fish the eddies or near the bottom. Save the fast whitewater for floating because the fish won't be there. With that knowledge and a little bit of luck, you'll have trout sizzling in the pan by evening.

GEOLOGY, FLORA AND FAUNA

Active pastimes like camping and fishing have an immediately perceivable appeal and connection with floating. But there are passive experiences moving along with you that contribute subjective dimensions of pleasure.

Knowing something about geology helps you understand the river, for the earth and the water move in a rhythm and harmony equivalent to a river and its bed.

The knife edge of water acting against rock keeps the river ever cutting down. Rainfall and the explosive power of frost contribute to the gradual collapse of sheer walls—lateral erosion. If the bed cuts through limestone, you'll see the results of chemical reaction; water and natural acids dissolve limestone and slowly eat it away, creating pockmarks and honeycombed caves high on cliffs where the river once ran.

If the river has cut through sedimentary rock, you'll be looking at a mirrored wall that reflects to infinity. Ages ago a river laid down those stratified slabs of sediment—fine silt and clays that *it* eroded from higher ground, then dropped as sediment in some quiet lake or Cenozoic sea. Now the river *you're* floating is doing the selfsame thing.

The trees along a river are a vital part of the picture too. High on canyon walls, roots reach deep into frost cracks, eventually prying rocks loose and contributing to the erosion process. A knot of verdant green on an otherwise dry hillside probably signals a spring, deep soil, and a paradox. Simultaneously, the grasses and brush growing there encourage and discourage erosion. Their roots eat into rock and erode it into soil; those same roots hold the soil against the effects of water and wind. Along the riverbank, the tree roots that split rocks apart now hold high

banks in place against the onslaught of high water.

They also provide a stable environment for burrowing and nesting animals—minks, otters, bank beavers, bank swallows and muskrats, not to mention moles, voles, field mice and insects. Eagles live on the high cliffs and prey on rodents and an occasional duck swimming in the river. Herons, otters, ospreys, mergansers and kingfishers prey on the fish. Fish eat smaller fish and aquatic insects. The rocks, the trees and the life that floats by are all connected to the river, and the river to them. Everything moves in cycles upon itself. Recognizing them might not be the most important thing about whitewater floating . . . but then again, it might be the whole trip.

COMMERCIAL FLOATS

One option open to the beginning floater skeptical of his ability, experience and even interest in running whitewater is to take a guided commercial float.

Outfitters ply most major whitewater rivers in this country, offering excursions that run from a day to a week, with prices in the neighborhood of $50 for a day (per party member) to $600 for a week (everything included except sleeping bag and personal items). You can book into one through any travel agent.

Don't get the idea that because these floats are "commercial" they're necessarily tame or posh. You'll eat good food, and the boatmen will do most of the chores, but otherwise the taste of spray and excitement will be identical to a trip you'd mount up yourself.

These guided trips are tremendous learning experiences. You get a firsthand look at how turbulent water behaves . . . and what it can do. The boatmen making these runs are usually delighted to function as teachers too. If you show interest they'll explain just what they're doing and why, and if you show aptitude, they'll probably let you take a turn on the oars, advising you about proper approaches and oar handling as you drift

Guides and outfitters regularly run many of America's best whitewater rivers on a commercial basis. "Commercial" doesn't mean "tame" though. Such operations are a good way to get your first taste of real whitewater . . . safely. *Photo by American River Touring Association*

along. The instruction alone can be worth the price of the trip.

WHITEWATER SCHOOLS

An even better way to get a solid background in running a river is to attend a whitewater school. Courses in whitewater navigation are offered in on-the-river classrooms, and subject matter includes extensive whitewater work as well as attendant river-running activities like camping techniques, river lore and first aid. A few of the larger river outfitters offer this type of instruction, though usually "students" take the course as an understood prerequisite to a job as a guide with that outfitter.

The American River Touring Association (ARTA), 1016 Jackson Street, Oakland, California, 94607, offers a full summer instruction program that comes closest of all to a real "school," with courses keyed to several levels of age, maturity and river experience. Offerings run from a thirty-three-day "Professional River Guide" course ($625, minimum age 19) to "The River Classroom" (two-day trips for $30, minimum age 14), with graded courses for all levels of whitewater interest and expertise in between.

KNOWING THE ROPES

A piece of rope is like a knife, or a flame, or a wheel. A very simple object in appearance which is nightmarishly complex when you delve into all its possible applications.

While a thorough knowledge of rope handling would be of immeasurable benefit to anyone running a river, there are a few twists that are required learning.

Throwing Rope Throwing a rope involves a bit of technique best understood by beginning with a straight piece. As you coil it in your hand, imagine you're wrapping it around a spool. Each circle should be approximately the same size, and you should twist it once for each curl you take in, to keep it from kinking.

The rope should be stored in such a way as to keep it lined up just the way it went into your hand, without coils falling over or working between each other, out of sequence.

When you throw the rope, use your off hand to hold on to the same end (the bitter end) you picked up when you first began coiling it. Hold the coils in your throwing hand, and toss them in a looping, haymaker sort of sidearm throw. The rope will uncoil in the air just as it went onto your hand, the coils closest to you uncurling first, and the line eventually laying out arrow straight.

If you're left-handed, don't try to throw a rope coiled by a right-handed person, and vice versa; you'll end up with a mess like a bird's nest.

Lining & Roping Long-lining around rapids requires snubbing. You should have a bow line and a stern line (for a safety rope), and both lines should be wrapped twice around something solid. The friction of the snubbed rope will give one man grip enough to hold even the heaviest raft against the current. Ease the craft along slowly; generally, it's unwise to let the craft gain momentum. An exception lies in suction holes and any water falling back on itself. There, you need momentum to carry the craft through, and you might also consider pulling hard on the stern line, using the bow line for your safety.

If your line isn't long enough to reach the length of the rapids, you'll need two lines on the bow. When one runs out, snub the second up tight on another solid anchor downstream and ease the raft down from there.

A particularly useful tool in long-lining is a cut pole. If you run into a riverbank protrusion like a tilting snag or boulder, cut a long pole and notch the end. Set the notch into the painter close to the bow, and you'll be able to push the raft out into the current and around the obstacle.

Knots

When working with rope, there are two ends or, more precisely, directions. The working end is the short end—the end you're working to tie the knot. The bitter end is in the opposite direction. The bitter end is not necessarily the other "tip" of the rope; in fact, it can be every inch of the line below the working end. "Running line" refers to that pale area between the bitter end and the working end.

There are eight knots you need to know as a boatman. The first is the slipknot. This is nothing more than a simple bow. It can be used in conjunction with several other knots when a quick release is advisable; for example, use it with a half hitch when you have another craft in tow, or when you have a piece of gear lashed down that you have to get at often, like an ammo case with cameras inside.

Slipknot To tie a slipknot, twist the rope into a loop six inches or more above the working end. Reach through the loop and grasp the running line immediately above the twist. Pull it through the loop and draw it tight. You'll have a bow that can be released with a jerk of the working end.

Double Half Hitch To see the advantage of all this, let's examine two versions of the double half hitch. This is a self-tightening knot used to secure rope to a fastening so the knot doesn't loosen or slip—such as gear to a raft deck. In the double half hitch the working end is wound around the anchor point, then around the running line and then passed through the loop formed. Wind the working end around the running line and pass it through the loop once more, pull it tight and you have a double half hitch. But you also have a knot that takes a lot of worrying to get out. If you'll throw a slipknot into your last hitch, a jerk of the working end will leave you with one half hitch—and easy undoing.

Bowline There are a few other places where the slipknot comes in handy, such as with the modified bowline. A bowline (pro-

71

SLIP KNOT

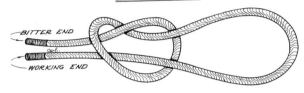

BITTER END

WORKING END

DOUBLE HALF-HITCH WITH SLIP KNOT

DOUBLE HALF HITCH

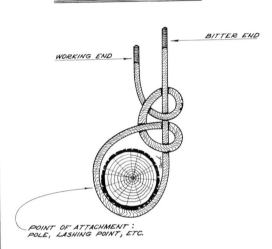

WORKING END

BITTER END

POINT OF ATTACHMENT:
POLE, LASHING POINT, ETC.

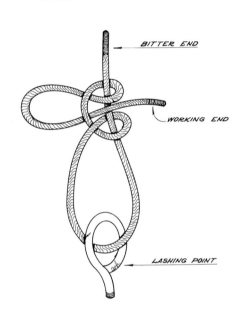

BITTER END

WORKING END

LASHING POINT

MODIFIED BOWLINE

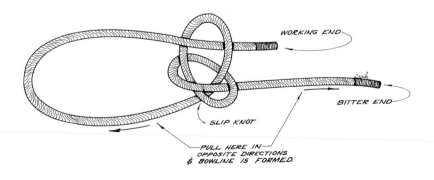

WORKING END

BITTER END

SLIP KNOT

PULL HERE IN
OPPOSITE DIRECTIONS
& BOWLINE IS FORMED.

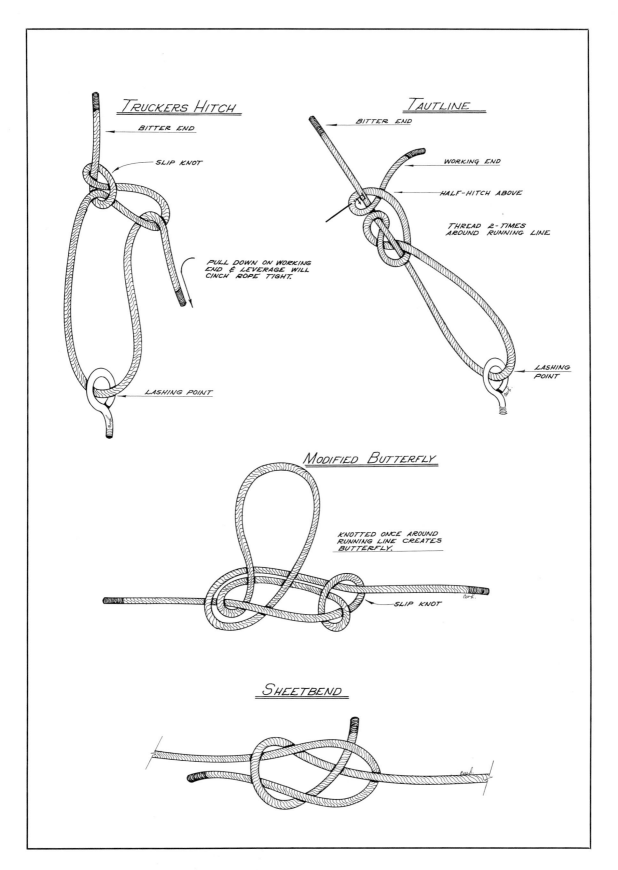

TRUCKERS HITCH

BITTER END

SLIP KNOT

PULL DOWN ON WORKING
END & LEVERAGE WILL
CINCH ROPE TIGHT.

LASHING POINT

TAUTLINE

BITTER END

WORKING END

HALF-HITCH ABOVE

THREAD 2-TIMES
AROUND RUNNING LINE

LASHING
POINT

MODIFIED BUTTERFLY

KNOTTED ONCE AROUND
RUNNING LINE CREATES
BUTTERFLY.

SLIP KNOT

SHEETBEND

nounced bole-in) makes a loop in the working end that will not tighten down on itself. It is used as a safety line for swimmers, as a hand-hold on the end of a painter, as a stepladder, a lashing point and a hundred other things around a boat. To tie a modified bowline ("simplified" would be a better term, as it is the simplest way to do this knot), make a slipknot a foot above the working end. Now insert the working end through the loop. Pull the loop tight by tugging in opposite directions on the running line, and you'll have tied a bowline.

Trucker's Hitch The trucker's hitch requires that you pass the working end through the lashing point, then back up to, and through, the loop of a slipknot. Grab the working end and pull against the slipknot; it gives you leverage to cinch down your lashing as tight as banjo string. Secure the knot by pinching the doubled-over working end at the loop. This will be enough pressure to hold the rope you've gained, so slack doesn't form again. Tie a double half hitch with a slipknot and your tight lashing comes free easily.

Slipknots also can function in a similar way to trucker's hitches anywhere along the length of rope, and here are commonly used as anchors for a web of lashings.

Butterfly If you don't want the slipknot to slip, pass its loop once around the running line from which it hangs, and draw the lashing loop through the double loops thereby formed. This knot, a version of the "butterfly," also may be used as a makeshift ladder.

Tautline The tautline is a sliding knot like the double half hitch, but it binds under tension. It's a good knot for tenting because you can easily adjust for sagging or tight canvas as weather makes it shrink or stretch. It's also good for any lashed load that needs frequent readjustment.

The procedure for tying a tautline is a bit complex, and more easily explained by diagram and trial and error on your part.

The working end is first passed under the bitter end at a convenient point above the lashing, then wrapped twice around the run-

ning line below the loop formed. A half hitch is then thrown above the existing knot configuration.

The principle is to thread a knot that angles down and binds when tension is put on the bitter end of the rope. It is a simple knot to tie—once you learn it. But the learning is the earning. Get yourself a piece of rope, a patient moment, and practice. It's worth it all; you'll find dozens of uses for this knot.

Sheet Bend The sheet bend is the most practical knot for linking two rope ends. It's as strong as any joining knot and comes apart easily. It is best understood as two interlocking loops. In your hands, loop the working ends of both lines to be joined and consider the pattern that would bind them thus. Hold one loop firm and thread the working end of the second rope through it, over the working end of the first loop and under the running line of that loop—the one you're holding stationary in your hand. Now bring it back through the stationary loop, parallel to the running line.

When you can do all these knots from memory, you're learning the ropes.

THE SHUTTLE SHUFFLE

There are a put-in point and a take-out point on every float, and when you reach the take-out point, you're going to have to have some means of transportation waiting. Getting your car or truck there is called the shuttle.

Experience has shown the wisdom of making the switch before you cast off. When you get off the river, even after a day's outing, everyone will be tired and beaten by the sun or the cold and damp, depending on how your weather karma held out. Waiting around for someone to pick you up, then going through the process of retrieving your vehicle, will prove a tedious hassle.

There are a number of ways you can make this switch. If your party has only one car, one person can drive to the take-out point and hitch back to the put-in point. Times being what they are, the advisability of this approach is questionable. You could stand with outstretched thumb for hours—perhaps all day—without getting a ride. If this is your only choice, look like a floater (like with cutoffs and a life jacket around your neck), or carry a fishing rod; ''floaters'' or ''fishermen'' are more acceptable passengers than a non-identifiable stranger on the side of the road.

You might also consider hiring a second car to make the switch, or hiring both a car and driver. Shuttle drivers are quite common along popular float rivers. Make inquiries at the local barbershop, bar or tackle shop.

Another possibility is to carry a small motorcycle with you, drop off the car and drive the bike back to the launch. You'll obviously have to return to the launch at the end of the float to pick up the bike, as will be the case when you bring two vehicles.

LAUNCHING

Getting your raft off a bar or rocky landing takes a special touch that you might have to explain to others. In most cases, it's advisable that you remain on the oars during the launch.

First, make sure that the raft bottom isn't hung up on anything. Get your passengers to sit on the tubes, with weight off their feet.

To get you off, the bow man must lift and push from shore, then leap into the bow once the raft is drifting free. It requires a little savvy and a lot of commitment. Once the boat is free and moving, the slice of water between boat and mate grows wide in a hurry, but once you get the knack the jump is dry and easy.

If there's difficult water downriver, you'll have to pivot the boat quickly to get into ferry position. You'll get the quickest pivot by turning the bow upstream, then into the river, even though you're turning nearly 270 degrees versus 90 degrees. This is because of the slower water next to shore; your stern will tend to drag as your bow catches the faster midstream current and you whirl around.

As you swirl away from the shore and ease into ferry position, try your oars on for size, turning the boat right and left, digging for slow water, then rising into the swift stuff. Feel their response and the water moving under you. You're in the saddle of a spirited horse, your oars are wired to the surges and eddies. There are colors to dazzle you, smells and sounds to delight you, and the air is cool and moist all around. Feel it, know it, get with the river.

Now you're rafting!

3 CANOEING
by Sam Curtis

Sam and Sue Curtis on the Gallatin River, Montana.   *Photo by Peter Bennett*

Morning has taken the chill from the air as you paddle lazily with the current, feeling your muscles limber in the sun. You're with the river now, silently passing a water ouzel who does his bobbing dance on a mossy rock. The trees move past in a line that becomes a curve.

Then the sound of wind rises; an involuntary shiver alerts your lulled senses to what's ahead.

The sound is water and it grows as you round the bend. A hundred yards ahead, the rapids. You scan the water, the rocks, the subtle slicks, waves and eddies. It'll go. The lip approaches and you're in it, stomach ballooning in your mouth, paddle doing what you've taught it to.

These sensations are a part of the lure of river running—the tug of resistance against your paddle, the cold spray on your skin, the montage of rocks, trees and sky etched against the insistent flow of water. To the uninitiated, these gut-level feelings must seem to be the essence of whitewater.

Experienced rivermen know better.

The sensations are there all right, but they build upon one another to form an experience that goes beyond mere sensuousness. A chord is struck that speaks to your instinct for harmony. You aren't an alien intruder bent on conquering a wild force; you become part of that force.

The desire to *work with* moving water is ingrained in every whitewater boater, but his craft too has to be compatible with the river.

It was primitive man who first sensed this need for harmony, and the evolution of the canoe reflects his desire to make a craft that responded to the rivers he ran.

Those first canoes were not the sleek craft we know today. The wooden dugout, although refined over the years, started as an ungainly flotation device that allowed its builder to ride on water without getting completely wet—one step removed from swimming. But primitive man wasn't dumb, and he dug out a dugout again. The process wasn't easy, considering he chopped, burned and scraped the innards out of cedar logs fifty to sixty feet long.

Yet each new log he hollowed added to the refinement of his new mode of transportation. He learned that by tapering the bow and stern, he could make his craft glide through the water more easily and with less splash. In order to make his canoe more stable, he came up with the idea of widening its beam. By filling the dugout with water, then heating it with fired rocks, he was able to stretch the wet and pliable wood outward on each side. Stout pieces of wood were then wedged from one side to the other to keep them spread in the desired position.

At its most advanced stage of development the dugout resembled the canoes of today, but it had a major drawback. It was heavy. If a man wanted to catch his supper from a river two miles overland from home, he couldn't carry his canoe.

The need for mobility resulted in the development of skin and bark canoes. Instead of building the entire craft of one piece of wood, a frame was fashioned with light pieces of wood and covered with animal skins or bark. Bark became popular in North America because the forested land provided the material needed for building and repair. The frame was made of cedar and was bound together with spruce roots. Roots were also used to stitch the bark of birch, elm or spruce tightly over the frame. Then spruce resin was applied to the stitching to make it watertight.

The bark canoe of the American Indian developed into many shapes and sizes depending on the practical needs of its owner. Small shallow-draft canoes were used in quiet waters for hunting and fishing and where frequent portages were necessary. In large, open lakes and along the coast, bigger canoes with high sides were employed.

I'm sure there are some Indians gliding through the waters of the Happy Hunting Grounds wearing a smug grin because the bark canoe was the craft that eventually opened much of the vast wilderness of the North American continent. It was the workhorse for that once booming business called the fur trade.

The classic two-man bark canoe was the miniature prototype for the North and Montreal canoes that traveled the waterways of the Canadian fur-trading routes during the 1700's and the 1800's. The Montreal canoes with their 36-foot length and 6-foot beam could carry cargoes of three tons and were well suited to the big water of the Great Lakes. But they were too large for the smaller waterways of the North Country. There the 25-foot North canoes came into play.

Voyageurs in Montreal canoes, laden with supplies and trading goods, would shove off from Montreal and work their way to Grand Portage on the western end of Lake Superior. The North canoes were filled with prime pelts from the rich fur country of Lake Athabasca, in what is now northeastern Alberta, and were paddled, lined and portaged to their rendezvous with the *voyageurs* from the east. Here the furs were exchanged for supplies after a combined journey that had taken the men three thousand miles across Canada.

It was during this period that canoes earned their place in the history of the frontier, and many of us think of the passing of that era with regret. Yet the water remains.

The vast chains of rivers and lakes sprawling over Canada contain half the fresh-water surface area of the earth. This mind-boggling fact explains why that land offers some of the best whitewater canoeing in the world. Many of its wild rivers flow through wilderness unchanged from the days of the *voyageur.* Some of the portages first used by Indians, and later by fur traders, are still visible and in use.

But Canada doesn't have a monopoly on water. In almost every state in the United States you can drive to roadside whitewater for a day of shooting rapids, or you can escape urban sprawl for weeks or months on a modern odyssey of *voyageur* proportions. Maine's St. John and Carrabassett rivers, New Hampshire's Mad and Saco and the Westfield River of Massachusetts are all white enough to tick-

le your knees. In New York State, the Tioghnioga and Grass rivers will give you an equal challenge. Minnesota's Kettle and Apple rivers, Wisconsin's Wolf River, the Potomac River in Maryland, the Arkansas and Colorado rivers in Colorado, Montana's Madison, the Cedar River in Washington State and the Kings River in California are all rivers that boast wild water.

You don't have to worry about paddling room, that's for sure. But why take to rapids in a canoe?

Elsewhere in this book a dedicated oarsman and an inveterate kayaker lure and cajole while touting the virtues of their respective craft; the raft is boisterous and good-humored, the kayak spry and temperamental; the raft wants big water while the kayak looks for the tricky stuff.

In comparison, the canoe is more modest, I must admit. The traditional undecked canoe is not a boat for heavy water; Class II runs are its limit. But what it may lack in daring, it makes up in sociability and versatility.

In most cases, the canoe is a two-man affair while the raft and kayak are one-man shows. The skill needed to perfect a finely tuned canoe team offers a subtle challenge. Each person must not only know what he is doing and why but also has to know the same things about his partner. It's a balancing act of control.

A canoe's versatility comes in its speed, maneuverability and carrying capacity. There's no doubt that a raft can carry more gear than a canoe or kayak, but it's a slow, ponderous beast with a lumbering gait. The kayak, on the other hand, is agile but carries only the meagerest load and is awkward in slow water. But a canoe can handle reasonable payloads and still maintain a fast pace while responding quickly to the paddle. These characteristics make it the classic touring boat, particularly where stretches of calm water have to be covered between fast runs.

Finally, I think in every canoeist there's a strong sense of heritage. Rubber rafts are products of industrial technology, and although kayakers like to point to the Eskimos as their ancestors, modern kayaking viewed in historical perspective has yet to reach puberty. But canoes have been running the waters of North America for hundreds of years. Indians, explorers, Maine woodsmen and western wranglers have paddled through enough history, down enough rivers, to offer impressive testimony to the craft's virtues.

So much for the soft sell. Let's get down to basics.

SELECTING A CANOE

Wood and Canvas For centuries canoe builders had little choice in materials—wood, wood and bark, and later wood and canvas. Today, a well-designed wood-and-canvas canoe made by a skilled craftsman is a sleek and handsome craft. For some folks, canoes will always be synonymous with these materials. But in light of newer methods of canoe construction, wood and canvas is not the best choice if you're primarily concerned with running fast water.

Wood-and-canvas canoes are susceptible to punctures and cracked planking and ribs. If the paint is scratched off in a brush with a rock, you'll have to retouch the scratch or the canvas will rot. Even under normal flat-water use, annual sanding, repainting and revarnishing are needed to keep the craft in top condition.

Two materials have been refined to the point where, for all practical purposes, they have retired wood-and-canvas canoes to the tranquility of calm water. The materials are marine aluminum and fiberglass.

Aluminum Canoes made of marine aluminum started being produced shortly after World War II. Alloying elements of magnesium and silicon are used to add strength and corrosion resistance to the aluminum and to allow it to be stretch-formed in the die of a hydraulic press. After the parts of the canoe have been formed, they are heat-treated to provide further strength.

Aluminum canoes are popular because of their durability and low upkeep requirements. Canoes made of standard-weight marine aluminum can take a great deal of rock-bouncing punishment. They aren't indestructible; some have been twisted into metal pretzels under the poor handling of indiscreet hotshots. But most of your mistakes will result only in a dent or an occasional puncture.

There are some drawbacks to aluminum. Its light weight—80 pounds for a standard 17-foot model—makes it susceptible to wind when you're on big water. You can get pushed into places you're trying to avoid if you don't take this wind factor into consideration. Prolonged contact with dissimilar metals such as bronze, iron and steel can cause galvanic corrosion, so these metals have to be insulated from the aluminum if you use them for installing accessories. Aluminum is also noisier than other materials when slapped by water. Despite these drawbacks, however, these canoes can't be beat for ruggedness and low maintenance.

Fiberglass The newest addition to canoe materials is fiberglass. Fiberglass canoes are formed in molds and are composed of glass cloth that is bonded together and strengthened with plastic resin. The form molding process makes it possible to produce fully decked canoes that have cockpits for the paddlers. These craft require delicate handling and advanced whitewater skills, but they can be made to perform tricky maneuvers in water that would swamp an open canoe. Decked fiberglass canoes are used for whitewater racing and in water above Class II in difficulty.

Fiberglass is more resilient than aluminum and will often pop back into shape after running into a rock. But in a hard collision it will puncture more easily than an aluminum boat. The decked models do have the advantage of being less susceptible to wind because they ride lower than do open canoes.

I feel aluminum is the best buy in an open canoe because of its superior durability, although there are also fiberglass models available. If you want a decked canoe, fiberglass is the thing. I should point out, however, that handling these canoes requires a great deal more skill and team coordination than you'll need in an open boat.

Canoe Designs

Although there are only two choices in materials, choosing a good whitewater design is another matter. If you've ever thumbed through canoe catalogues, you know that these boats come in all kinds of shapes and sizes. A look at some basic designs will be helpful here.

Let's say your primary interest in a canoe is speed. The design to look for would be a long craft with a V-shaped bottom; it would have a narrow beam and would be sharply pointed fore and aft. The length and shape of the bottom would provide efficient tracking so you could concentrate on forward strokes without spending all your time trying to keep the craft on course. The narrow beam and pointed ends would reduce friction and let you slide through the water easily. Realize, however, that such a radical design has its price; this canoe would be fast, but it would be unstable and lack maneuverability. You could use it only on a fairly straight river that had few obstacles.

If you wanted maneuverability instead of speed, you'd need a short canoe with a flat bottom as you look at it from side to side. The keel line, the bottom of the canoe from bow to stern, would be rockered. It would have no keel, a wedge that runs down the center of the bottom from bow to stern. In this design the length, bottom shape and absence of keel let you slide sideways easily; the rockered keel line makes for more responsive turns. This would be a good boat for tight places but it would be hard to keep on course in open water.

Finally, assume your only concern is stability; you don't care about speed or maneuverability. Yet another design is needed. You'd want a long boat with a broad beam; it would have a flat bottom and a straight keel line with a keel.

Each of the three designs I've mentioned concentrates on one quality at the expense of others and none of them would be suitable for all-around whitewater use. But the exaggeration of their designs does provide guidelines for buying a canoe that will work best for you.

Start by deciding how you want to use your boat. There are three general categories that most whitewater aficionados fall into.

Two-Man Open Canoe

The first group includes those of us who want to have another paddler along and who like to take off for three or four days in a craft that will handle well on rivers *and* lakes. We like the exhilaration that comes in making a well-executed run where we've worked as a team and can feel it in the response of the canoe. But we take to water for more than wild rides; the hatch of flies, scarlet lichen on black rocks, quiet pools where cutthroat laze—the

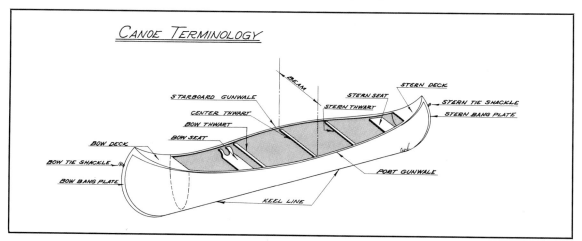

CANOE TERMINOLOGY

BEAM

STERN DECK

STARBOARD GUNWALE

STERN SEAT

STERN TIE SHACKLE

CENTER THWART

STERN THWART

STERN BANG PLATE

BOW THWART

BOW SEAT

BOW DECK

BOW TIE SHACKLE

PORT GUNWALE

BOW BANG PLATE

KEEL LINE

entire fabric of the river's world has brought us there. Occasionally we enter a race sponsored by a local club, but it's done more in the spirit of fellowship than in the drive of competition.

If this is the kind of canoeing you're looking for, your best bet would be a 16- to 18-foot canoe with a flat bottom; it would have a slightly rockered keel line and a shoe keel; the beam would be broad. Each of these features provides an important quality.

Length A 16- to 18-foot canoe provides the carrying capacity needed for two people plus camping gear, but is still short enough to allow good maneuverability in whitewater suitable for open canoes. A 17-footer offers the best compromise between capacity and maneuverability.

Flat Bottom A flat-bottomed canoe rides higher than one with a rounded or V-shaped bottom; this means greater carrying capacity and less tendency to plow through the water. Also, a flat bottom will slide sideways more easily than a round one; you'll want this sliding ability on whitewater.

Rockered Keel Line With a slight rocker to the keel line, you'll be able to pivot the canoe easily because there is less water resistance on the hull at bow and stern. The drawback of this design feature is that wind catches the upsweep of the bow and stern, making the boat hard to handle in breezy weather.

Shoe Keel The standard keel depth on flat-water canoes runs close to an inch and helps keep the craft on an even course. The shoe keel is only half an inch deep. It's a compromise keel that allows you to keep a true course on calm water while still letting you sideslip easily in whitewater.

Broad Beam The beam, the width of the canoe at its widest point, should be 35 to 37 inches in a 16- to 18-foot canoe. This width along with the flat bottom keeps the craft riding high. The taper of the canoe to bow and stern should be gradual. For example, a well-designed 17-footer has a beam of 36 inches; at the stern thwart the width is 3l inches, and at the stern seat the width is 22

inches. The proportions are the same in the bow. These dimensions provide proper buoyancy at bow and stern, allowing the canoe to ride over waves. A craft with a sharper taper would knife through waves, shipping water more easily.

These are the features to look for in an open canoe to be manned by two people, but maybe you'd rather go it alone.

One-Man Open Canoe

You're still interested in the excitement and subtleties the river has to offer, yet you prefer to have full responsibility for handling your craft. You fit into the second category.

You'll want a shorter canoe than that used by two people, but one which has the same design features. A 14- or 15-footer is a good boat for solo work. Don't consider anything shorter than 14 feet. As the length of the canoe diminishes, so do its stability and high flotation. The shorter a canoe gets, the more taper it will have at bow and stern, assuming it has an adequate beam to begin with. This sharp taper not only reduces its buoyancy but it also makes the craft more tippy. That is why a canoe under 14 feet is difficult to handle in rough water. It rides low and requires too much attention to stabilization.

C-1 Slalom

So far I've been talking about open canoes—craft that are suitable for water no greater than Class II. But there's a lot of water rougher than that, water which roars around boulders, swirls into eddies and then falls away to form standing waves big enough to eat a six-man raft.

Contrary to popular literature and visions of canoeing grandeur, this kind of water is not the stuff to tackle in open touring canoes. Specially designed competition racers, with full decks to ward off incoming spray, are the right tools for this stage of the paddler's trade.

As the term "competition" might indicate, these are finely honed craft, their engineering defined and limited by regulations set down by the International Canoe Federation. The people capable of handling these boats form the third group of whitewater paddlers.

There are four types of decked canoes to consider: the C-1 (one-man canoe), slalom and downriver, and the C-2 (two-man canoe), slalom and downriver. As the terms indicate, the slalom canoes are designed for use in close-quarter maneuvering; the downriver models are designed for speed in a straight run where obstacles pose few problems.

The C-1 is often mistaken for a kayak, but the distinction is clear: In a C-1 you kneel and use a single-bladed paddle; you sit in a kayak and use a double-bladed paddle.

The C-1 slalom boat is small and light; it measures 13 feet long and 2 feet wide with a weight between 30 and 40 pounds. As in all these canoes, the relatively small length, width and depth are effective only because the craft is completely decked and because you are enclosed by a spray skirt. The spray skirt fits over the rim of the cockpit and around your waist, preventing water from getting into the canoe.

The C-1 has a rounded hull and rockered keel line without a keel. The design is ideal for its intended use in running slalom courses where you have to maneuver through gates, pairs of wooden markers suspended above the water, while at the same time negotiating rapids. The challenge is increased by the fact that you have to take some gates backwards and you must paddle upstream to pass through others. A slalom course requires a snaky boat and the C-1 fills the bill.

C-1 Downriver

The C-1 downriver, on the other hand, is built for speed. Its 14-foot length and V-shaped hull with straight keel line make it a good tracker. Both bow and stern are sharply pointed, with the bow taper starting behind the cockpit. It's an unstable craft with little maneuverability, but it's been engineered for one purpose—getting down a river fast.

C-2 Slalom and Downriver

The two-man versions of the slalom and downriver boats have design characteristics similar to their C-1 counterparts, but they're longer. The C-2 slalom is from 15 to 16 feet long with a 32-inch beam; it weighs 45 pounds. A downriver C-2 runs 16½ feet with a 32-inch beam and weighs 50 pounds. The bow and stern cockpits in these canoes are equipped with seats hung from the cockpit rim and with thigh and toe braces.

Recently, some manufacturers—Old Town and Easy Rider, to name two—have come out with completely decked two-man canoes that have cargo cockpits amidship. The Old Town model meets the International Canoe Federation's competition requirements, and it's a good compromise if you want to race and tour but can't afford two different boats. The carrying capacity isn't as great as the bigger open canoes, but this model is suitable for extended trips where gear is kept to a minimum.

Whether touring or racing in teams or solo, your own whitewater ambitions will dictate your choice in canoe design, but before sinking any money into a boat, back up your choice with the advice of an experienced paddler. Local canoe clubs or whitewater organizations can help you and may even let you try handling different canoes to get a sense of their feel.

PADDLES AND ACCESSORIES

When you're on a river, a paddle is your power and you'll need a good one, one that floats, one that won't break when you lay into it and one that's built to take the demands of whitewater.

Paddle Materials

Paddles come in wood, aluminum, fiberglass, plastic, and combinations of all four materials. Wooden paddles have a resiliency not found in the synthetic materials, but they're heavier and will tire you more easily. Straight-grained ash or maple should be your choice here. Get paddles that are laminated as opposed to ones made from a single piece of wood. The laminated models are far more durable and less likely to crack under heavy use.

Synthetics The two virtues of paddles made of synthetic materials are their lightness and the fact that they need no maintenance. Make sure the shaft of the paddle is hollow and watertight so it will float should you drop it in the drink.

Paddle Designs

More important than the material used in your paddle is its basic design. The blade should be 7 or 8 inches wide with a square tip. Both of these features give power to your stroke. The grip should be squared or T-shaped to allow a firm grasp and precise angling of the blade.

When considering paddle length, your strength and reach are more important than your height. But as a rule, the paddle should reach your chin when the tip of the blade is resting on the ground. You'll want a paddle two or three inches shorter than this for a decked canoe, since they ride lower.

Thigh Brace

Although not provided by canoe manufacturers, foot and thigh braces can be installed in open canoes to allow more versatility and you'll need them for "bracing strokes," strokes where you have to lean out over the water. The thigh and toe braces help you become an integral part of your canoe.

The simplest method of making thigh braces in an aluminum canoe consists of riveting a metal ring two inches in diameter to the keel line about four inches back of the point your knees hit when you're kneeling in paddling position. This ring will be the bottom anchor for the brace. Attach it with a piece of hardened aluminum, one inch by four inches, using two rivets on either side of the strip. Drill the rivet holes with a #21 drill and use $\frac{5}{32}$-inch rivets.

The brace itself consists of a webbed belt an inch and a half wide and long enough to be fastened to one side of the seat thwart, looped through the ring and then pulled taut and attached to the other side of the seat thwart. Buckle attachments on either end of the webbing work well because you can easily take the brace out when it's not in use, and you have the added benefit of being able to adjust the tautness of the brace.

Toe Brace

To keep your thighs pressed tightly against the webbing, you may find it necessary to install toe braces under the seat. Use blocks of wood three inches wide and two inches high screwed to hardened aluminum strips that are riveted to the bottom of your canoe in the way I've described.

Follow the same installation procedures in a fiberglass canoe, but form your anchor strips of fiberglass and resin, and epoxy them to the bottom.

The exact positioning of the anchor rings and toe braces will vary according to your physical idiosyncrasies, so be sure to install them to fit your particular paddling position. If you're going to wear a canoe it should fit well.

Spray Deck

Along with toe and thigh braces, spray decks made of pre-shrunk canvas or rubberized nylon can be found on some canoes. The spray deck has hooks every six to eight inches along its edge that are fastened to eyes riveted to the outside of the gunwales. To prevent water from puddling on the material, you can put bowed pieces of wood from one gunwale to the other so the spray will run off. The cockpits in an improvised spray deck should have a strip of wood or plastic sewn in around their edges so they'll accommodate a standard spray skirt.

When you get right down to it, I'd say a manufactured decked canoe ends up being safer and cheaper than one you fix up yourself. There's always the danger in an improvised model of having a wave pull off the bow fasteners, leaving you in a tangled mass of material as water gurgles around your armpits.

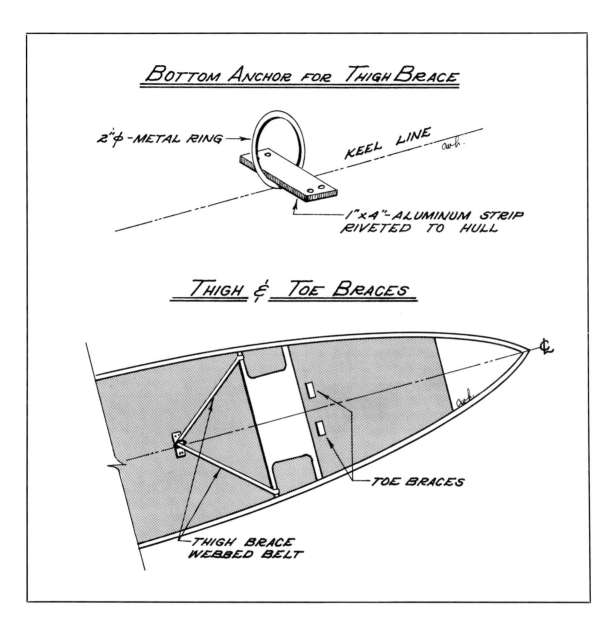

BOTTOM ANCHOR FOR THIGH BRACE

2"∅ - METAL RING →

KEEL LINE

1"x4"-ALUMINUM STRIP RIVETED TO HULL

THIGH & TOE BRACES

TOE BRACES

THIGH BRACE WEBBED BELT

Life Jacket

Get a good life jacket. It's a basic safety item you should always wear on whitewater. Some states require the use of Coast Guard-approved jackets, but just because it has their backing doesn't mean it's suitable for rough water. The buoyancy of a life jacket depends on its thickness and surface area; consequently, the bigger and thicker the jacket, the more flotation it will offer. Unfortunately, that increase in flotation is coupled with a decrease in freedom of movement. You've got to make a calculated compromise. Most boaters find that a jacket rated at 40 pounds buoyancy is about as bulky as they can take and still have the freedom of movement needed to handle the paddle. In the rough water a decked canoe is capable of running, you'll want that much margin of safety. For the water you'd run in an open canoe, 20 pounds of buoyancy is adequate.

Another fact to keep in mind is that you'll want a jacket that will keep you floating face up in the water. To do this the jacket has to have at least 25 percent more buoyancy in the front than in the back.

Painters should be secured so they can be pulled out with a slight tug.   *Photo by Sam Curtis*

A life jacket works for your safety. For the safety of your canoe equip it with painters—⅜-inch nylon lines twelve to fifteen feet long attached to bow and stern. These lines are invaluable when you have to go after a swamped or runaway boat; they allow you to pull from a distance. Painters should be coiled and secured to the bow and stern decks so they can be pulled out with a slight tug.

Wet Suit

I will discuss clothing in more detail when I deal with touring equipment, but there are some special items to consider even if you aren't in a touring situation. The first is a wet suit. When you're canoeing in high and cold waters of spring runoff, or any time the water and air are cold, these neoprene suits are indispensable. A ³⁄₁₆-inch-thick wet suit will serve you well in all but the coldest situations, and it won't cramp your paddling style. In addition, a wet suit will add a degree of buoyancy to your body if you land in the water.

Knee Pads

Another item that classifies loosely as clothing is knee pads. The bottom of a canoe is hard on the knees, and pads are a welcome, soft cushion. You can get knee pads of the variety used by gardeners in most hardware stores, or you can improvise your own. Some canoeists glue rubber pads directly to the bottom of the canoe, but if you shift your position they aren't always where you want them to be.

Okay, you've got the gear; you need the know-how.

THE NATURE OF THE BEAST

As a kid growing up in Connecticut, I spent all the time I could at a pond near my home. The main attraction was an old wood-and-canvas canoe my father had bought years before. My friends and I would spend hours paddling the shoreline in search of snapping turtles and frogs. We'd never had training in canoe handling, but we'd learned that certain strokes got us where we wanted to go. Our maneuvering was graceless, yet it made no difference on the quiet water of a millpond.

Then one summer two of my cousins and I decided to take the canoe down a stretch of the Housatonic River. I had enough sense to kneel down in an attempt to keep my weight low in the canoe, but that's about the only thing I did right. From my stern position I first tried to use the paddle as a rudder. The canoe didn't turn and we bashed off the oncoming rocks. Then we decided we'd have to get up more steam in order to steer. That worked a little better until I tried to avoid a rock and swung the stern broadside right into the thing. Over we went.

The adventure was my first hint that any whitewater aspirant had better have a clear understanding of how and why a canoe can be made to respond.

Center Pivot

First, you should understand that when you turn a canoe it pivots at the center. This means that when bow and stern paddlers are using strokes of equal power the canoe will turn away from the paddle side of the stern paddler. It does this because the stern paddling position offers greater leverage than the bow position since it's further from the central pivot point. The stern man has to alter his stroke to compensate for this veering tendency if he wants to keep the canoe traveling in a straight line.

The canoe's center pivot characteristic has some important implications when you shoot rapids. Consider the course of a canoe making a left turn on flat water. The canoe is moving in a straight line, but when the stern man executes the turning stroke, the stern slides to the right of the line as it pivots on the center. This movement makes little difference to the lake paddler, but when you're dodging rocks in tight quarters there's a problem. A rock comes up close on the right; the stern man initiates a basic stroke to turn to the left; the stern slides to the right, and before power

strokes can move the stern out of the way—crunch!

Basic still-water handling just doesn't work in whitewater.

The Myth of Steerage Way

So what do you do to avoid that rock? Here a major myth of canoe handling should be laid to rest. You do *not* have to be going faster than the flow of water to be able to maneuver a canoe. Steerage way, the forward speed needed to make a craft respond to the rudder, is only necessary when in fact the stern paddler is using his paddle as a rudder. In this case, maneuverability depends on water resistance against your stern paddle. That resistance is obtained through forward movement. But rarely will you use your paddle as a rudder in fast water; steering doesn't provide the quick handling you'll need.

In the case of that rock coming up on the right, you can sideslip the canoe to the left with a "pry stroke" to the right and a "draw stroke" to the left. (Both of these strokes have the blade deep in the water parallel to the canoe. In the pry the paddle is pulled against the gunwale and literally pries the canoe to the side. The draw starts out from the canoe with the paddle being drawn toward the gunwale.) If you have to move a greater distance to avoid the rock, you could use a back ferry—back-paddling the canoe at an angle to the current.

The point is that forward movement is by no means a prerequisite for maneuverability.

BASIC STROKES

That first whitewater venture on the Housatonic taught me some things about a canoe's center pivot and the inadequacies of using my paddle as a rudder. So I patched up the canoe and lugged it back to the pond. Our river fiasco hadn't frightened me off; as a matter of fact, I was itching to return. But I wanted the skills to work with the river, not against it. That time of flat-water training paid off and I discovered that even the simplest strokes have their subtleties.

Forward Stroke

For example, the forward stroke looks easy enough, but how you hold, position and power the paddle are matters that make the difference between a powerful, effective stroke and one that will do little when you need it the most.

To start with, you've got to hold your paddle the right way. Someone who wraps his fingers around the shaft of his paddle just below the grip and holds his other hand well up from the blade isn't going to fare well in rough water. The grip is there for a purpose and you should grasp it firmly in the cup of your hand with fingers curved over the top. Your lower hand should grip the shaft as close to the blade as possible without feeling awkward.

By holding the paddle this way you get the best leverage, your paddle being the lever, with your lower hand the fulcrum or fixed point on which the paddle turns. Your upper hand is used to push the weight of water on the blade. The closer the fulcrum, your lower hand, is to that weight, the less energy you expend on the stroke. The lever example is apt here because your lower hand should remain as fixed as possible on the forward stroke; you push with your upper arm; you don't pull with your lower.

When you start the forward stroke, put the blade deep in the water in front of you and at a right angle to the keel line. Since it's the resistance between blade and water that does most for the power of your stroke, the more surface area pulling directly against the water, the more effective the stroke will be.

As you push the blade through the water, it should be parallel to the keel line. If it parallels the gunwale it will describe a slight arc away from your line of forward movement, losing some of its power. During the stroke the shaft should be vertical when viewed from the rear. Don't use a long follow-through because once the blade is opposite your hip it starts to push up toward the water's surface, adding little to forward movement.

Finally, the stroke should come from your whole body. The lower part of your body—feet, knees, thighs—make you an extension of the canoe; the upper part—arms, shoulders, back and stomach—packing the punch to the water.

As I said, the forward stroke has its subtleties. But my comments on those fine points are not intended to make you abandon ship. Hopefully they'll give you a sense of the importance of precision in any stroke you use. If you work toward that precision in the basic strokes, mastering the advanced ones will come more easily.

Back Stroke

The other two basic strokes to perfect at the outset are the backstroke and the J stroke. The backstroke is your power in back-ferrying, in slowing forward movement and in softening an inevitable confrontation with a rock. The stroke is started behind your hip and your upper arm is pulled toward you. You may find you're able to get more power by rotating your upper hand so your palm faces you, but in my experience the change makes little difference.

J Stroke

The J stroke is the move used by the stern man to offset the veering tendency caused by his position of better leverage. This stroke starts the same as the forward stroke, but at the end the blade is pushed away from the canoe at a right angle to compensate for the stern's side drift. The pattern inscribes a "J."

STROKES FOR WHITEWATER FOLKS

The forward, back and J strokes are basic to any kind of canoeing. But in whitewater you'll have to learn to do a lot more with your paddle to be up to the demanding situations posed by rock gardens, eddy fences and waves. To learn the advanced skills, nothing beats the tutelage of a weathered riverman, someone who can recognize the beginnings of bad habits and coach you on the tricks of each stroke. It's far better to get your first dunkings, and you'll get plenty, in sight of an experienced hand than to go splashing off for wild water in an attempt to learn on your own.

Grumman Boats is in the process of compiling a Learn-to-Canoe Directory that will list by states the organizations which teach whitewater canoeing. To get a copy, write to Grumman Boats, Marathon, New York, 13803. This will be the best way I know for finding a coach.

The explanation of strokes that follows will not make you a whitewater whiz; only years of paddling will do that. But I hope it will give you a sense of the variety of maneuvers you'll need for tackling a river. Here are the strokes—their principles and purposes. Understand the concept; then head off to the pond for those long hours of practice.

Draw Stroke

The draw stroke is used to draw your canoe sideways for short distances. Start the stroke by putting your paddle vertically into the water as far out as you can reach and at a right angle to the canoe. Keep the surface of the blade parallel to the keel line. You'll want to thrust the blade deep as you draw it toward the gunwale. Water has to be pushed under the hull to make this stroke effective; any that boils against the side wastes energy. As you draw the paddle close to the canoe, be careful that it isn't pinned against the side by the momentum of the water. As you quickly push your upper arm forward the blade will knife out to the rear.

When using the draw, the force of surface water against the hull will cause the canoe to tip away from your paddle side, allowing you, with knees bracing the canoe, to lean out for a more powerful stroke. But at the end of the stroke you'll want to be centered back over the canoe or you'll get a quick tip to the paddle side. After a few soakings you should have the hang of it.

Diagonal Draw

This is a draw stroke that is angled 45 degrees to either bow or stern. Angled to the stern, it will move you backward, or at least

slow your forward progress, while also moving you sideways. It will move you forward and sideways when it's angled toward the bow.

You'll find this stroke particularly useful when you're paddling solo. In that case, your center position in the canoe—over the pivot point—lets you turn the canoe left or right while drawing it sideways.

Cross Draw

In shallow water where you can't push your paddle deep, the cross draw can be used. It necessitates switching your paddling side, and in tight maneuvering those few lost seconds can work against you. It also puts you in an unstable position, which is risky in turbulent water. But in shallow, medium water it does have its place.

To start the stroke you swing your paddle to the opposite side of the canoe without changing your grip. Hold the length of the paddle almost parallel to the water with the blade facing the canoe. Put the blade in the water in front of you about 30 degrees out from the keel line; then push it toward the bow with your upper arm. You have to push water in front of or just under the bow so you'll want to make the stroke as far forward as possible, but reach only with your arms to do this. Keep your body centered over the canoe. If you don't, then hope the water's warm.

Pry Stroke

The pry stroke has an effect that's the reverse of the draw; instead of moving the canoe toward the paddle side, it moves it away. Use it on the canoe side opposite the draw when you want quick sideways movement. With this stroke, you begin by pushing the blade under the canoe parallel to the keel line with the shaft resting on the hull next to your knee. With the blade deep in the water and your top hand out over the water, you literally pry the canoe away from the paddle side with your arms, shoulders and back. Here's one stroke where your bottom hand should slide up on the shaft, since the hull of

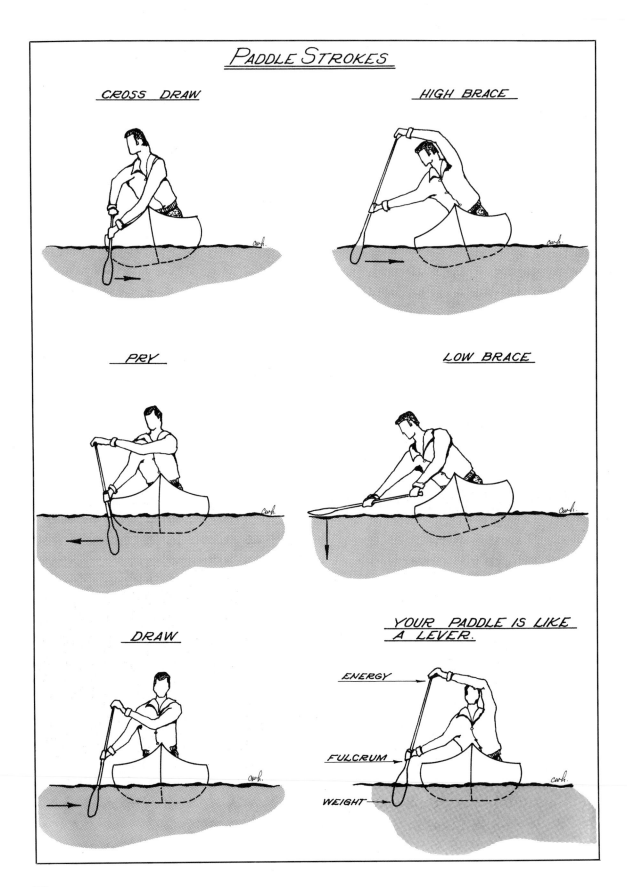

PADDLE STROKES

CROSS DRAW

HIGH BRACE

PRY

LOW BRACE

DRAW

YOUR PADDLE IS LIKE A LEVER.

ENERGY

FULCRUM

WEIGHT

90

the canoe becomes the fulcrum instead of your lower hand. The strength of the pry depends on starting it as far under the canoe as possible and on not pulling the paddle much beyond the vertical position. You can make a quick recovery by knifing the blade backwards out of the water in the same manner used in the draw.

Keep your knees well braced and your hips limber on this one; the pry will tip the canoe towards the paddle.

Sweep Strokes

These turning strokes are used on stretches of river that don't require very quick maneuvering. The forward sweep, if you're in the stern, starts at a right angle to the canoe and is swept in an arc to the stern. When you're in the bow, start the stroke in front of you next to the canoe and sweep the paddle in an arc out to a right angle. Whether in bow or stern, the forward sweep will turn the canoe away from the paddle side.

The reverse sweep traces an arc in the opposite direction from that of the forward sweep. In the stern start the stroke next to the canoe; in the bow start it at a right angle to the canoe. This stroke will turn the canoe in the direction of the paddle side.

Sometimes the forward sweep and the reverse sweep are combined in the same maneuver to make a responsive turn. For instance, a forward sweep in the right stern and a reverse sweep in the left bow will do a fast job of getting you pointed to the right.

Two variations of sweep strokes are used for two specific situations. When setting the angle for a back ferry, the stern man can use a reverse sweep that is levered off the hull in a manner similar to the pry. By using the hull as the fulcrum in this situation a great deal more power is added to a maneuver that calls for muscle.

The second variation is called the C stroke, which is used when you're paddling solo from the center of the canoe. Use it to turn the canoe to the paddle side. Start the stroke in front of you and out from the canoe, pull the paddle in towards the gunwale in an arc, and then push it out behind the pivot point so you end up describing the letter "C."

This solo paddler is beginning a C stroke to get his canoe angled downstream. *Photo by Old Town Canoe Company*

91

Brace Strokes

Before I'm struck between the eyes with a double-bladed paddle, let me say that brace strokes were first used and perfected by kayakers, and the intensity of those folks comes through in the strokes. Braces, although relatively new to canoeing, have become indispensable for top-rate whitewater maneuvering. But a note of caution: When using a brace you've really got to be an appendage of your canoe. Don't try these strokes without thigh and toe braces.

The low brace is not only a defensive stroke, one you use when tottering on top of a wave, but it's also used aggressively to maintain stability when you're crossing boundary lines between currents of different speeds and directions.

Positioning for the low brace has the paddle blade on the water at a right angle to the canoe with its surface parallel to the water. Your palm should be facing up on the grip and the wrist of your other hand should be directly over the shaft in a vertical position. Vigorous downward pressure with your lower arm and upward pressure with your upper arm actually braces your body against the water as you lean out of the canoe and use your hips and knees to stabilize the boat. You'll have to throw yourself into the stroke and have faith that hanging over the side will actually help when you're in rough water.

The high brace combines bracing action with drawing action. Here your upper arm is held high and almost straight above your head. With the blade deep in the water, your lower arm pulls the paddle toward the canoe. When the stroke is done right, the canoe will be leaning sharply toward the side the paddle is on, but the bracing action, along with the use of your knees and hips, keeps the craft from going all the way over. When you feel you need more righting action, pull harder on the paddle or switch to a low brace.

For reasons I need not enumerate, perfect these braces on the old millpond.

The bow paddler is using a high brace to stabilize the canoe and to pull in close to the boulder. (Upper Hudson.) *Photo by Grumman Boats*

Some Comments on Team Paddling

All the strokes I've described here are part of river canoeing. Once you've got them ingrained in your head and muscles and can use them with near-instinctive ease, you're well on your way to working with the rivers you run.

There's only one problem. Most of the time you'll probably want someone else along to man your bow or stern. And you'll want that person to have paddling skills comparable to yours. One good way to form a well-balanced team is to find someone who wants to go through the learning process with you—husband, wife, friend or relation. Chances are your skills will develop at an equal pace and you'll have the added benefit of working as a team from the outset—a benefit that will really pay off when it comes to that balancing act of control.

As you practice strokes and maneuvers, take turns handling both bow and stern positions so you'll feel at ease in either. Also get used to using each stroke on both sides of the canoe. As a rule, you don't switch paddling sides when running whitewater because it wastes valuable time. But there will probably be times when you're canoeing with a person who can only paddle well on one side or in one position. So if you can develop versatility in your skills you'll be able to accommodate a greater number of partners.

Whenever you do take to the river with a new partner, make sure you've agreed upon who's going to paddle on what side and settle on some basic commands. Most whitewater paddlers use the word "okay" to mean don't do anything. Other than that a simple "forward," "back," "left" or "right" should do.

Finally, make sure you both agree that the bow man is the captain. He's the guy who sees the water the best, so he should make the decisions on what maneuvers are needed.

WHITEWATER TECHNIQUE

In the last section I talked about strokes as individual movements. But on the river a pry reverses to a draw as you snake among rocks and boulders; your forward stroke flattens to a low brace as you top a wave. Your strokes blend together to harmonize with the water's twists and turns. To achieve this kind of grace you've got to be able to read the water well. Chapter 1 of this book sets forth the principles of water dynamics; you should study it thoroughly. I've made no attempt, in the following discussion, to duplicate information already presented in that chapter. My intention is to explain the maneuvers used in a canoe when confronted with the varying water conditions and obstacles you'll find on a river.

Channels

A river isn't one flowing mass; it consists of various channels that are often flowing in different directions and at different speeds. As a rule, your best route will be the channel with the largest volume of water, because that's the path meeting the least resistance—the fewest rocks, boulders and plugs. But before you slip into a channel, check its full course. You'll have to do this from shore, if you don't have a good view from the canoe. One channel may appear to be the best route at first, only to meet downstream obstructions which you can't avoid after your initial commitment. When you can see this happening, pick a less obvious but safer channel at the outset.

Keep the canoe parallel to the current, once you are in the channel. Positioning is achieved with the use of draws and pries. The stern man is responsible for letting the bow know which strokes are needed to maintain alignment, since he can see the situation without looking over his shoulder. If you don't move parallel to the current, the hull of the canoe will be exposed to obstructions and to the water's potential capsizing force.

Changing Channels

Sometimes you'll find it possible to change channels in the course of a rapid, and you may be forced to do so to avoid obstructions or mean water. Use a back ferry to make that change unless it's so short you can do it with draws, pries or sweeps.

The back ferry is accomplished by paddling backwards at an angle of about 30 degrees to the direction of the current. This is an exception to the rule of moving parallel to the flow of water. The maneuver is initiated by the stern man with a draw or pry stroke that moves the stern in the direction you want to go. The exact angle of canoe to current will depend on the speed of the water. Fast water calls for an angle of less than 30 degrees; slow water for an angle of more than 30. Maintain your angle with draws, pries and sweeps interspersed with your backstrokes.

You're going to find times when you won't be able to back-paddle as fast as the current. So you'll still be going downstream as you move across-stream. Learn to judge your rate of downstream travel in relation to your rate of cross-stream travel, so you can tell whether you'll be able to reach your desired destination before being smashed into the obstacle you're trying to avoid.

Trial by water is the only way to perfect this kind of judgment.

River Bends

Another exception. This one is to the first commandment that says follow the channel with the greatest volume. Water reacts to the laws of centrifugal force when it comes to bends in the river; the greatest volume moves to the outside of the curve. Unless you do something, you'll be moving right along with it and you can easily get forced into the bank or into obstructions along the bank. Avoid these traps by using a back ferry to keep in the shallower, less powerful water on the inside of the bend.

Big Waves and Suckholes

Stay away from these in an open canoe for simple reasons of safety. If you take on much water, your boat becomes a sluggish beast. Swamping is suddenly more than a possibility; it's downright probable.

Even in a decked or covered canoe, carefully evaluate stretches of river with waves or suckholes before you decide to attempt a run.

When waves get really big you won't be able to paddle over their tops, and you'll get rolled back into the trough. Any large volume of water going over a dam or ledge will form a suckhole that could trap you and your boat in its rolling, aerated turbulence.

Obstructions

Two obstructions that are particularly dangerous are fallen trees and wire fences. Trees that are lying in the river have usually been toppled by a swift current which has undermined the roots. The same current can force you into the fallen tree because the water flows through its branches without being diverted. A canoe isn't going to flow through branches, and grabbing on to them will only hasten an upset. Play it safe: stay away from the thing in the first place.

Wire fences are more insidious; they're difficult to see. Most people who've put fences across a river warn boaters by placing red flags or large signs on the wire. Other landowners haven't been so thoughtful. When you're canoeing unfamiliar waters, ask local folks about possible fences.

A river's most natural obstructions are rocks. When it's here a rock, there a rock, you won't have many problems in avoiding them if you can see them. But when it's everywhere a rock, rock, your problems may not seem so simple. Negotiating a rock garden requires the use of draws, pries, cross draws and sweeps in quick succession. And you'll need precise coordination between bow and stern, or crunch—bubble, bubble—burp . . .

Those underwater rocks present a different challenge; they can really catch you unprepared. Don't let any riverman get away with claiming he's never had his teeth jarred by the force of a skulking sleeper. The river has its way of keeping you on your toes, so keep your eyes on the river. Know what the humps, ripples and V's are subtly saying and take the hint.

Eddies

To the uninitiated, eddies seem innocuous enough—just little backwater pools that don't have much to do with running a river. Nothing could be further from the truth. Eddies provide rest stops and observation points in a strenuous run, and they provide fun for the paddler who wants to play with the effects they have on his canoe and test his skill.

Of major importance to the boater is the eddy's boundary—the line between slow-moving water going upstream and swift water flowing downstream. To get in and out of an eddy, this line must be crossed; and the crossing has a rude surprise for the unsuspecting.

Eddies are caused by obstructions, and a canoe must pass the obstruction before entry can be made. Assume the obstacle has just been passed and you execute strokes that turn the bow into the eddy. First, this puts your canoe broadside to the current and its capsizing force pulls on the hull. This in itself can bring a quick end to the maneuver. Second, if your bow somehow manages to enter the eddy, the canoe is immediately spun around by the opposing forces of water on bow and stern; the bow is pushed upstream, the stern is pushed downstream. The canoe either swamps or continues downstream backwards.

There is some savvy connected with working eddies.

Back Ferry The safest eddy entry involves the use of a back ferry. Back-paddling is begun before you reach the obstruction that forms the eddy. The canoe must pass close to the obstruction; as soon as it has been passed, the stern man pries or draws his end of the canoe into the upstream end of the eddy. Then both paddlers use backstrokes to pull the entire canoe into the calm water. Once the stern has entered the backwater, the force of the downstream current on the bow also helps to push it in.

The back-ferry entry is effective and allows for tight control. But in very powerful currents, it's difficult to use because backstrokes are inherently less powerful than forward strokes. Try as you will, there are places where you simply won't have time to back into

an eddy; you'll be past it before you can complete the maneuver.

Eddy Turn At these times, a forward entry—called an eddy turn—has to be used. Both paddlers paddle forward, angling toward the obstruction so the bow passes it as closely as possible. As soon as the bow enters the upper end of the eddy, assuming the stern man is paddling on the eddy side and the bow man is paddling on the side away from the eddy, the stern man leans into a low brace. At the same time the bow man uses a pry stroke to bring the bow up into the eddy; he immediately follows this with powerful forward strokes to pull the entire canoe into quiet water. Precise strokes and coordination must come into play as the canoe crosses the eddy fence. The bracing stroke is necessary to the maneuver to counteract the opposing forces of water on bow and stern.

When the eddy is on the other side of the canoe, where the stern man is paddling on the off side and the bow man is paddling on the eddy side, different tactics have to be used. The approach is made in the same way, but as soon as the bow crosses the eddy fence, the bow man leans the canoe into the turn with a high brace while the stern man continues to paddle forward. As the stern swings downstream, both paddlers use forward strokes to pull the craft all the way into the eddy.

Once you've gotten into an eddy, you also have to get out, and the problems caused by current differentials are the same. In moderate water, it's possible to back out. Good momentum is needed, and the canoe must be at a shallow angle to the current or your stern will be caught and spun downstream. The canoe should be almost parallel to the downstream current and close to the eddy fence before the stern man sets the angle for the back ferry. As soon as the angle is set, both paddlers must back-paddle with powerful strokes. If the current is too strong, the canoe will be pushed back into the eddy. If the angle is too large, the stern will get whipped downstream and you'll have to use stabilizing braces to prevent an upset.

Peel Off A bolder and more exciting method of exiting from an eddy is the peel off; it's like an eddy turn in reverse. The canoe is pointed bow upstream and at a shallow angle to the current. Both paddlers use powerful forward strokes to get the bow across the eddy fence. When the bow enters the current, the bow man paddling on the upstream side uses a pry stroke to help the current spin the bow downstream. The stern man uses a low brace on the other side, leaning the canoe downstream so the current catches the hull.

When the paddling sides are reversed, with the stern paddle upstream and the bow paddle downstream, the stern man paddles forward while the bow man, on crossing the eddy fence, uses a high brace to lean the canoe downstream into the turn. This forward exit is exciting, for the canoe carves into the current like a hawk circling on the wind. You know you're in tune with the river.

Forward Ferry You're not always going to want to peel off from an eddy. You may want to cross the river to another eddy or paddle upstream from one eddy to another. For both these situations the forward ferry comes into play. This maneuver starts the same as the peel off, with powerful forward strokes used to cross the eddy fence. The upstream angle of your canoe should be as close to parallel with the current as possible so the force of the water on the bow doesn't spin you into an unsuspected peel off. Continue with forward strokes at a slight angle to the current once the entire canoe is out of the eddy. Be prepared for the buffeting effect as you cross the line; you may have to use a fast brace or two between forward strokes, but once you've gotten into the current the forward ferry is surprisingly effective.

The Rough Spots

Being able to select the best channels, avoid obstructions and use eddies are the nuts and bolts of whitewater canoeing. But when obstacles, eddies and shifting channels come combined with really heavy water, you may have to get out and walk.

The amount of water flowing in a river directly affects the nature of any rapid. In low water, a rapid may be shallow and easy to run. The same spot can be a boiling nightmare of haystacks and suckholes when the water is high.

Standing waves, or haystacks, are particularly hazardous for the open canoe, because in attempting to run them you'll ship water. You may be able to skirt the waves by carefully selecting your route, but even decked-canoe teams must thoroughly evaluate the situation before deciding to make a run.

Dams, ledges, boulders—any obstructions in heavy water—pose problems. A great surge of water going over a dam or ledge causes a frothy back roll as it plunges to the riverbed. The water becomes aerated and lacks buoyancy, and the roll-back can easily dump you out of the canoe and trap you.

In addition to these particular problems, heavy water increases the capsizing force of current differentials. Eddies are more difficult to enter and exit and can become swirling whirlpools of whitewater instead of quiet, safe backwaters.

If you've settled on an open touring canoe, you've also got to settle for Class I or Class II water. Leave the rough stuff to raftsmen and paddlers with enclosed boats. A raft bounces back into shape when it's bent, and enclosed boats can float bottom up without shipping water. The traditional open canoe has neither of these virtues. So remember your modesty.

Let's face it, no matter what kind of canoe you've got, there's some water that's too hairy to run!

POLING, LINING AND PORTAGING

As a whitewater devotee, your main pastime will be running rapids, but there are going to be times when this won't be possible, safe or practical. You may have to pole or line your canoe up or down a stream when the water becomes too shallow, turbulent or obstructed. Extremely rough stretches will force you to portage—to carry your canoe and equipment overland.

Poling

This is a traditional technique used in an open canoe. Poling is used in shallow water where you can't get adequate paddling purchase or where a rock garden won't give you enough paddling maneuverability. You'll need a ten- to twelve-foot pole about an inch and a half to two inches in diameter. This you can cut from the shoreline forest in remote wooded areas. But I prefer to carry one with me and eliminate the needless cutting of trees along my route. I use a ten-foot spruce pole and have attached a metal disk to its butt to prevent the wood from splaying against the river bottom.

To keep your canoe aligned with the current when poling, the downstream end of the canoe should be lower in the water than the upstream end, whether you're going with or against the current. Have the heaviest paddler stand at the downstream end, or if you're solo, stand just aft of the center thwart when you're going upstream and just forward of it when you're going down.

Poling Upstream In poling upstream, bow and stern men kneel or stand and place the butts of their poles firmly on the river bottom a foot or so behind them. Your hands, which should be gripping the pole about two feet apart, slide in a shinnying fashion up the pole and push the canoe forward. You and your partner can push from alternate sides or from the same side. Keep pressure on your pole with both hands—backward pressure to keep the canoe moving forward and lateral pressure to control stability and the course of direction. For constant control, one pole must be in contact with the river bottom at all times.

Poling Downstream There will be times when you'll want to pole downstream, particularly when you need precise control. Here the opposite procedure of going upstream is used. Place the pole on the river bottom *ahead* of you, and shinny your hands *down* the pole. In very fast water a quick succession of brief contacts with the bottom is more effective.

An alternative to these two downstream methods is to use the pole as a drag. Trail the pole behind you with one hand grasping it two or three feet in front of your body as you face the bow and the other hand grasping the pole next to your body. When you want to break, force the pole to drag on the bottom by upward pressure of your forward arm and downward pressure of your other arm.

Effective poling requires skill and practice. It isn't a technique for the novice with a canoe full of gear in swift water.

Lining

Lining Upstream Lining is a good alternative to poling when paddling is impossible but portaging isn't necessary. It can be used for both open and decked boats. You'll need two fifty- to sixty-foot painters attached to your canoe—one to the bow tie shackle or front seat, the other to the stern seat or thwart. Attach the painters to bow and stern grab loops in a decked model. To line upstream, the bow is pushed out into the current until the force of the water on the hull starts to push the canoe away from the bow lineman. At this point, both bow and stern linemen draw slack from their lines and start pulling upstream. Keep the bow slightly further from shore than the stern so pressure of the current on the bow allows an even course as you pull. If you let the bow swing too far out, excess water pressure on the canoe makes it difficult to pull. When you pull the bow too far in, the current catches the far side of the canoe, swinging the bow downstream. Both bow and stern linemen should keep an eye on the position of the canoe in relation to the current and should adjust their lines to keep it on a steady course and to avoid rocks and snags. If the bow does get out of control, let it go until it has swung downstream and is again parallel to the current before you start pulling again.

Lining Downstream In lining downstream, hold the canoe back against the current just enough to give you some control. The lines should be tied to the stern towing shackle and the bow seat or thwart if you've got an open canoe. Control in downstream lining depends on angling the stern instead of the bow.

When you're traveling solo you can line a canoe by handling both bow and stern painters and by using the same techniques employed in team lining.

There may be times in a boulder-strewn river when a combination of poling and lining or poling and paddling will provide easiest progress. Here one man handles both lines while the other remains in the canoe to guide it around obstacles with a pole or paddle.

Portaging

So far all the situations I've discussed haven't necessitated taking the canoe out of the water, but some rapids can't be run, poled or lined; they're just too damned big. This is where the portage comes in. Portages aren't pleasant but they do give you a renewed perspective on the river and your canoe. Instead of sliding with the current or curving into an eddy, you have to huff over solid ground lugging your ungainly canoe and your gear. Although your portages probably won't come close to approaching the grueling, cargo-laden trudges required on the nine-mile Grand Portage and the twelve-mile Methye Portage of *voyageur* notoriety, they are part of what whitewater's all about.

Making a portage can be an efficient, smooth-running affair or it can be a chaotic and exasperating experience. Knowing what has to be done, how to do it and who's responsible for doing what are key factors.

On reaching a portage head, one man should steady the boat in the water while the other removes the gear. Some canoeists partially beach their canoe, but this practice isn't too wise since pulling a loaded boat on shore causes undue stress and wear on the hull.

The ease and swiftness with which a canoe can be unloaded depends on whether everything is in its proper place. A craft littered with an assortment of fishing tackle, clothes and food is a backbreaker to unload, and if you swamp, it's like a burst popcorn machine—everything spews out in the water and bobs on downstream or sinks to the bottom. Keep all your gear consolidated in packs or bags.

Open Canoes After unloading, lift the canoe onto shore and secure the paddles. A small block of wood cupped to fit the contour of the center of the paddle shaft and attached to the bottom of the center thwart a few inches from the gunwale will make it easy. To attach a paddle, slide it under the thwart, press it against the side of the canoe and push the center of the shaft into the cup of the block. The grip and the tip of the blade press against the curved canoe sides and the block keeps it in place.

Just leave your paddles inside the boat if you've got a decked model.

Before starting out with packs and canoe it's wise to reconnoiter the portage trail. A well-used portage presents no problems, but there will be times when you'll be traveling on infrequently used trails in remote regions; you may even have to make your own trail. In either case, take your gear over first, returning for the canoe once you've checked the trail's condition; or if one man can handle the gear, have him go first, selecting the easiest way, followed by the man carrying the canoe.

On short portages, you can carry an open canoe by turning it over and resting the center thwart on the back of your neck and on your shoulders, although this won't feel very comfortable. On anything over a quarter of a mile, an improvised or commercial carrying yoke should be used.

Carrying Yokes Many canoe companies, like Old Town, Grumman and Chestnut, have yokes for open boats that you can buy fairly inexpensively. There are aluminum yokes with attached cushions to pad your shoulders. These yokes either slip over the center thwart or take its place. Wooden yokes take the place of the center thwart and are contoured to fit around the back of your neck and rest on your shoulders.

An improvised yoke can be constructed in a matter of minutes using two paddles and some cord. Place the paddles on the stern and center thwarts with the tips of their

This is the way old-timers hoist a canoe to their shoulders. The paddles have been tied to the thwarts to make an improvised carrying yoke. *Photo by Peter Bennett*

blades extending about a foot beyond the center thwart and angled slightly toward the gunwales on either side. Tie the paddles securely with cord at each thwart. Positioned in this manner, the blades of the paddles provide two flat surfaces which rest on your shoulders with your head in between.

There are innumerable ways of getting a canoe from the ground to your shoulders, but only one way is considered right by old-time canoe men. Using this method, you stand beside the canoe at its center thwart, grasping the thwart with both hands next to the near-side gunwale. The canoe is then hoisted from the ground so the bottom rests on your thigh. At this point, slide one hand across the thwart toward the far gunwale and flip the canoe with a jerk of the arms and a shove of the knee up and over your ducked head so the carrying yoke rests on your shoulders. Sounds easy? . . . No? . . . Well, it comes close to being natural after some practice. The trick is to use quick coordinated movements similar to those a weight lifter uses. Don't try to drag it up; jerk it, using momentum, muscle

flow and a prayer that you don't get a hernia.

An easier method, but one that's looked on with scorn by those old-timers, consists of walking yourself under a canoe that's already over your head. Stand at the stern of the canoe and grasp it with one hand on the bottom and one on the top of the stern. Lift the stern over your head and at the same time pull your top hand down and your bottom hand up, rolling the canoe over so the top of the bow is resting on the ground. Now walk, moving hand over hand along the gunwales, to a point where you can slip your shoulders into the yoke. With your hands holding the gunwales in front of you, give a forward bob like a water ouzel; the bow will raise off the ground and you're ready to go.

Decked Canoes Portaging a decked canoe requires different tactics. A C-2 is most easily carried by two people, one grasping the bow grab loop, the other the stern loop. The advantage here is that both people can also carry packs. With a C-1, stick an arm inside the cockpit and rest the rim on your shoulder. You'll probably want to use a folded shirt for pad-

It is easy to walk into your carrying yoke, particularly when you have some assistance. The author's wife is carrying a waterproof "black bag," which is ideal for keeping gear dry. *Photo by Peter Bennett*

ding. Portaging a C-1 by yourself makes it almost impossible to shoulder a pack, so you'll have to make two trips.

The man carrying the canoe on a long portage will want to rest periodically. With an open canoe, lean the canoe in the crotch of a tree or against a sturdy branch and place the stern on the ground. You can duck out from under the craft without having to roll it off your shoulders and then put it back again. On portages over a mile the man with the canoe should change cargoes with the pack carrier, since different muscles are brought into play for each of these loads.

Once you've reached your destination, place the canoe in the water parallel to the shore. You can literally throw the canoe into the water, assuming you can flip it so it ends right side up. The canoe's light weight—

though you might not agree at this point— plus water displacement makes for gentle water/canoe contact, unless you throw it on a rock.

When you reload your gear, put the heaviest packs on the bottom amidship so the canoe is trim fore and aft and side to side, and try to keep all your equipment below the level of the gunwales—no problem if the canoe is decked. The final positioning of packs should be done with both people in the canoe so you're sure you have the level trim wanted for running whitewater.

Once you've shoved things around to get that even trim, secure the packs in an open canoe with two-foot pieces of nylon cord having O rings on one end and quick-release snaps on the other. Put the cord through the packs' shoulder straps and then around a

Prepared to get on with it. *Photo by Peter Bennett*

thwart. The snap does away with complicated lashing and knots that are fingernail breakers when wet; it also allows for quick gear removal if you should capsize.

TRIP EQUIPMENT

When you're really hooked on rapids, you often find a stretch of water that's close at hand and adopt it as your own backyard whitewater, usually spending the day running it and returning home at night. But there comes a time when you yearn for rapids more remote and challenging. You want to follow a fast river for three or four days, maybe several weeks. So you thumb through river guides and a trip starts to take shape in your head.

Whitewater trips where you carry everything you need to be self-sufficient let you fully experience the subtleties and excitement of the river—from finding delicate fern fronds around your evening camp to hearing the roar of rapids on the morning breeze.

But a trip like this takes planning.

Start with a look at the carrying capacity of your canoe. The manufacturer says your 17-foot model will carry 1,000 pounds. That means you and your buddy, each weighing around 175 pounds, can carry a whopping 650 pounds of gear! This kind of figuring leads many a would-be *voyageur* to pile his canoe with everything but Grandma's rocker. And the canoe sinks.

Unfortunately, figures on carrying capacities are deceiving for the whitewater buff. First, some manufacturers tend to be rather optimistic when it comes to how much their canoes can safely carry. Second, these figures indicate maximum carrying capacities on calm water, not whitewater.

Experienced canoeists follow the "minimum of six inches freeboard" rule of thumb. In other words, there should be at least six inches between that part of your canoe riding lowest in the water and the water itself. On really frothy trips even that margin of safety is cutting it close.

It's important to pare down your equipment while still maintaining high standards for safety and a degree of creative comfort. Such items as first-aid and repair kits, painters and life jackets, should go along automatically. But there are other things needed for a comfortable trip, and these change with the idiosyncrasies of each paddler. Norm Strung, for instance, wouldn't think of shoving off without a flask of martinis to mellow his evening musings; that's basic to *his* comfort. I prefer bourbon. Another friend takes a pound of licorice. You may need a pillow, a Monopoly set or a bagful of fishing gear. If you've got to have it, take it. But remember, the water's white and you want to ride high.

Backpacking Gear

Modern backpacking equipment is ideally suited for whitewater use. Lightweight two- to four-man tents run only five to ten pounds. A good down sleeping bag adds only two or three pounds. Freeze-dried and dehydrated food cuts down on the bulk and weight of canned goods. If you use these items, personal and community gear, excluding canoes and paddles, shouldn't average over forty pounds per person for a week's trip.

Packs

Perhaps one exception to the use of backpacking equipment is the backpack itself. The metal frame found on most modern packs is made for carrying sizable loads over long distances. But, sitting in the bottom of a canoe, it can be a nuisance. The metal frame tends to gouge, scrape and bang the bottom, not particularly damaging to aluminum but possibly harmful to fiberglass.

Duluth Packs and Pack Baskets The two traditional canoe packs appropriately come from states boasting fine paddling waters—the pack basket of Maine and the Duluth pack of Minnesota. The typical pack basket is about eighteen inches high, fifteen inches wide and ten inches deep, with a flat bottom and attached carrying straps. It is woven of wood slats, usually ash. An optional waterproof cover is available. The advantage of a pack basket is that it protects breakable items and its wide mouth provides easy access. The Duluth pack is a large canvas sack usually two and a half feet high with closing flap, shoulder straps and tumpline—a strap attached to the top of the bag that goes around your forehead, putting much of the pack's weight on your neck muscles. Unusually heavy weights can be carried in this manner by someone experienced with the pack. It takes some getting used to, however, and a Duluth pack can be torturous if you've never tried one. Its virtue, though, is that it can be crammed with any number of items and still conform nicely to the canoe's bottom.

Unfortunately, these two packs are getting hard to find. Some outdoor suppliers like Herter's and R.E.I. still carry them, but if you can't find them or feel they aren't the packs for you, there are some alternatives.

Rucksacks, Duffelbags and Black Bags
Rucksacks (pack bags without frames), duffelbags with a single carrying strap, and surplus rubberized Army packs (black bags) are all suitable for canoe use. The black bags require no waterproofing, but all the other packs should be lined with a double layer of large plastic bags—the kind used in garbage cans. You may even want to protect individual items by placing them in smaller bags.

Clothes

When you get around to packing your clothes, take shirts and pants that won't cramp your movements. Short pants are comfortable until you get sunburned, so include a pair of baggy blue jeans or khakis. Take along a loose-fitting long-sleeved shirt too, something like an old work shirt, in addition to T-shirts.

Other than following the rule of looseness, clothing should be suitable to the weather conditions you can expect. Wool is a good insulator when wet, so it lends itself nicely to whitewater travel, especially in northern climates. Choose rain gear with an eye toward its drawbacks in the event of swamping. Long draping outfits like ponchos are impossible to

swim in; take a rain jacket instead.

Footwear

For footwear, the rule is flexibility. Your feet get curved, curled and twisted when you are kneeling in a canoe, and you want a shoe that will do the same. Low-cut tennis shoes are ideal. The holes that soon develop in the canvas make convenient water drains and the fabric dries quickly. You can use soft-soled leather moccasins, but they slip off easily and take longer to dry. In any event, leave hiking or street shoes at home or in your pack until you want to explore the river country on foot.

In General

Other items of equipment you carry should include those things used by backpackers—light tent and sleeping bag, flashlight or candle lantern, waterproofed matches, food and first-aid kit. Whitewater canoeists can safely carry more than the backpacker, but safety considerations—primarily the effect of weight on canoe control—should be the major determining force.

All other equipment concerns have to do with your canoe. On the checklist for trip gear, include one life jacket per person and one spare paddle per canoe, plus two fifty- to sixty-foot lengths of ⅜-inch lining ropes. A carrying yoke and pole are optional for open canoes.

A canoe repair kit is a must.

CANOE REPAIR

A lame canoe, it can happen. Faulty judgment, bad water, wrong timing, any of these can send you into a collision course. Be prepared for the results.

There are a long and a short to repair kits. The short version consists of a roll of silver-backed duct tape—the stuff home heating contractors use to seal joints in heating ducts—and epoxy. These two items can be used on both aluminum and fiberglass for stream-side repairs on day trips where access by road is available.

For punctures or small cracks, thoroughly

dry the surrounding surface and cover the area inside the boat with duct tape; it's very sticky and holds well. Then mix up enough epoxy to fill the hole from the outside. Once the mixture sets up, you'll be able to get to your take-out point.

If you've really bashed up your canoe, forget about temporary repairs. Call it a day. Hitchhike to your car, and take the old crippled craft home for an overhaul.

That's fine when the road's nearby, but if you're fifty miles from the nearest tire track, tape and cement isn't going to do the trick. You'll want the long repair kit for long trips in remote waters. The contents are different for aluminum and fiberglass.

Repair Kit and Repairs: Aluminum

A complete aluminum repair kit consists of the following:

Roll of silver-backed duct tape
Epoxy
Three sheets of 6016 aluminum alloy with T-6 temper
Rivet kit
Rubber mallet
Hand drill and #30 and #21 bits
Metal file
Four $\frac{5}{32}$" bolts with nuts
Screwdriver
Pliers
Tin snips
Roofing cement or rubberized caulking compound

Any major encounter with an immovable object, whether rock, boulder or tree, will probably cause two things—a dent, and a hole or crack.

Attack the dent first. A hard blow with the heel of your hand will often pop out a large one. For smaller ones and dents that have creased the aluminum, you'll need the rubber mallet. First turn the canoe so the dented part is resting on soft ground. Then start pounding out the dent from the outside edge, working in circles toward the center. If the keel or gunwales have been bent, put a block of wood—tree limb, stump, whatever's handy—

on either side of the bend and go at it with the mallet. Stomp on it with your foot if you have to, or get a person on either side and pry the bugger back into shape. It's not a delicate operation, but take it slowly, checking to make sure you aren't causing more damage.

After you have something that comes close to the old canoe shape, check for punctures or cracks. Drill a hole at each end of any crack with a #30 bit; this will prevent it from running further.

Next, cut an aluminum patch to fit over the area so its edges extend at least two inches beyond the damage on all sides. After forming the patch to fit the contour of the hull, position it and drill a hole in each corner of the patch and through the canoe. Use a #21 bit. Secure the patch with bolts. This is simply to hold it on while drilling and riveting.

You're ready for drilling the rivet holes. Again using the #21 bit, make holes one inch apart and half an inch in from the edges all the way around the patch. Remove the aluminum and file off burrs on boat and patch.

Finally, smear roofing cement or rubberized caulking compound on the inside of the patch and bolt it back on. Rivet all the holes with $\frac{5}{32}$-inch rivets, leaving the sealing of the four bolt holes until last.

Repair Kit and Repairs: Fiberglass

The repair kit should include the following:

Large piece of 10-ounce fiberglass cloth
Large piece of fiberglass mat
Polyester resin
Catalyst (hardener)
Duct tape
Epoxy
Scissors
1" putty knife
Paintbrush
Wood file
Coarse sandpaper
Paper cups
Acetone and rags for cleaning

Any dents in fiberglass can be sprung out with your palm or fist; the holes aren't so easy.

First, you'll want to dry the area and use the file and sandpaper to clean and rough up the surface for effective patching. Do this on the inside of the canoe if you can. Sometimes it's impossible in a decked model, and you'll have to settle for a patch constructed from the outside.

Large holes should be filled with putty, which you can make by cutting fiberglass cloth into fine shreds and adding resin and some catalyst until you have a stiff glop. Back the hole on one side with duct tape and fill the other side with the mixture.

Once you have this solid backing for the fiberglass patch, cut three pieces of glass cloth two inches larger than the damaged area and cut one piece of glass mat an inch larger than the cloth.

Place these four pieces over the fracture, with the mat going on last. Then, using the paintbrush, thoroughly soak all layers with resin to which catalyst has been added.

Once the mixture starts to gel, you can stop mucking around and let it harden. Sand off any burrs once it gets hard. If it's absolutely imperative that you get back to civilization quickly, at least let the patch cure for an hour after it hardens. It would be better to wait eight to ten hours.

This is the time to be philosophical. Call it a "rest" day, and turn on to the plants and animals that inhabit the river's world. Otter tracks in the mud, willows cropped by feeding moose, the crusty beginnings of insects under rocks. And at the heart of this kaleidoscope of life and color, the prime attractor. Bush, bird, beast, bug and you, all part of the flow of water.

4 KAYAKING

by Earl Perry

There go the ships; there is that Leviathan whom thou hast made to play therein.

—Psalms

Photo by Roy Cromer

The first kayaks were built by the Eskimos of seal and walrus skins, which had been gummed by old women to proper suppleness, then split and sewn over keelsons of wood and baleen. In them hunters dared the gelid northern seas seeking food and the materials for more kayaks. Since none of these hunters could swim (having no place to learn), a brush with the flukes of a whale, a comber taken at the wrong angle or a blast of wind meant a capsize from which one must either do an Eskimo roll or die of hypothermia. While the reasons why we kayak have changed, the punishment (reward?) for a mistake can still be the same.

FOLDBOATS

Copying the design and construction of Eskimo kayaks, the Germans created the foldboat: skins in the one have become treated canvas, and bone ribs have become a light structure of wood. Foldboats, however, are scorned by most "real" rivermen, for while they are surprisingly rugged and nearly as stable as rafts, they have all the maneuverability of a fired bullet; when once they start down a rapid, only God and solid objects alter their course. Although they carry a lot of gear and can ride immense water (Alexander "Zee" Grant was the first to kayak the Grand Canyon using one, though he rigged it with sponsons), they can do so only so long as the watercourse is straight and requires no large evasions. They are really useful only for their portability; they fold up into a compact, relatively light bundle. David Roberts, the climber and fine writer, used one to get out of the Alaskan wilderness after one of his climbs; the small bundle fitted well into a plane and the river required no more spry a craft. But because foldboats are not quite sturdy enough to absorb the crashes their unwieldiness causes, I shall ignore them.

DOWNRIVER BOATS

Downriver or wildwater boats are reminiscent in shape of the Eskimo's kayaks. Con-structed of fiberglass or plastic, they are relatively long, about 14′7″. Older models use a V bottom to serve for the keel they lack; the more recent ones can be thought of, seen in cross section, as an omega inverted (℧). There is a rough marine law which states that the greater the ratio of length to wetted width, the greater the speed of the hull. Since international regulations specify a minimum width for the deck, the ingenuity of the designers conceived this shape to pass the regulations and still preserve a minimum width, not much wider than a telephone pole, where the boat meets the water. Certain of these boats are Swedishform and certain are fishform; this means the widest point at the waterline is respectively behind or in front of the paddler. Since the best racers I know would commit themselves only to the modest observation that "both types are represented among the top boaters," I suspect the distinction is important mostly as a convenience for displaying kayakers' pedantry, a matter of sound and fury which will perhaps engage the reader in long delightful arguments on the banks of rivers yet unseen.

All flourishes of nugatory learning for the moment stifled, the beginner ought to know that speed and tracking (the ability to continue in a straight line after one ceases to paddle) are the fortes of these boats; maneuvering is not, and neither is rolling. They are boats made for a very specific and perhaps limited task—the descent of a given stretch of river as fast as it can be done by hand; therefore, they have as little relation to most kayaking as one of Breedlove's salt-flat, jet-powered racers has to a Lotus.

SLALOM BOATS

Most kayakers prefer slalom boats, or at least hybrid whelps of slalom and downriver boats. Since it is all too likely, I understand, that a hybrid will display the worst characteristics of both parents (every miscegenated half-downriver, half-slalom boat I ever used upholds me here), it is better to stick with a plain slalom boat. Originally designed to slip about through gates suspended above the waters of particularly bad rapids, forwards, backwards, upstream and down, they have (as seen in cross section) smooth oval or round hulls which roll up into low and rounded decks. They are 4 meters (13′2″) long and 0.6 meter (approximately 23″) wide. Like the downriver boat mentioned above, they are now made of fiberglass; the egg-like rigidity of the oval cross section has replaced the whalebone ribs of the first kayaks, and God's own resilience in the skins is replaced by smooth laminations of woven glass. This very smoothness—for slalom boats are a whirl of curves blending into one another everywhere but at the tips—fathers their uncanny agility. They can be spun, thrust, twisted and rolled easily, for they weigh only about 20 to 35 pounds. Beyond the relative slowness of such craft (though they still can almost match a motored pontoon) and the small space for gear, they have but two disadvantages. With their low decks and consequent low volume, a great bursting wave can momentarily sink the whole craft, and with their unrockered (rockered means bent up at either end) tips they tend to pearl (from the surfer's term "pearl diving") when driven straight into waves of any size but the smallest; their nose plunges into the wave, and some time is required for the air in the boat to extricate it. But these are minor objections, detailed merely out of duty; slalom boats are the ultimate river craft. Their water-strider ability permits them the smallest and steepest of rivers alike with the giants: a young fellow in 1973 successfully sneaked into Cataract Canyon on 65,000 cubic feet per second, a stage the great motored pontoons of the professionals rightly fear. While he courted death and risked arrest (he had no permit), he made the passage and a point: the slalom kayak is the most versatile of river craft.

Like a fine pair of skis, or a really accurate rifle, the capacities of a slalom boat seem to linger just in advance of the capabilities of its owner. A beginner, if he manages not to wreck his new boat in the first year, or even in the first day, will for years be ferreting out lurking abilities in the boat, mastering them and discovering that more remain.

KAYAKERS AND OTHER BOATMEN

Before I discuss the process of buying or, as is more usual, making a kayak, it might be well to have a general and exaggerated discussion of what kayakers are like. Let all qualifications be stated at first: there are many kayakers, many personalities and therefore many reasons to kayak. Still, there are things to be said about kayakers as a group. First, in essence—an essence we all seek consciously to avoid—the real pleasure of kayaking is in having a chance to be killed in beautiful and noble surroundings. The government is trying either to remove such possibilities or at least to gather them all to itself, so no man may nobly die save in war (if then), but kayaking still offers a chance. If one believes that at the intersection of life and death, there is certainly strength and possibly meaning to be found, then one will begin to see, if not a justification, yet still a reason for kayaking; those who think this a batch of nonsense are better advised to clutter the highways and not the river. Or at most (apologies to my co-writers) let them sink their money in rafts. For raftsmen (and I have not only been one, but was a professional for many years) tend to be a more placid group, with hulking slabbed shoulders and swoops of belly curling down past their belt loops. They have a taste for the easy living that their rafts carry for them. You find them mellowing out around their blazing white-man fires, savoring cold beers and massive rare steaks. But a kayaker you find huddled about some shrunken matchstick of a fire, chewing energetically at the mucilaginous husks of his brown rice. He is the Cassius of the river, and his lean and hungry look is not solely the result of the tiny carrying capacity of his boat. No, he could, by setting that astounding technological imagination he has to work (and be assured that fiberglass kayaks are designed, not by obscure fiberglass engineers in unaccountable shadow corporations, but by kayakers themselves), attain some way to carry his own rare meat, if he wanted. He does not want to. He is (I am, you may be) that finest of masochists, one who does not enjoy the pain so much as the attendant sense of personal righteousness. He is, at extreme, a fanatic, and stokes the fires of his eyes, not by feeding his flesh, but by mortifying it. His muscles are not those of a raftsman, great smooth cannonballs under the flesh, but thin stringy masses that when stressed by a stroke stand out like the grain on ancient and weathered wood. Like D. H. Lawrence, he believes, really believes, hell, *knows,* that the more machinery you interpose between the world and your senses, the duller your senses become.

In camp a raftsman may award himself a nap. A kayaker will go scrabbling up towering canyon walls and cascade down after dark, full of enthusiasm for the experiment of whether he can subsist on roast cactus. He can. On the river the raftsman, though he may be so powerful in the shoulders as to be able in flustered moments to snap a 14-foot hickory oar, is generally found lounging on the soft pneumatic tubes of his raft. He may spend whole long lazy minutes deliberating whether he will hit a cliff or get caught by an eddy. He does this, not because he is interested either way, but because it is a nice, fatalistic sort of question which will resolve itself in a minute anyway. If the river sees fit to lodge him in the eddy and rotate him for a while, he does not mind. Planets and galaxies and electrons all rotate, so he is in good company. Rivers and their raftsmen operate by the principle of minimum work; both have a stated quantum of energy which they expend as slowly and as uniformly as conditions permit.

A kayaker, on the river, can seldom be seen motionless, for when he ceases to paddle he feels vague guilts and is soon scooting about the water again. He may flail furiously back upstream to inspect a cliff he will have forgotten in another minute, or race off downstream to dally for hours in the next rapid. He will paddle down it, and paddle back up it. He will run it backwards to see if he can tip over end for end; he will run it sideways to see if that big hole will eat him; he will run it to punish himself. A kayaker is the sort of person who not only skips his lunch, but spends his lunch hour jogging; he takes his sauna baths with real snow.

One might get at the comparison, again, with all qualifications assumed, by opposing an English gentleman, a stately, portly, dignified gentleman accustomed to the amenities of liqueurs and massive spitted roasts, to a gaunt Puritan of Cromwell's army, nourished on coarse wheat bread and God's own truth, directly vouchsafed.

It is said that Roger Williams, before he established the principle of religious toleration, grew so fierce in his purity that no one in the world except his own wife could be worthy of sharing communion with him. Now kayakers, sometimes to an irritating extent, indulge and love this same sort of individualism: it is one of the reasons for taking up the sport. It is a sport almost purely individual and therefore, not very paradoxically, permits the rarest and strongest of friendships to spring up. A raftsman may not like *large* groups of people; we surely hated the old-time circus trips in Grand Canyon, when we shared the canyon with 175 dudes and the attendant motors, boats, stoves and gear, while cooking amidst a subway press of folk and defecating in rows upon the beaches. But in the main, with rare and unhappy exceptions, a raftsman likes his boatload of people. A kayaker loves his boatload of himself. He will be killed by no one but himself, should he be killed; he will as a rule kill no one but himself by his mistakes. The kayaker has intense responsibility for himself, but for his friends, who are like him, almost none.

Strength is a reason to take up the sport; so is emulation; I tend to think of them as discreditable justifications, but pleasant adjuncts to kayaking. For strength you can get in a Vic Tanny's, and emulation you can indulge watching television; to come to kayaking solely for these is to debase the river itself. But justice is another matter. It is one of the prime gifts of kayaking. For there comes a moment in certain rapids when skill and the situation are in tenuous balance. Your efforts, at their maximum, have brought you to the point where effort is unavailing and chance rules; a wave which you cannot anticipate or time may or may not burst, so you may or may not finish the rapid upright; in a big enough rapid, you may or may not finish it alive. The superstitious may use such a moment to assess the state of their karma; for me it is valuable as a moment almost of surrender. It is one of the few chances we have on this side of the grave to experience nonhuman and perfectly indifferent justice. One is at the peak of one's skill and strength, yet the outcome is not to be commanded.

I have yet to mention scenery; it is there. Perhaps it is even true that it is deeply rewarding sometimes. But on a real river, the kayaker will debouch at the take-out with a photographic memory of the river itself (all those who are destined to be boatmen have this sort of memory; you can read *Life on the Mississippi* by Twain for an early confirmation of the fact). He will remember where he ran and where he would have run and where he never should have run at all, yet on the banks he will remember only a jumble of rocks, willows and towering silver heaps of driftwood. This is all the scenery he has noticed, for the river has required his eyes. When David Yeamans and I injudiciously kayaked Westwater Canyon years back, we flushed out of the last rapid and were surprised to find we had been running a chasm comparable to the Inner Gorge of Grand Canyon, and that above it were sinuous tinted tiers of crimson sandstone that rose in palisades and conchoidal fractures for a thousand feet. A kayaker comes to love the river itself, and when it grows so dull he must look at mere cliffs, even if the Grand Canyon itself furnishes them, he will feel a little disappointed.

Now, assuming that those I intended to filter out by the concentration on death and devastation above have ricocheted back to the sections on rafting and canoeing, it is correct to add that not a kayaker in thousands actually gets killed, and that if at base that may be why one practices the sport, still kayakers are usually extreme in their safety precautions, and lose less than the raftsmen, whose sport is the safer. Now let me enter the discussion of buying and building kayaks.

BUYING A KAYAK

New Boats

Large sporting-goods stores in large towns, the kind that cater not to plebeians such as we hunters, but to purists such as we backpackers and bicyclists and fishermen (*fly* fishermen, of course), will generally carry kayaks if the area they serve has any rivers. The "Boats" section of the yellow pages can help. Boston has many dealers; Berkeley and Denver are meccas for the sport; so are certain Eastern colleges like Penn State and Dartmouth. *American Whitewater* magazine and *Downriver* magazine list sellers and affiliate members who can direct you to kayaks. The most recent addresses I can get for these magazines are: *American Whitewater,* Box 321, Concord, New Hampshire, 03301; and *Downriver,* Box 366, Mountain View, California 94040. If your sporting-goods stores cannot help you, and you cannot get to these magazines and their advertisers, find a river with rapids and sit on the bank until a kayaker comes by. Hail him in and pump his brains.

The kayaks available from such sporting-goods stores will likely be of the slalom type. Ask for it. Do not bother with hybrid types, good for touring as the salesman will say, or boats for beginners. You want the hottest boat you can get, unless you are rich. Buying a good beginner's boat just means having to scrap it in a year or so, when you are no longer a beginner, and then you have wasted its price. Better to get an expert's racing slalom boat and have it chew on you for a while; eventually you will be able to handle it, and will have bought only one boat instead of two. Such a boat will run $200 to $500, depending on whether it is made by a starving craftsman trying to get through college or a kayak factory in Europe. It will likely be adequately designed and adequately crafted. Do not get a boat constructed with chopped mat glass. This is glass chopped up and sprayed with resin into a mold; it is both heavy and weak. The boat will come with a spray cover and some flotation, though not nearly enough. Most of the good boats are constructed of fiberglass cloth. A new model is worthy of mention. This is the Riverchaser or Hollow-form, used by the kayak patrol on the Middle Fork. It is made of frisbee material and is almost overly flexible while remaining nearly indestructible. This boat is now (Summer 1975) for sale in Denver for $250 and is a good buy for the affluent beginner and the expert who must run a lot.

Used Boats

More attractive than the buying of a new boat to most kayakers, who tend to think of themselves as rational consumers or even cheapskates, is to buy a used boat from someone in a nearby club. Depending upon the greed of the seller, the ignorance of the buyer and the condition of the boat, the price will be from $30 to $250. This is probably the best, and certainly the cheapest, way to enter the sport, for the boat if wrecked is a smaller loss, and the beginner will be many months and rivers before he transcends even the modest capacities of a battered and patched old hulk that weighs fifty-five pounds.

Equipment

Even getting a good buy on a used boat, one must count on a considerable outlay to enter the sport, about as much as if one were to begin to ski from scratch. And almost none of this outlay can be safely skimped. The boat must have float bags so it will not sink when dumped; these run from $5 for old inner tubes to $27.50 for the combination gear and float bags manufactured by Whitewater Sports in Denver. These should be bought by anyone who conceives of an overnight trip at any time in his career. There must be a paddle, from $10 to $30; I prefer about 86 inches but the paddle should not be over 92 or under 78 inches. I prefer a slightly spooned blade, others a flat blade, and a few top men rely on a heavily spooned blade for river use. There must be a wet-suit top of neoprene foam if the kayaker plans to boat in the spring or in the water excreted from the bottom of a dam; for really cold weather, a full wet suit with pants, booties, mittens and even perhaps a hood is important; all of this, depending on thickness, custom tailoring and whether the suit is full or partial can shift the cost between about $30 and about $140. You should buy a helmet if you plan to boat anywhere besides a swimming pool, and a good helmet if you plan to boat anything worse than Class III water; the expense—$5 for a useless used hockey helmet and up to $75 for a high-grade motorcycle helmet—will seem paltry the first time you roll up with a deep scoring in the helmet. Check pawnshops for bargain helmets. And most important of all, you must have a life jacket. Since certain regulated rivers require that it must be Coast Guard-approved, saving expense dictates buying this type initially, at about $10 to $35. It should give you about 20 percent of your body weight in buoyancy; the 33-pound-buoyancy Mae West type is best. A word of caution is in order. Many a self-styled expert will denigrate the need for a life jacket; *he* has never needed one on the dinky little technical rivers he has run, or never needed a large one. And, he will tell you, your own body will furnish some buoyancy (it will if your body is fat) and your wet suit will furnish some (it will, from 3 pounds for a ⅛-inch sleeveless top to 10 pounds for a ¼-inch full suit). Furthermore, he will say, you may need to ditch the life jacket to swim out of certain holes.

Do not believe him. You are not an expert. You may never even get to be one if you take his advice early on in your career. And finally, his advice may hold for races and steep, tiny rivers. But it is just this sort of expert who dies like a dude when he faces the flooding rivers in Idaho and Colorado, or the huge rivers of the Southwest and far Northwest, where the volume runs from 10 to 200 times as much as he has ever encountered in California or back East. Dick Hertzler of the kayak patrol on the Middle Fork, who ran this year on water up to probably 35,000 or 40,000 second-feet (cubic feet per second), wears the largest life jacket he can buy with a wet suit as extra insurance. I myself have risen from the depths below a ten-foot hole, so slowly and so battered, so panicked and so unable to breathe, think or swim, that the 40 pounds buoyancy I wore seemed nearly inadequate. When you yourself are an expert and competent to argue such points, you may do without a life jacket or wear some puny aggregation of air bubbles trapped in vinyl. You may live to repent. Until then buy a large jacket whose cloth covering is nylon and hold your peace.

All this adds from about $65 to $320 to the cost of the boat, before one takes that first paddle stroke in the river, depending on whether you go for the old hockey helmet and a 79-cent dry suit (a non-buoyant rubber suit worn over a wool sweater with elastic at the wrists, waist and throat) or the top-of-the-line equipment from the most expensive of shops. But you can, of course, justify the purchases to your spouse and children as they grind on canned chili and soybean hamburger by suggesting that all this ancillary equipment will last five to thirty years and can thus be amortized at only a few dollars a year. If you are shrewd, you can even borrow a trick from the dam builders and do a cost-benefit analysis. You take the cost of the equipment and balance it against an entirely arbitrary figure some ten to thirty times as great, and prove to your spouse that while you have to *pay* $250 for the equipment, you will be getting some $5,000 to $7,500 in the benefits of health, strength and even, if you are shameless enough to carry it off, increased marital fidelity, so you cannot afford not to buy it. The cost-benefit analysis ratio is highly favorable. Your spouse, who is a citizen and therefore must have been convinced by the Bureau of Reclamation when it used exactly the same arguments to murder Glen Canyon and dozens of other rivers, will surely have to be convinced when you use them. A man can do anything with figures, and might as well, since his own government sets him the example.

BUILDING A BOAT

The last of all the choices, between buying new and buying old, is to build the boat yourself. It will be, unless you are a total klutz, a better boat than you could buy; what does some gnome in the Black Forest, wine bibber along the Seine or dope smoker in California care about your boat? *You* care about your boat. There are kits available, such as from Plasticrafts in Denver; they contain everything you need to make a kayak and run some $85 to $110. Or you can rent the mold if you find a satisfactory one and can afford the rental and freight fees. Then purchase all the materials (being a member of a club may rain discounts upon you) and get to work. This usually runs $90 to 225, though it may still be possible even with inflation to get one finished up in California for $80.

Health Hazards

Those who like to do it themselves, or at least trust themselves more than anonymous craftsmen, and who have never worked with fiberglass, may find this alternative appealing. If you are one such, let me try to blunt your enthusiasm, for while I build my own boats, and have assisted at the construction of twenty or thirty of them, it is not a task I would wish upon a bureaucrat. So, if you like to work on cars, imagine working on a completely impacted, rusted muffler for three days with no progress and a steady rain of gasoline and powdery rust in your face. If you have ever had to empty the porta-potty, a task we professional boatmen have been at for years, you might imagine that task magnified into three days, and undeodorized by the pleasant philosophical reflections on mortality and corruption, or the amiably scatological ribaldries in the manner of Swift and Rabelais, with which a boatman beguiles the hours each morning while he hoses away the evening's dinners. No, here there are no unarguably "organic" redolences; the fumes, in fact, are poisonous. Your lungs are filled with fumes and glass, your skin is filled with glass dust and its surface burnt with resin.

This is not an exaggeration. There lives many a worker now (for a while) whose lungs are punctured with asbestosis or whose abdomen rots with mesothelioma, who thought a job in an asbestos factory was a fine and lucrative way to raise a family. Painting the radium dials on watches was a fine way to earn a living some years back; ask the man whose mouth is now a putrid mass of cancer from licking the brush to get a fine point on it. It is known that inhaling glass fibers of the minute size that float in the air above fiberglass can cause silicosis, a disease in which the glass punctures the alveoli of the lungs, reduces their surface area and eventually makes a walk of three paces too strenuous to be completed. It is said that the aroma from the resins that impregnate the glass causes impotence and temporary personality changes. It may also be a cumulative poison. So each boat a man builds shortens, by how much no one knows, the time he has to run it. And no one does know; we are given these gifts by unknown chemists in unknown corporations. We can take these technological gifts in good faith and remark that everyone has to die sometime, or we can be suspicious. God knows what the side effects of these chemical gifts are; the chemist and I do not. So when I say it is best to lay the boat up with "adequate ventilation," it is best that you agree. If you can, do it outdoors, out of direct sunlight, with a breeze blowing. When you come to sand the boat, or to lay the uniting strips of glass down the line between the hull and the deck, and must insert your head into the cavity, hold your breath, wear a respirator for when you forget and inhale, share the work with your friends, and do not stay at it very long. Keep all your skin covered, wearing dishwashing gloves and even a bathing cap, since if resin gets on your skin you will burn almost immediately. You can remove resin with acetone, but it is so volatile it extracts the moisture from the outer layer of your skin, leaving a whitish scurf.

I have embedded in an appendix the materials necessary for constructing a kayak. I here assume you have no guide, no one who has built a boat before, to assist you. If this is the case, before you buy the materials, before you pass from contemplation to action, send off to Wildwater Designs, Inc., Penllyn Pike and Morris Road, Penllyn, Pennsylvania, 19422, for a booklet entitled *Boatbuilder's Manual*, by Charles Walbridge. The price is $3.00 as of this writing, but the book is invaluable. All that I have to say is based on my own experience, and I also recommend that you read Mr. Walbridge's detailed and cogent remarks on the subject. With this caveat, and the further caution that those who have bought a boat may not be entranced by the pages to follow, let us begin.

Mold Preparation

I assume all the materials have been selected and assembled, measured and cut. Be sure your shop and your person are protected by layers of plastic and clothing before you begin, for even acetone or MEK (methyl iso-butyl ketone, a potent solvent) is ineffective against hardened resin. So, set the molds on a pair of sawhorses, wax them three to six times with a carnauba wax, and when this has been buffed smooth, paint, wipe or spray on the mold release; let it dry between each coat. Put on the mold release in several layers, for if it fails you may wreck your boat or be assessed for mold damage.

Mixing Resin

Put your coloring in the resin before you mix any of it with the catalyst. This will insure uniform coloration in the boat. Then, from the colored gallon, extract no more than a quart for your first attempts. Following the manufacturer's directions for the materials and temperature you deal with, mix catalyst

A section of glass cloth, rolled up from both ends when it has been cut to length, is laid in the boat. By marking a center line on the mold and on the cloth, little glass is wasted. This double roll makes the cloth easier to handle, and permits wrinkles to be worked out toward each end. *Photo by Earl Perry*

with the resin. If you mix up more than a quart at a time at first, you may find the pot setting up faster than you can use it, or worse, not setting up at all. This can be serious, for while the resin will harden itself in about a year, even a week of setting the sticky lay-up in front of heat lamps is more time than most people can bear. I have found that a piece of coat hanger bent into a T and spun by a power drill for a minute provides an adequate mix of catalyst with resin. If you are doing a gel coat, which offers a little extra weight, smoothness and protection, paint it evenly in the mold, with no bubbles or puddles. Usually it is customary to start with the hull mold; it is easiest.

Saturating the Cloth

When the gel coat is dry (if you opt not to use one, begin here) mix up another quart of resin, pour a workable amount in the mold, spread it with the squeegees, plasticaters, brushes, or rollers, and put in the cloth. This can be done by putting in one end and simply unrolling the whole cloth until it reaches the other end, but I have found it safer to roll each end of a layer of cloth up to a previously marked center line which is matched with a center line on the mold. Then the cloth is unrolled gradually in each direction, as each section is impregnated with the resin. The Scylla and Charybdis of the job are using too much resin, which makes a heavy, weak boat by ponding and floating the glass (this is unexpectedly called making a bubble) above itself; and using too little, which causes pinholes in the finished boat. Pinholes are dealt with by adding and working in more resin; bubbles are dealt with by scraping away the excess of resin that has floated the glass and depositing it in a drier area. If you get bubbles that do not vanish when you have removed the excess resin, they are likely caused by folding, warping, pulling, stretching, tweezing or generally mishandling the glass cloth. Try to correct this by lifting the cloth and relaminating it, working the wrinkles out from the center to the sides and from the midpoint to the ends. Adamant wrinkles may be cut with a scissors into two flaps, one of which is flattened and the other of which is laid upon the first. This is an unsightly and debilitating procedure for the boat which should be avoided if you can.

When a layer is properly laminated, it will have no wrinkles in its weave, no sparkling irregularly shaped rectilinear patterns that indicate a dearth of resin. It will be a uniform dark color through which the mold sometimes can be seen. When one layer is done, either do the next or lay in the reinforcements at stern and bow. Remember, these should overlap gradually so an excess of rigidity does not afflict the finished boat with stress cracks at the margins of the reinforcements. A good source for reinforcements is the set of four right triangles of glass which overhang the mold, two at each end, from the previous full layer. However, it ought to be pointed out that very many layers of reinforcements so increase the weight of the boat as to cancel gains in strength with losses in agility. I have put in as many as four layers of reinforcements on a four-layer hull and created a battleship. Each end of the boat, however, should have an extra layer or two.

The deck presents a few more problems, since it is thinner than the hull and contains the cockpit, or coaming, the rounded lip around the seat opening to which the spray cover will be attached. When the first layer is impregnated there will be an oval of unimpregnated glass in the coaming area. Allowing two inches of excess that will be stuck down in the coaming area, cut out this oval in the middle of the boat. The remaining overhang is cut radially every two to four inches about the margin of the coaming area, so it

will lay in properly over the rolled areas of the mold, without wrinkling. If, as is normally the case, the coaming is not part of the deck mold, simply stick the glass down into the ravines of the area as best you can, making the radial cuts where necessary.

Several layers of reinforcement are necessary in the coaming area. A rectangle of glass about 26 inches long and about 8 inches wide is laid across the boat behind the cockpit to distribute the load the paddle puts there as you enter the boat. The whole area near the coaming is reinforced with a piece of cloth cut to look like a square with triangles attached to opposite ends. The points of these triangles extend past the coaming area a foot or two toward either end. There should be at least one layer, maybe two, of bias-cut strips (strips cut some 3 to 4 inches wide by about 6 inches long, whose weave runs at a 45-degree angle to the rectangle of the strip) which are laid in the coaming area; the bias cut permits them to bend without wrinkles in the wavy terrain near the coaming. Each end should have a reinforcing patch; the one in the bow should be larger since it is most stressed by doing end-for-ends.

When the last layer is in the deck, you may apply the final reinforcements. There are a number of types. The first is simply a rope of about ⅜-inch diameter running out to each end from the coaming area, glassed in by a rectangle of cloth as long as the ropes and some 8 inches wide. Or one may use bomb tubes, a sort of Masonite conduit about 1¼ inches in diameter that is said to have formed part of the viscera of certain bombs; unfortunately no one who has not seen them can help you find them. They are glassed in just like rope, and because they have threaded plugs in their ends, they carry maps nicely. Or you can make L ribs of glass by taking an angle iron, covering it with waxed paper and laying a few layers of glass upon it. After curing, trimming to the proper length and cutting away excess width, you can place the resulting "angle glass" along the medial line of the deck with a layer or two of glass along its length to cement it to the deck. Or, finally, you can simply take rectangles of glass, wet them with resin, set them in the boat in whatever pattern appeals to you (Walbridge's drawings suggest a chevron) and push them up into little ridges. They will look much the same as a rope reinforcement, without the excess weight of the rope itself. All this can be done after the boat has set up solidly, but then you must sand it for a good bond, whereas while it is still soft you may simply add the reinforcing ribs without the extra effort of sanding.

Trimming the Laminate

Another task which goes more easily before the laminates have completely set up is the trimming. This should be done when the laminate, or resin-impregnated glass, is stiff but not stony. Each mold will have an irregular fringe of glass projecting above it. This must be cut away with a very sharp knife, which may well be ruined by the process. Do not delaminate the glass or tear the laminate away from the mold. This can best be done by putting the cutting blade and arm inside the boat and cutting toward the outside. If you damage the mold, you may be made, as you deserve, to pay for it, so be as gentle as you are accurate.

Seaming the Boat

We approach the foulest and most fateful of tasks, the joining of the two halves. I have heard it said that if both halves are still a little wet, though hard, it may be possible to do the joining without sanding or rasping, but I have my doubts. I let them set up hard, put on a respirator, then circumambulate each half, rasping down to the glass fibers and to a line two inches below the top of each mold. When this is done the two molds are bolted together through the flanges of each (if you have a mold without flanges remove the two halves of the boat, line them up and tape them together; see that you do not have a mold without flanges ever again), and the boat is inside its halves ready to be joined by strips of glass tape.

Take up a four-foot-long stick with a nail and brush on one end, paint in a strip of resin along the crack at the bottom of the two halves, attach one end of a piece of glass tape to the nail, thrust it out to the end of the boat, detach it into the resin track and begin using the brush to stick it down. If you cannot see, attach a clamp light in the coaming area beside your head. If you can avoid it, do not burn your head on the light. Even with your respirator do not attempt to breathe inside the boat. Some run a strip the whole length of the boat; I have found this cumbersome and run each of the three strips in two pieces—six overlapping strips per side. Others soak each strip in resin before they attempt to insert it; such wet floppy tapes always deviate off the crack for me but you may do better. Take a lot of time, try to inveigle your friends into aiding you, and do not breathe. The task's wretchedness can only be learned, not described.

When the three layers of strips, each a little wider than the one beneath it, are all in, let them cure well, turn the molds over and do the other side. While this final seam cures you can lay up the seat and foot braces.

Bracing Systems

There are so many permutations of each that several possibly confusing paragraphs follow to discuss them all. Let us start with the simplest: Seat and coaming are integral and come off a single mold. Wax it and apply the mold release. Using the scraps from other processes and some regular glass, lay it up. You will want at least three layers at the bottom of the seat, five at the sides and four around the coaming. Bias-cut strips are necessary around the coaming. If you have a choice between a high and low seat mold for the boat, the criteria are these: high seats have better visibility and make the boat harder to roll; low seats produce an easier roll and less visibility. Since a beginner usually doesn't know what he is looking at anyway, I suggest the low seat for him and the high for an expert.

A coaming will often be separate. Lay it up,

The technique of seaming a boat is illustrated here on molds furnished by Plasticrafts of Denver. After the laminates of the hull and deck have cured and have been trimmed, the molds are bolted together through holes in the flanges, and a seam of glass tape laid in to join the halves of the boat. The molds are either hung from the ceiling or balanced on their side, so one seam is at the bottom. Glass tape, stuck on a nail on a stick, is extended out to the end of the molds, flopped off and stuck in a track of resin painted over the seam.   *Photo by Earl Perry*

cut it at one point to get it off the mold, and consider the seat. For when seat and coaming are not integral, the seat must be created. Usually a polyethylene foam block, glued with Barge contact cement or an epoxy to the bottom of the boat and sculptured to the gluteal contours of the boater, will serve perfectly well. But such a seat requires hip braces. The easiest and strongest way to make these is to lay up on waxed paper two rectangles perhaps 7 by 12 inches, each of which when trimmed will run up from the side of the seat to the lateral edges of the coaming. To lock these in place it is best not merely to glass them in to the top and bottom of the boat, but to run a sort of shaped strut out at 90 degrees from them to the sides of the boat where the

uniting seams have been laid.

Foot braces come in various types. The simplest method is to take L-shaped shelf brackets and bolt or rivet them to the sides of the boat. The bolts and rivets leak a little, and eventually pull through unless they are backed, on the outside of the kayak, by an unsightly metal bar. Another variety is the glass or aluminum perforated anchor. Two plates, one for each side of the boat, are drilled to accommodate a transverse shaft which will serve as the brace itself. The glass rectangles, after drilling, are glassed to the boat, when it has been removed from the mold, by several strips around their perimeter; the aluminum strips, also after drilling, are bolted to the boat. A shaft with a collar which is at once slightly larger than the shaft and slightly smaller than the receiving hole is run between two of the holes. When the shaft is positioned, its collar is slid into a hole and a bolt run through both collar and shaft to lock it in place. The bolt had better be of stainless steel, or you may never get at your forward dunnage and float bag.

The simplest system and the safest is to take a block of Ethafoam at least four inches thick and cut it to a plug which slips into the boat exactly as far as one's feet require. It should be channeled at top and bottom to let water run past and to admit the passage of an inflation tube for the front float bag. While such a brace does not permit access to gear on a tour, it adds both flotation and rigidity to a boat, and obviates the danger of passing right through a foot brace and being jammed in the boat.

A combination seat and coaming mold is shown in this picture in working position. In such a mold, the sides of the seat serve as hip braces and must be reinforced with a couple of extra layers of cloth. The coaming, or rounded lip, must be at least four layers thick. Because of the abrupt bends in the coaming, bias-cut glass strips, which will stretch around corners without wrinkling, should be used in laying up the coaming. *Photo by Earl Perry*

A separate coaming mold is shown here. The break in the mold permits the coaming, when it has cured, to be removed from the mold. It is best to tape the gap closed before construction, and saw through it later with a hacksaw. Bias-cut strips must be used everywhere on this mold and in addition a separate seat and hip braces must later be fabricated to go with it. *Photo by Earl Perry*

Removing the Boat from the Mold

We have wandered a little, and by this time the boat should be ready, after some long hours of curing, to emerge from the mold. It should feel hard to the touch. If it is not, leave it and heat it until it is. When the moment comes, tap about inside the molds with a rubber hammer or a 2x4. Use no metal. A boat is free of the mold when it crackles and turns a lighter color than it was. Unbolt the molds and try, by gentle tapping and the insertion of tongue depressors (not screwdrivers, which in exuberant hands can score the mold), to remove one half of the molds. When it comes free, take your tongue depressors to the other half. Walbridge cites some folk who have overcome problem releases by pouring water between the mold and the boat and freezing it overnight. This ought to work if a frost is provided. But far, far easier to have used a lot of wax and a lot of mold release; far cheaper too, if you end up cratering a mold to get your boat out of it.

Installing the Bracing Systems

Now come a variety of instructions about readying the boat. The installation of most of the types of foot braces discussed above must be delayed until the boat is out of the mold. So too with the seat and coaming. You must have a proper seat installed before you can approximate to a decent foot-brace position. So let us deal with that first. If the coaming and seat are integral, glass them in after sanding down to the fiber. This is easiest done by placing the coaming in position, fill-

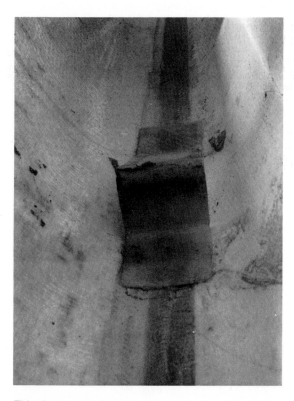

This simple glass foot brace is very similar to the shelf-bracket types discussed in the text. Five or six layers of glass are placed over a right triangle of 2x4's protected by waxed paper. When cured, the right triangle of glass is glued or glassed on to the seam by its overhanging flanges. This system permits access to the front float bag. *Photo by Earl Perry*

The perforated anchor foot brace permits access to gear and a variable position for the brace itself. Long plates of glass are cured, trimmed to shape by a saber saw and bored to accommodate a transverse shaft. The plates are attached by glass around their perimeters. The radiator clamps permit a sliding sleeve of aluminum conduit to extend into whichever hole is chosen, and when loosened permit the brace to be telescoped in and removed for access to gear. *Photo by Earl Perry*

A completed customized seat. Blocks of Ethafoam have been glued in beside it to lock the seat into the boat. Large black patches of neoprene foam provide a tighter fit and a measure of comfort. A back strap is attached with shock cord to give some stretch for relaxation. Not shown are the Ethafoam blocks under the seat which keep it from flexing and tearing the coaming away from the boat. The black lines are carbon fibers, an extremely expensive reinforcement. Unusual on this boat is a thigh brace, which appears in front of the seat and just under the coaming, and permits an even more solid fit of kayaker to craft. *Photo by Earl Perry*

ing in cracks with Cab-o-sil or automotive putty and laying strips of glass roving (painfully unwoven by hand into segments perhaps ⅜ inch wide and 4 inches long) all around the coaming, from both inside and outside. A little clear freezer wrap (not Saran Wrap) or waxed paper, stretched over the glass while the laminate is still wet, will save much sanding later by smoothing the surface of the glass which bonds the coaming to the boat. If the seat is not attached to the coaming, glass in the coaming, create the seat, whittle it to your dimensions, sit in it, glue it in and try to position your foot brace.

When you have found the proper position for the foot brace, install it. If it is an Ethafoam block, you must whittle it until it jams in snugly at exactly the chosen position. The other types are placed against your feet as you sit on the seat with your knees pressed against the top of the kayak, your actual heavy-water kayaking position. Slide your feet back and forth until the foot brace is exactly as far away as you want. With one of the foot braces, which is adjustable by virtue of the holes you have drilled in it, try to have the center hole in perfect position, so that the other holes permit use by your dainty wife or elongated husband. I am the first to realize how tricky this is, but you must get it right or endure an uncomfortable boat as long as you own it.

When the seat, coaming and foot brace

A racing foot brace. This nonadjustable system is a pipe glassed in to the boat. The vertical rib of Ethafoam, which reaches to the front of the boat and is paired with a similar rib behind the seat, furnishes a small measure of flotation and great strength; such a boat can be jumped on where the rib supports the deck. No float bags can be used with such a system, and carrying gear is difficult. *Photo by Earl Perry*

are in, it is time to consider a back brace. Walbridge mentions a simple piece of slack strapping run from one side of the seat to the other, or from one hip brace to the other. This system is well adapted to racing, since leaning back against the strap will sink the stern of the boat beneath troublesome gates. A system devised apparently by Dave Morrissey of Colorado is superior for touring and heavy water. This provides support to your back on those rare, slow, slouching days when you need it, access to your gear and strength for your boat. On the floor of the boat, running across the long axis of the boat, glass in two ⅝-inch sections of rope, just behind the seat. Just behind the coaming, on the deck, glass

in two more. Two slots are thus created immediately behind you, into which a padded rectangular chunk of plywood just the width of the two slots may be wedged. Since a paddler, at least in good water, is normally leaning hard forward, he will usually take but little support from this, but it keeps the deck and hull from collapsing together, and since it can be popped out by a hammer blow from your fist, permits access to the stern dunnage bag on a tour.

At this point one may put in the knee braces. The simplest system is to buy a couple of gardening or wrestling pads from a sporting goods store; these have the advantage of offering a certain amount of protection to your knees in sudden swims. But boats intended for heavier use or finer control will want sturdier braces. One may glue to the boat deck, where the knees touch it, pads of wet-suit foam. Or one may attach ridges of glass to the deck, against which the inside of the knees may be pressed, and then pad these ridges with wet-suit material. This last I favor, since it permits the knees not merely to press against the deck, but to be clamped toward one another.

Finishing Techniques

The boat must have its end pours of resin. It should be stood on end against a tree or the like, a little sawdust or glass scrap jammed into first one end, and when this has cured, the other end, and two to three inches of resin poured over the scrap. Any more than this adds weight with very little strength. When one end cures, do the other. When both have cured, drill through the resin-filled end (do not hit the main cavity of the boat) and run a grab loop of nylon through the hole. It can be spliced (nylon does not splice well) or tied with a fisherman's knot or sheet bend; the loop should just admit a very large hand. This you will use to swim the boat to shore, to portage it and to tie it to your car.

Along the outside of the boat there will be an ugly seam. You can sand it down, fill it with resin and lay down another strip of glass tape for a little extra strength. Clear plastic freezer wrap pulled tightly across the glass tape will make a handsomer seam. Or you may simply fill the crack with resin and lay a racing strip of 3-M or colored boat tape (of which there is more in a moment) along the seam, assuming that you like racing stripes. You must install your flotation bags, behind the seat and in front of the foot brace, and tie in a sponge to bail with. Those who do not mind the weight, and worry that normal float bags are weak, may use the instant-mix foams to pour some flotation into either end. If the seat is integral with the coaming, it will hang loosely into the boat; it can be fixed either by ramming Ethafoam blocks beneath it and to the sides, or by making a cardboard template across its front, providing for drainage by leaving a waxed stick on the hull beneath it, and pouring the instant foam from the rear onto the template. As the foam expands, the seat is locked in place; when the stick is removed, water can drain past it to be sponged up.

The Spray Cover

Nothing remains but the spray cover. If some hierophant has initiated you into the sacred mysteries of a sewing machine, and you do not fear to feed it very sturdy materials, you can make your own. They come in two types. Both types are snug about the coaming—so snug that the coaming must be velvet smooth to keep from cutting them. One type simply cinches in about your waist; the other, snugged like the first with elastic at body and coaming, has a section like a stovepipe hat which rises high on your chest and is kept there, not just by its elastic band, but by a set of suspenders. If you are an initiate to the gods that inhabit your sewing machine, you can doubtless make your own patterns and thus your own spray cover. If you are not, I suggest going to an upholstery shop which has the patterns for your particular boat. Some use Naugahyde for this; it is, I suppose, thought to look "sharper." I think either nylon neoprene or some of the nylon-cored vinyl fabrics are both lighter and easier to use on a

cold day. A spray cover, however attained, should run $10 to $20.

Many have gone to wet-suit material spray covers, which offer considerable ease of construction compared to the other types, since they need merely be glued together with wet-suit cement. One makes the pattern, leaving enough material where it will contact body and boat to be folded and glued over elastic cord; then one glues it, feeds in the cord through the holes left for the purpose, ties off the cord, glues the holes closed, and is done. This type of spray cover, being more malleable, is blessed on a cold day; it also furnishes a pound or so of flotation in a swim.

INTO THE POOL

So the new kayak, all bullet-shaped and pristine, is ready to be blooded. I assume you have not only readied all the ancillary equipment, but even, in an excess of tender concern, given the boat a few coats of carnauba-content wax to make it faster and protect it from the sun rot that gradually kills all kayaks. Do not bother, no matter how seductively it seems to be addressing you, to take it out on a river unless you are already an experienced riverman and can read water like a theologian can read Hebrew. Above all, do not wait till the spring and try it out on a flooding icy river embossed with rapids. I have seen a kayak, even in flat gentle water, survive only five minutes of its maiden voyage, and be reduced to a heap of drift glass and sodden shiny scrap. Take it to a warm pond or a swimming pool.

For even if you are an experienced rafter, and have dipped oars from West Virginia's New River to the Rogue in Oregon, or an expert canoeist who has bent blades from Canada to Mexico, a kayak is a different proposition. It has all the oily capriciousness of a greased pig in a county fair. While a raft's squatting bottom furnishes it stability so it needs only to be shifted about the river into attractive places and away from unfortunate ones, a kayak draws its agility precisely from its instability; that which saves the expert endangers the novice. You must fight, not just to put it where it belongs, but to keep it upright in the process. The least current jets, the difference of a few degrees on a paddle angle, even turning your head, will be enough to dump you when you are fresh to the sport.

Entering and Exiting the Boat

Lay the paddle transversely across the boat just behind the coaming, with the extended blade flat on the shore. One hand, which supports most of your weight, is on the paddle shaft, holding it up against the coaming, while the other, behind your back, is a little nearer the shore, though still over the boat. Move one foot into the boat. Then, supporting your weight on both hands, move the other foot into the boat. Your legs should be straight, with your butt in the air above the rear of the coaming. You are not stepping into the boat, but sliding into it. Stiff-legged still, slip both feet forward to the foot brace, bend your knees up until they touch the knee braces and finally drop your butt onto the seat.

The immediate sensation, particularly if you put the spray cover on right away (which is done by hooking it over the lip of the coaming behind you, then over the far front and finally over the sides), is claustrophobia, for you feel wedged in. In fact, if you do not feel wedged in, you had better shift foot braces, reglue knee braces and narrow the hip braces until you do. The tension of your leg muscles should lock you into the boat. It should feel like an appendage of your body, as if you were a fiberglass satyr.

One thing should be settled first. While it is (egregiously) possible to be pinned in a kayak, and I discuss the possibility below, there is many another hazard with which you can fill your nightmares that outranks this one. You must learn right away that you can exit from the boat underwater, can even do so very rapidly. Therefore, without trying a stroke, push out from the shore and tip over; your panic will, at the cost of a little damage to the innards of your boat, have you out in a flash.

But rather than thrashing about, kicking fetally at the insides of the craft, put your hands at the sides of the boat by your hips and shove your head down and forward. You will emerge. In some cases the new spray cover will have very small, constricting sphincters of elastic about you and the boat. Then it will be much harder to exit. Cure this by stretching the cover: hang weights on it and leave it on the boat when you are not using it. If it still does not pop off when it must, sew a loop of nylon cord or strap to the front of it. This should run from the inside of the spray cover around the lip of the coaming, down past the elastic band of the cover and up to where you can reach it. A tug on this lifts the front of the spray cover right off the coaming so the whole unit can come free.

Techniques

Now we come to the actual paddling of the boat, so let me insert a few warnings and disclaimers here. I can write descriptions of each stroke, and of their combinations, which seem correct and elegant to me, to expert kayakers and to you when once you have mastered them. But to you now, as an autodidact with no experience in this least forgiving of boats, they will probably seem baffling, especially as they are far from your experience in whatever other craft you have run. They will not feel right at first even when you do them correctly. So get a teacher, even if you must drive miles to find him, for his example will supersede my words. Spend a winter in a pool with him educating you to keep the boat upright and to move it about with finesse before trying to go down the river. I have been thirteen years and perhaps 15,000 miles attaining a competence in reading the river. It is a difficult enough task without learning to deal with all the caprices of a kayak at the same time. Your time in the pool will condition you, and while you may not need to be in flawless shape to run a kayak, it is a kindness to yourself and your friends. And for the final caution let me plumb the reservoirs of language used by millions of coaches and tell you that since it is far easier to train up a good habit than to root out a bad one, practice very slowly until the form of a stroke is ingrained in your muscles. When you are perfect, seek speed.

The Forward Stroke

I have divided the strokes into traveling and stability strokes, and deal first with the first category, specifically the forward stroke. Before trying this one you must learn to feather the paddle, since one blade is at a 90-degree angle to the other. (Nonfeathered paddles are a dude rig, worth neither purchasing nor using.) One wrist, called the fixed wrist, grasps the shaft of the paddle near its blade, and is kept straight when that wrist's blade is

paddling. When the opposite wrist is paddling and has its blade in the water, the fixed wrist is cocked back 90 degrees and the shaft of the paddle rotates through the loose hand. If you are right-handed you will likely keep your right hand fixed, so when you paddle on the right, the right wrist will be straight, and when you paddle on the left, the right wrist will be cocked back. The loose or unfixed wrist is always straight. Now, to paddle forward, put the blade in the water close to the boat, as far forward as you can comfortably reach when you lean forward; the arm closest to the water, the lower arm, should be straight. The upper arm, left on a right stroke, should be pulled well back with the fist at about eye level. Keep the lower arm straight as it moves

The forward stroke, demonstrated on the Arkansas. The lower arm, in this case the left, is straight and rigid. This kayaker uses his right wrist as his fixed wrist, so it is cocked back to feather the upper blade and put the left blade in the water in position for the stroke. The right arm will punch forward while the left remains straight as the stroke is continued. The kayaker's helmet is adequate for this Class IV rapid, but his life jacket is not. *Photo by Roy Cromer.*

along the boat, for as long as possible, and bend only at the end of the stroke if a little extra power is needed. Most people's fault in trying to paddle a kayak is to take their power from pulling on the lower arm, as if they were trying to hand-over-hand up a cable in the river like a steamer. But a little reflection will show that by pulling on the lower arm the biceps is stressed and constricted, whereas by punching with the upper arm and keeping the lower straight, the whole upper body tends to rotate toward the stroke, distributing the strain among the great muscle groups of the upper back and stomach—the triceps, trapezius, lattissimus dorsi, deltoids and rectus abdominus. And as the body rotates a little toward the stroke the boat tilts very slightly to that side and thus turns a little toward the opposite side. A linked series of such strokes, each slipping parallel to the long axis of the boat, the fixed wrist alternately cocking and uncocking, the paddler leaning gently out to each successive side as he strokes on that side, and the boat describing a series of delicate linked curves much like a skier's wedel pattern, is how the boat is paddled forward.

The Backstroke

The backstroke is used first to force the boat back onto the course it should have taken in that swinging, flowing series of concatenated forward strokes, when it has suddenly failed to answer to its guidance systems. Most novices make this as a timid little correctional stroke, but a real backstroke is a mighty thing. It is done thus: Put the lower paddle blade well behind you with the flat of the blade parallel to the surface of the water, close to the boat. This will leave the upper arm stretched forward across your chest and stomach, until its hand is several inches above the opposite side of the boat. Make sure that the lower elbow, back behind you as you lean back, is directly above the paddle shaft. Jam the lower arm down and forward (*not* out to the side) while you pull the upper arm back. If you have started the stroke by

leaning back, your upper body will move forward with the stroke and finally lean back again as the lower arm surfaces and gives the boat a final thrust back. The paddle blade under the water describes a sort of U and emerges up in the forward quadrant. Remember at the start of the stroke to shove the blade toward the bottom of the river, rather than dipping a dainty corner in somewhere beside you. This stroke should be leaned on, even though it will tip you over at first when you try to do so. When you have mastered it and are moving quickly forward, it has the power to swap one end of your boat for the other.

The Draw Stroke

The draw stroke is also a stroke that must be leaned on. Canoeists will know this one; its purpose is to move the boat directly broadside, without any forward or backward motion. It also capsizes beginners frequently, but since many hundreds of tip-overs are cemented into the masonry of a really solid kayaker, you may as well collect a few dozen learning this stroke. It is most valuable not in itself, but as a prelude to the bracing strokes. The wrists, for a draw stroke, are rotated back until the paddle blade to be used is roughly parallel to the surface of the water. The upper hand is over the head and the lower hand, controlling the parallel blade, is extended out to one side. The blade goes into the water directly out to the side of the kayaker with its width parallel to the long axis of the boat, and is pulled in to the side of the kayak. It is a sort of traveling stroke, but since it is not along the long axis of the boat, but transverse to it, the boat is pulled sideways toward the blade. At the end of the stroke the blade must be slid out toward the stern, so the path of the stroke is thus an L whose long side pulls the boat over and whose short leg slides the paddle out. This stroke should be leaned on.

Front and Back Braces

Such are the three basic traveling strokes. Variations on these are the braces, which are effective when rightly done against heavy water. These come with a confusing congeries of names—front, back, high, low, sculling, and so forth. If there is a front brace, it is just a strong forward stroke, taken and perhaps held an extra moment longer than a normal forward stroke would require, just as the boat submerges into a great wave. The back brace too bears a strong affinity to the plain backstroke. The paddle, again with the lower arm directly above the shaft, is shoved flat against the surface of the water. But the stroke is not carried through its full U; the back brace is a pressure against the surface of the water much like the pressure of your hand on the ground when you have tripped and are breaking a fall. And the back brace is done slightly further away from the boat than the backstroke proper.

Setting up for a reverse gate, a draw stroke aligns this kayaker. This is technically a front-quadrant draw stroke, since the kayaker must pull the nose of his boat to the left to get it safely through the gate. The hand over the head is cocked sharply back to enable the lower blade to take purchase in the water and draw the boat over. A draw stroke is normally leaned on more than this, but the narrowness of the gate would invoke a penalty if the boater leaned much more. The helmet is marginally adequate, the dry suit useful in a race with warm water and the lack of a life jacket foolish. *Photo by Roy Cromer*

The Low Brace

The leaning braces are much the most important of all the braces. They too help to counter the capsizing force of the waves by pressing the flat surface of the blade on the water. In fact, the low brace is merely a sort of transposed back brace. The hands are in the same position, but the flat of the blade is shoved against the water directly beside the paddler, rather than behind him. This brace should be leaned on; as you snap your hips, the boat should be tilted right up on edge before the paddle blade strikes the water and rights it to a vertical position.

The low brace and the extreme lean a kayaker must learn appear in this photograph. So great is the lean required here to keep the boat from being capsized by current coming from the right of the picture that the elbow cannot be kept above the shaft of the paddle. *Photo by Roy Cromer.*

The High Brace

The high brace is begun much like a draw stroke. The upper arm is above the head with the wrist so cocked as to present the flat, lower blade of the paddle to the surface of the water. The boat is tipped up on edge and the lower, bracing blade stretched far out into the area beside the paddler. But instead of pulling the blade through the water as in a draw stroke, the flat is smacked against the surface, the hips are snapped hard and the boat is brought back to a vertical position. You should practice leaning the boat out more and more upon these braces, until your lower armpit is wetted by the pool and you can still brace handily back up.

The Sculling Brace

The sculling brace is a protracted high brace. The wrists are cocked back, the high arm is over the head, and the flat blade of the paddle, instead of smacking the water once, is made to scull, or describe little figure-8 patterns upon the surface. As the paddle sculls, the boat is leaned heavily out upon it.

These braces should be practiced, especially upon your weak side, until you think they are rock solid. Then get a friend to help you. He stands in waist-deep water behind you and by tipping the boat to one side or the other forces you to brace it back up. Because you cannot see him, the practice is a modest approximation of what the river will be doing to you later. As great waves are about to hit you from the side, you brace away from them, presenting the smooth bottom of the craft to defy their purchase; as great waves do hit you, you brace through them and with a snap of the hips, right the kayak.

Combined Strokes

The Sweepstroke When a beginner finds the kayak warping off course, as he always does, he resorts to a timid correctional backstroke; this works, but it cancels his forward momentum and is thus an offense against the minimum-work principle by which the river itself works. There are a number of other strokes that will adjust the course without stealing momentum. The first is a variant upon the simple forward stroke, the sweepstroke. This is also called a "C" stroke. A plain forward stroke travels close along the side of the boat; it would be represented by an I. But if one makes the path of that stroke a C, if one starts the stroke close to the side of the kayak, sweeps it well out away from the side of the boat and completes it by bringing it close into the stern, its pattern like a crescent moon whose horns point toward the boat, then it will turn the boat away from the side the stroke is taken on. And if one combines this stroke with a lean on it, it provides a quicker turn. If one then takes the final step, of continuing the lean while one paddles alternately on both sides, the boat will describe a long gradual turn, much used in wildwater racing.

The Climbing Draw One of the most useful and graceful of these combined strokes is the climbing draw. Now the draw stroke pulls the whole boat to the side because it is taken right beside the paddler. But if you plant a draw near the nose, the nose will be drawn over; near the stern, and the stern will shift. This is the principle of the climbing draw. If the boat is moving fast (and the faster, the more efficient the stroke will be), one leans forward and out to plant what is a hybrid stroke between a draw and a high brace. Both wrists are cocked back, and the paddle enters the water up in the front quadrant with the front edge of the blade further from the side of the boat than the rear. The nose begins to turn toward that blade. When the nose has turned almost enough, the paddle is swept in to the side of the bow to move it the final few inches, the wrists are uncocked to straighten the blade, and the stroke is completed with a simple forward stroke which propels the boat off in its new direction. The path of the stroke is thus an L, but it is an L on its side; the short leg of the L attracts the nose of the boat into a new direction, and the long leg then drives it in the new direction. When one is hurtling along backwards, the inverse of the stroke works; the stern is drawn over by a stern-quadrant draw, and the boat is then powered away with a backstroke.

The Duffek Turn The Duffek turn is another stroke which combines momentum and a brace to guide the boat. It is named after Milovan Duffek, a Czech kayaker whose techniques, developed in the early 1950's, enabled first Walter Kirschbaum and then himself to win the world championship. This is a turn created from the hanging brace. The boat, as with the climbing draw, must be moving fast for this stroke to work. So, accelerate the boat until it is moving as fast as your strength and the pool's dimensions admit. By taking a hard sweepstroke on the side opposite the one you are about to turn toward, you begin the turn. You then lean harshly toward the inside of the turn and plant a high, hanging brace. This move is invariably and correctly compared to a man running down a street and grabbing a lamp pole. Even as he swings around the pole, you will swing around the planted flat blade of your paddle. When you have come about some 90 to 180 degrees and the turn is completed, you finish the turn and stabilize yourself with a snap of the hips, for you have never been out of the position of the hanging brace throughout the whole turn.

A permutation of this turn deserves to be mentioned. It can be done backwards. Of great use is the same turn, done either forwards or backwards, from a low-brace position, with the shaft of the paddle across the chest rather than above the head. This permits a particularly hard lean and a particularly strong brace. Finally, all these strokes can be ended, not with a paddle brace, but with a draw stroke to one end or the other of the kayak, if one needs more rotation than the simple turn itself has provided. You might, for instance, do a turn going backwards and finish it by a draw to the stern of your craft, spinning it even more.

The Rolls

Practicing All of the bracing strokes and hanging turns exact a suppleness of hips so great one almost needs to consult certain vulgarly written marriage manuals to get an idea of it. One thinks of the sensuous woman rolling her hips about like ball bearings. But this same fluidity of the sides and hips is as necessary to roll the boat back up after it has capsized as it is to brace it. The best initial practice for a roll is to get over to the side of the pool without a paddle and grab the gutter with both hands. Lacking a pool, have a friend stand beside you in the water holding a paddle in his hands. You grab the paddle by the shaft with both hands, and it serves the purpose of the gutter of the pool. You may lean your whole weight upon it. Then flip the boat as far over as you can and right it with another snap of your hips. You will fail if you do not have your knees locked against their braces and your feet firm against their rest. You should be able to go over all the way and flip back up all the way. If your hips cannot take it and your external oblique seems about to snap like a frayed cable, that is too bad. You must torture your hips until they can take it. The idea is to strengthen the hips so much that almost no pressure on the side of the pool or the shaft of your friend's paddle is necessary to right you. You will quickly find, especially if you are a man and have not a woman's lowered center of gravity, that this is best done by rolling the hips violently while keeping your head under water as long as you can. You should try to force your head to be the last part of your body to emerge. While you are over, your body will be rotated toward the gutter, but as you press down with your hands and snap your hips you should curl forward from the waist toward your knees. If you try to keep your body oriented toward the front of the boat and keep your hips rigid, you will find this exercise very difficult and rolling the boat later almost impossible.

There are several sorts of rolls, all of which are easier to do (especially if you have a teacher) than to describe or visualize. The main rolls (I will mention some variants) are: the long paddle or recovery, which is most powerful and reliable but leaves you in a poor position when you surface; the screw roll, which requires no changing of hand position on the paddle and thus brings you up in

The similarities between the high brace and the Duffek turn are illustrated by this picture. As the kayaker passes the eddy fence from the current, he leans upstream, away from the eddy current he enters, and plants the paddle in a brace. His velocity, combined with the upstream press of the eddy on his bow and the downstream rush of the current on his stern, swing him sharply about. The figured deck of the kayak comes from laminating a paisley cloth in with the glass. *Photo by Roy Cromer*

shape to paddle on immediately; and the no-paddle roll, which so far as I can see has marginal utility for loosening the hips, considerable utility for impressing young kayakers, and next to none on the river. If the rapid is bad enough to strip the paddle from the hands of an experienced man, it will do him but little good to surface without it. Better just to bail out and see about saving the self and boat, unless you know one of your friends is about to make a dramatic paddle toss to you.

The Recovery Roll Let us take them in order, starting with the easiest, the recovery. Let me add first, however, that it is most use-ful to get a nose clip to safeguard your sinus-es from chlorine or pond scum, and goggles to teach you what you are doing, for you are going to have to tip over and sit there unpan-icked for long seconds deciding what you are to do. If you try to go over and spurt back up like a kitten from a toilet bowl, you will create bad habits for which you eventually pay. Hav-ing a friend handy to pull you up when you make mistakes will save a great deal of time otherwise siphoned into dragging the boat onshore, tipping it over and, by lifting alter-nate ends, bailing it out. The theory of a recovery is simple; you have been using the side of the pool as a rest from which to right yourself when you have tipped over, and now the paddle will replace it. Sitting upright in the pool, the paddle is slid through your hands to one side until both hands are on or near a single blade. The outer hand is on the tip of the blade itself; the inner hand is on the shaft near it. This blade is close to your chest and parallel to it, and the other blade extends well on out to the other side upon which you will recover.

When the blade held close to your chest is parallel to the altitude of your chest, the extended blade is parallel to the surface of the water. Tip over toward the extended blade. As you fall over let the extended end of the paddle, the end you are not holding, float up to the surface. To keep it up on the surface, you will find yourself half twisted toward it and leaning up toward it, just as you were when using the side of the pool for practice. This is fine, since in a river it means your draft will be reduced, so if you strike a rock while upside down it should theoretically be with your chest or shoulder rather than your face.

Once you are over, stop and observe your position. The long end of the paddle should be at the surface, and the blade in your hands still close to your chest. You are about to lever yourself up with a scissoring motion. The hand close to your chest is pulled up; the hand on the shaft is simultaneously shoved down. If all goes well the blade will remain quite close to the surface throughout the stroke, and you, by flipping your hips strongly and keeping your head submerged as long as possible (even ducking it at the last moment), will pop back up. The most common causes of failure are "losing a knee," thus failing to keep the lower half of your body tightly braced in the boat; and failing to start the paddle motion with the blade right up at the water's surface. If you do this you will complete the roll, if you can complete it at all, with the blade way down underwater.

The great disadvantage of this type of roll is that when you do surface, presumably with half a furious rapid still awaiting you, your paddle is in a wretched position to finish it, since one hand is still grasping a blade close to your chest and one is still on the shaft near that same blade. Neither is ready for that dramatic paddle brace which will save you from the next wave. For just this reason I once made a series of recoveries in Hell's Half Mile on the Green, rising from each only to be knocked under the next wave before I could prepare a paddle brace to counter it, at last arising, after traveling 300 feet mostly underwater, on the fourth roll.

The Screw Roll So while the recovery is the strongest and easiest roll to learn, it does have the disadvantage that, having learned it, you may be tempted to use it in the wrong place. Better to start by learning the screw roll. It is more difficult but you will arise from it ready for the next part of the rapid, since it requires no repositioning of your hands on the paddle. Another advantage it is said to have (happily I have never been forced to try this out) is that while you are underwater the placement of one of your arms guards your face from being smashed on the rocks. Here are the words on how it is done for a roll to the right, from which you will surface on the left. Swing the paddle to your right until the shaft is parallel to the long axis of the boat and a few inches out to the right side of the kayak. Each arm is straight, the right slightly behind you and the left crossing on a diagonal in front of your chest and stomach. The left blade is parallel to the surface of the water. Tip over and gaze. The left blade is parallel to the surface of the water, and your right hand will still be on the shaft near or slightly above the surface of the water.

Shove your right hand away from you; in the upside-down position you will be shoving it up into the air, above the bottom of the boat a little. Now when you come to roll, much happens at once. The right hand is kept mostly fixed in the air by your side. The left, which is up by your right knee on the surface, sweeps the paddle broadly out in a quarter of a circle through the front quadrant until it reaches the area directly to the side of the boat. All the while the blade must remain very close to the surface; this means your left arm will pass by your face. Your left biceps should scrape your nose.

At the same time your left blade is describing this quarter circle on the surface, you are flipping your hips. This should lift you at least halfway out. You should find yourself with your paddle out to the left in the bracing position, your body mostly under and your kayak nearly righted. Your right arm will be over your head. If the sweeping arc of the left paddle blade has been successful, you need only make a paddle brace and pop up. Those who have practiced their paddle braces extensively may well find there is no need for the initial quarter-circle arc; they will be able to go completely over and roll back up with no more than a paddle brace. Another variant on this roll might be called a sweep roll. Instead of a quarter-circle arc with paddle brace to complete it, the blade is swept all the way back through a half-circle. The boat, by a flip of the hips, is righted during the first part of the sweep, and the kayaker emerges as the paddle continues its broad sweep to the stern. This variant has particular utility in a race, since the final part of the sweep, as the body emerges, has terrific power, and accelerates the boat away without much loss of time.

Here are the common faults which make such an elegant move a thrashing failure. Many, panicking, do not get all the way over before they start their strokes, and thus end the roll with the paddle so far under it cannot be braced upon. And, if you have failed to snap your hips during the arcing stroke on the surface, you will also end with the paddle blade too far underwater to brace on. Many fail to lean toward the opposite knee, toward the right knee on a roll up on the left, and toward the left knee on a roll toward the right side. And most, at first, do not remember to keep their knees, feet and buttocks solidly locked into the boat. If you are not locked in by the tension of your lower body, you will never do anything but lever yourself out of the boat when you begin to exert the paddle.

The No-Paddle Roll The no-paddle roll can be done with either one or two hands; the technique is roughly the same. When you are upside down, turn your upper body toward the surface on the side you want to surface on, reach both hands (or one hand) up as close to the surface as you can and begin sculling with them as you flip your hips. When you are nearly up give a final snap of your hips and shove your cupped hand(s) down against the surface. This should bring you up, for that last hard, cupped push with the hands is the equivalent of the pushes against the gutter of the pool which have brought you up many times in the past.

DOWN THE RIVER

When you have a reliable roll on both sides it is time to take the boat out on the river. For while it is possible to kayak without a roll, the only ones who can really get away with it are those who can already read the river very well, and those who have a great deal of natural stability. And even these will swim a good deal, to the annoyance of their companions. No, at base, if you cannot roll there will be a certain stiffness to your relation with the river, a residual quantum of fear which will lock your hips and freeze your reflexes at regrettable moments; you will be no more than a man in the water and not a porpoise; you may have power but you will never have grace.

Let us assume it is all together: the new boat, the new equipment, the new skills, the new strength and conditioning, a river somehow still undammed, undiverted, unadorned with Wild Goose Ranchos, uncluttered with litter and power plants. Get a guide, get someone who has run it before. Do not think that because you have "conquered" the municipal plunge, you can "conquer" the upper Arkansas. In the first place, flowing water, no matter how sluggish, is infinitely more tricky than still, and in the second place, no one but a fool ever talks of conquering a river. You had better begin thinking in terms of permission;

if your skills are great enough, and your luck, a river may permit you to descend it. You do not govern a river, even if you are the Bureau of Reclamation and think to ruin it with a lake; what you call a victory, whether gained with a kayak or a vast and hideous concrete plug, is only an evanescent concession. When you are dust and Lake Powell, "the jewel of the Colorado," looks much more like a mud flat than a gem, the river will still be flowing. In perhaps 10,000 years the glass of your kayak will be starting to form sand grains and Glen Canyon Dam will be a waterfall or a rather spectacular rapid full of rounded concrete boulders and steel reinforcing bars; the river will still be flowing.

The river is so much older than you and so much longer-living that it makes any comparison between its life and yours similar to the comparison between your life and that of one of those insects that hatches, flourishes and dies all in a summer's day. And it is bigger too. To get a feeling for this let us glance at some figures. In the days before a series of dams upstream wasted its tributaries and rendered its waters salt, the Colorado River at Lee's Ferry, Arizona, averaged some 20,000 cubic feet per second, day in and out, year after year through the paltry sixty or seventy years of record. In glacial times it swelled; through the cyclic droughts of prehistory it shrank. Now that 20,000 second-feet is by most kayakers' standards a big river, though by the standards of the North Country it is unspectacular—the Columbia has run about 1,750,000 second-feet at flood stage. But let me try to make 20,000 second-feet take on meaning in more homely contexts. Take an average swimming pool, 30 feet wide, 75 feet long and perhaps averaging 6 feet deep. The volume of one and a half such pools would have to pass a given point every second to fill the measure of such a flow. There will be, every second, just shy of 1,300,000 pounds of water in such a river. Now you and your kayak will weigh about 200 pounds; the ratio is not favorable.

Let us take another unfavorable ratio. If you have turned over and come out of your boat and have not equipped it with float bags, the boat will then hold about 1,000 pounds of water. If the river is flowing a mere 10 feet per second, which is probably a low figure for a river of this size, and your kayak finds you between itself and a rock, it will strike you with about 10,000 foot-pounds of momentum; not unlike interposing yourself between a creeping sedan and a brick wall.

Let us return to the Colorado for a glance at relative sizes. Your boat is just over 13 feet long. The river may very easily be 400 feet wide, with an average depth of 5 feet and average velocity of 10 feet per second. Not perhaps very impressive looked at as averages, but that depth of 5 feet could conceal a maximum depth of 20, and that average velocity of 10 might mean a velocity, out in the center where you are, of 20 feet per second, or about 13 miles an hour. Very slow in a car; quick on a horse or bicycle; and appalling in a raft or kayak.

Therefore, if you come to kayaking thinking to vanquish nature, give it up. Your mind may be divorced from nature, but your body is not. You are subject to it; you cannot win, and if you try you will eventually lose either your traps or your life. You can only learn the laws to which you are subject and obey them; this is the only "victory" you are permitted. You must learn to run your kayak by a sort of jujitsu. You must learn to tell what the river will do to you, and given those parameters see how you can live with it. You must absorb its force and convert it to your uses as best you can. Even with the quickness and agility of a kayak, you are not faster than the river, not stronger, and you can beat it only by understanding it. You cannot personify it and you cannot scorn it; you can only love it and comprehend it. It is impersonal, insuperable and just; it will give you what you deserve because it cannot give you anything else. You must see that you deserve well of it, for though it is not your enemy it is remorseless.

The Eddy Turn

All this is easier to understand in theory

than in practice. For it is all very well, and very easy to say, "See what the river is doing and take that as your base," but it is not easy for a novice to gain understanding of a river. The best source for that is an articulate guide. Failing that, the chapter that begins this book is a good place to start. Since I am happily absolved of teaching the reading of water, let us simply proceed with getting the kayak out upon the river and safely down it. Pick an easy river at a moderate stage; you want no more than an even 10-foot-per-mile gradient and no more than a 5,000-second-feet flow. You want no truck with rapids or even very fast water yet. You will need a driver to get your vehicle to the end of the stretch (10 to 15 river miles is an adequate first day), or a second car to spot at the end of the trip, or a resolve to hitchhike back up when you have finished the run. Then, with float bags tightly inflated and life

jacket tightly cinched, select an eddy and put the boat in the water, aimed upstream. You will enter the boat as you have entered it in the pool. Paddle up the eddy until you strike the main current, and swing through a 180-degree turn into the surging body of the river.

This is the time for all the leaning the pool or pond has taught you. As you cross the eddy fence and encounter current flowing the opposite way, you are vulnerable. The clutch of the current will take purchase on the upstream side of the boat and roll it in a flash. If you lean away from the current you enter, the jet of water will wash harmlessly beneath the hull. To do this, you must plant a hanging brace and do a Duffek turn, as you hopefully have learned in the pool. With the boat tilted downstream and your downstream armpit washed by the river, you will swivel rapidly about and be set.

Having passed through an upstream gate on a slalom course, this kayaker demonstrates the classic eddy turn. The gate is in an eddy and the boat enters the current (from right to left) leaning away from it on a strong high brace; the upper arm is cocked back and the lower blade provides a pivot point about which the boat will rotate. This is also called the Duffek turn. *Photo by Roy Cromer*

You debark from the river in just the opposite fashion. Enter an eddy from the main current and again lean away from the current you penetrate. Since the eddy is running upstream, you lean upriver. The eddy's force on the front of the boat, coupled with the press of the main current on the tail, will throw the boat into a fast 180-degree turn; aimed upstream, you may then draw the boat over to the shore and, placing the paddle behind you, clamber out. Should you try to stop pointed downstream, by grabbing a tree branch or the like, the current will rush you out to the limit of your arm, tilt you upstream and capsize you. One can scarcely stress it too much—lean away from the current you enter.

Strategy in Rapids

Now the running of a kayak in rapids is again a matter that fits well into words, and with difficulty into experience. One can, and I will, put the key strategies into a couple of sentences. You take your maneuverability from your velocity relative to the current—on a large river, by outspeeding it; on a small and rocky river, by slowing down and back-ferrying, or paddling backwards at an angle to the current. You avoid rocks, as a novice you avoid holes, and you avoid waves of a size large enough to eat you. In flat water you cleave to the outside of a turn to steal the excess velocity cached there, but in rapids, since that same velocity creates the biggest holes and complications (only the largest

Gathering momentum with a forward stroke, this kayaker heads for a drop. To see why he sought speed, consult the opening picture of this chapter. High velocity is a must for hitting heavy water. *Photo by Roy Cromer.*

boulders can resist such velocity), it is best to enter a curving rapid toward the inside of the turn.

Transferring these simplified words from a page into action—there is the difficulty. When is a wave large enough to eat you? You must be eaten to learn it. How do you avoid a hole? All the strokes above will not help until you can see that swelling mound of water with the bubbling calm below it far in advance. And to do that you must see thousands of holes, and watch thousands upon thousands of skeins of currents, until you know exactly where a patch of water selected by your eye or inhabited by your boat will go, not just a few feet, or a few yards, or a few rods, but for hundreds of yards downstream. You can learn a little of it by systematically tossing logs into various currents at the top of a rapid; you can learn a lot of it in hours with an expert; you learn the most of it by doing. And some of it, or most of it, you may never learn at all, for there are those who are completely uneducable, and all of us who are partly uneducable, in the ways of moving water. In the back of the mind there is always the receding mirage of absolute competence and absolute knowledge; each ledge or pitch of ability reveals pinnacles beyond it to be scaled; each descent of a bad rapid brings the mind and body closer to the final melding of ultimate skill with ultimate possibility—the Ultimate Run, the Limit of Possibility! No man has *yet* made it; no man knows all about the river; beneath the shallow mines and tunnels of our current skills and knowledge lie vast sunken chambers and galleries of lore that a man might just reach if his strength and brains and luck and judgment all cohere. No man knows it all, and this is one of the deepest pleasures of kayaking.

A Glance at Physics

Before we move to the plain of techniques for the river, there are ravines of simple physics to be bridged. The current may be thought of as an infinitude of vectors, each with direction and velocity. A skin of water on the absolute perimeter of the bed, thickness to be measured in molecules, does not move, and stays in adhesion to its particular particle of rock, but all the rest moves. Just beneath the surface near the center of the stream is the vector of greatest magnitude; there the current is fastest. Upstream vectors lurk in the eddies; toward the margins of the stream are smaller vectors where the proximity of the bed slows the flow. The mass of the current is everywhere shot through with tiny corkscrew vectors of turbulent flow.* There are diagonal vectors of helical flow on the surface and deep beneath it. Vectors in the breaking waves plunge straight down; vectors deflected from the upstream face of rocks jet straight up.

The kayak too, because it has direction and velocity, may have a vector drawn for it. Since vectors may be summed or subtracted, if the kayak is paddling faster than the current its vector is added to the vector of the current which floats it. A roundabout way of saying that if the current is moving five miles an hour, and the boat is moving four above it, the kayak moves nine miles an hour.

Since a vector delineates velocity, it also comprises time. Let this same kayak be paddling upstream at his steady four miles an hour in the same five-mile-an-hour current; at the end of an hour it will have been carried but one mile. Paddling across the current, he will have traversed four miles and have been carried five down what must be an Amazon of rivers. His actual path is of course a diagonal, the hypotenuse of a triangle whose other two sides are formed by the vectors of his motion and the current's motion.

Let us now beset the kayaker with an obstacle to see the relevance of all this. If it is a certain distance away from him, it is a certain time away from him. If he paddles directly down the current toward it, he shortens the time which separates him from it; he thus strikes it harder and sooner. If he paddles

---

*Vectors, technically, do not curve, so a corkscrew vector is an absurdity. I have let this stand, however, since the actual case—a corkscrew current bristling with tangential vectors like a spiral staircase with slanted treads—is not so easy to visualize.

directly up the current, his collision is still inevitable, but it will be delayed and gentler when it happens. If he paddles directly across the current, he may miss it, for that is the attitude in which, for his effort, he moves the furthest away from it. He will thus consume as much time as if he had drifted without paddling at all, but he will fill that time with the most lateral motion. This is, incidentally, why the best raftsmen tend to enter rapids broadside.

Aim the kayak at an angle downstream. The vector of its motion (we are setting aside the current momentarily) thus has two components; one is his downstream velocity and the other, attached to the tip of the first, is his lateral velocity. Part of his four miles an hour is absorbed in downstream motion, part laterally. Attaching the current vector to the end of the kayak's two vectors (since it has been sweeping him downstream all the time he angled across it), we find he has again shortened the time between himself and the obstacle while moving but little away from it.

And this has advantages, especially, as I said above, on big rivers. By paddling thus you shorten the time a hazard affects you. This is why a kayaker or a raftsman about to pitch from the crest of a cavernous trough or suckhole will paddle or push forward on the oars as hard as possible straight into it. He may just gather enough momentum to lance through it without being tipped over or sucked back up into it.

Say the kayak takes the same angle, aimed slightly across the current, and back-paddles. This is the back-ferrying position. There are again two components to his vector; one is upstream and the other is lateral. The upstream component partially cancels the current, so he is lengthening the time between himself and the hazard. And if he expands the time available to himself, he expands the time for the lateral component of his velocity to operate. If, for instance, a kayaker is one second away from a rock, and is able by back-paddling at an angle to increase that one second to five, he will have five sec-

onds of lateral motion to use to escape it. If the lateral component of his back-ferrying is two feet per second, by the end of his five seconds he will have moved ten feet laterally through the current which is taking him down upon the rock.

If he gains enough seconds for his lateral velocity to operate by all this back-ferrying, he will slip past the rock. Even if he doesn't, he is still in better shape than if he had elected to paddle forward at an angle, for he will at least hit the rock slowly and perhaps not stave in the nose of his boat. Thus the rule that small rocky rivers exact a lot of back-ferrying. Most Western kayakers are a little weak on this maneuver, because their rivers do not much insist upon it. But on the Eastern rivers, the prevalence of rocky ledges and very obstructed channels quickly educates boaters into a competence at back-ferrying. Having seen a number of boats wrecked by Westerners whose first impulse faced with a rock garden was to throw on the power and race forward, I can advise learning and using this skill.

But suppose it is not a rock, but rather a large hole he has elected to miss by back-ferrying. He may, given the efficiency of the maneuver, get past it. If he doesn't, and is drawn in, he has compounded his error by back-paddling. For he is moving slowly relatively to the water, and may thus not have enough velocity to punch through the dead water in the wash. He will be eaten. Hence the rule that on large or very high rivers where the rocks are mostly flooded under, a fast and aggressive forward stroke is best.

But all this has so far presumed an uncomplicated stream, its currents all parallel, moving in a smooth thrust down to the sea. None of this artificial simplicity is found in a rapid, where the currents run in all directions. It is upon these currents that the kayaker depends; he must learn to read them down to the quarter of a mile an hour, down to fractions of a second. He may, for instance, have to reach down below the surface to find slower water in which to plant a turn. He may have to locate an eddy, not behind a projection on

KAYAKING & OBSTACLES

DRIFTING

PADDLING FORWARD

PADDLING BACKWARD

PADDLING LATERALLY

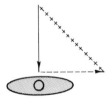

PADDLING FORWARD AT AN ANGLE:
TIME IS SHORTENED.

PADDLING BACKWARD AT AN ANGLE: TIME IS LENGTHENED.

① 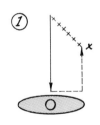   ②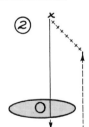

LEGEND

———————→   CURRENT VECTOR FOR A GIVEN TIME.
- - - - - →   KAYAK VECTOR FOR THE SAME TIME INTERVAL.
+ + + + +   ACTUAL PATH TRAVERSED BY THE KAYAK.

NOTE: THAT WHEN THE KAYAK IS PADDLED AT AN ANGLE
IT REQUIRES 2- VECTORS IN A RIGHT TRIANGLE
TO REPRESENT ITS MOTION, AND BOTH MUST BE
ADDED TO THE CURRENT'S VECTOR.

cwh.

the shore, but behind a rock, and use it to turn himself. He may even have to reach over the top of a rock or the crest of a hole to find the current differential that will turn his boat for him. But it is in recognizing and playing these minute current differentials, a momentary slackness caused by a deeply buried rock or a reflex wave as the water sluices past an exposed boulder, that an expert is separated from a novice.

Braces on the River

The Forward Brace It is now, in the rapids, using the current differences between eddy and wave, even between one part of a wave and another, that all the braces that were so long in the learning and required so many dunkings, come into play. Most often used is the forward brace, since it is little more than a forward stroke. When a great wave breaks on the front of the boat in a cascade of murk, when you are trying to breast the reflex wave combing out diagonally from the edge of a hole, the boat may stall on the face of the wave and perhaps do an end-for-end (endo) backwards if it is not impelled through and over the crest. One must force a paddle blade through the crashing water that tops the wave to the rapid downsloping smooth water on the back of the wave. For the paddle, planted in that fast and solid water behind the wave, is like a ledge to a climber, and will let you pull the whole boat on through the powerful break.

If you wish not to penetrate, but to skirt parallel to such a wave, there are two strategies, both of which employ side braces. Since the force of the water pouring down the face of the wave and onto one whole side of the kayak will capsize it, you may (as with the forward brace) simply reach through the crest and hold the brace until the boat cruises past. This if you are sure to hit the wave pretty solidly. Or, if you will pass a little further away from it but still parallel, try bracing away from it. This will present the smooth kayak bottom to the tumbling purchase of the wave, and while it slips off the hull the kayak slips past.

The Back Brace The back brace of course substitutes for the forward when you have reversed, by choice or by the river's fiat, and must try to break through a wave in reverse. It also has some use when traveling forward, in a wilderness of eddies, fountains and whirlpools.

But, to discuss the back brace in such a situation, we must see the area a little first. It is a mistake to simplify currents too much; one begins to think of currents flowing down and eddies flowing upstream as crudely and directly as the arrows a boatman sketches on the sand to instruct his greenies. The thrust of the current is down to the sea, not as if the sea were calling it down, sucking it away to the base level of the world, but as if some impulsive force in the river itself were jamming a great tongue of water down through all the obduracies of rock and backwater. And that great tongue never rests and never duplicates itself; seen from one vantage it flows for moments with an excess of force, as if intent to ream out all the resistance and slackness in the water below; the next moment it abates. Its quickest water oscillates irregularly from side to side like the slow and potent sweep of a rattler's tail. The eddies that impede its journey are never static either, flowing with alternate power and weakness, crashing one moment in eddy surf against the shore and the next receding away from the bases of the rocks. When that great tongue of river meets the quieter water of the eddy it peels vast scrolls of water away from the eddy and sets them whirling. And as these scrolls rotate they involve yet more water from current and eddy within themselves, until sometimes a whole segment of the river's main flow seems to have been diverted off into a lateral spin and is lost in a maze of whirlpools. Then the segment of flow succeeding may shift off into an eddy on the opposite shore, till all the river's surface is a labyrinth of vortices and fountains.

Now such whirlpools, when they are large—and such phenomena as these are mainly big-river attributes—are real if transi-

Two strategies for dealing with waves are illustrated here. The kayaker has reached through the froth of the wave to solid water to plant his brace. And, since the main body of the wave is to the right of the picture, he has leaned to the left, in order to present the smooth bottom of his craft to its force. The brace is a typical forward brace, different from a forward stroke only in the amount of lean it supports. *Photo by Mary Cromer*

tory hazards to a kayak. There really *is,* just as ignorant locals have been telling boatmen since John Wesley Powell took to the Green River in 1869, a "suck" so big it can take a boat right under. On a really big river (40,000 to 45,000 second-feet) I have had the side of a 27-foot pontoon go under crossing the eddy line. Captain Gray, to boatmen the most famous steamboat pilot of all time, who took a 175-foot steamer through Hell's Canyon, reports having the Columbia River suck a gigantic log raft from beneath him and hold it under for 200 yards. This same river has taken ten-man rafts under in the whirlpools; their occupants were grown men and not fourteen-year-old boys such as Gray was at the time. This is, of course, a giant river. Even at lesser flows there will be strength in a whirlpool to take the tail of a kayak under three or four feet, until the boat is almost on end, and make it move like the axis of the earth through a wobbly and somewhat frightening precession. At such times a back brace will help. You cannot really paddle out of such a thing, because you cannot break its suction; the river in its endless variation will quickly break it for you and send you on; the back brace merely tries to assure you will be released upright.

Fountains

Below, beside or even above such a whirlpool will be a boil or fountain; these are also found behind rocks or points, and sometimes appear in midstream due to deflected current jets from submerged rocks or from sand-dune or anti-dune formations working out. Those behind rocks and near whirlpools, being most violent, are of most interest, for such a fountain, blooming up from the deep, is another real though ephemeral hazard. A boat caught in the trembling center of such a hydraulic is merely lifted violently as if God's own elevator had taken it up. One caught on the margins will be flung into a surfing position and will slide forwards, backwards, sideways, away from the writhing mound of water until it chooses to subside. Now it is at the extreme

edges of a fountain that a kayak may have difficulty, for there, where the fountain meets the current, secondary whirlpools may form. And there is another curious feature about the edges of fountains, unnamed so far as I know. At the edge of a fountain the water is flowing steeply down, so by friction it carries the water of the main current under with it, forming a downsuck as steep as a cliff and as narrow as a knife. The kayaker finds himself, as it were, in a little canyon of turbid water whose walls, on every side of him, are plunging under. And there is no real way to brace, though of course you are most enthusiastic in trying. Should you lean away from one sinking current, the opposite one takes purchase on the boat; lean away from that one and the first is ready. All the practice in the pool with someone behind you tipping you suddenly one direction and as suddenly to the other may pay off in such a spot; if not, a fountain of this sort, or at least its attendant features, rarely grips you more than a few memorable seconds.

Big Waves

When you deal with water capable of producing such hydraulics, you will likely have to deal with heavy waves. These I would call waves from a true five to a true fifteen feet high; a wave is measured not by laying an imaginary tape up the face from trough to crest, but by developing an imaginary line connecting the lowest points of the troughs and extending from that line another which pierces the waves right up to their crests; that second line is the height. It should be pointed out that measuring waves from the shore is far more reliable than your excited guesses after running them; a mere five-foot wave is big; it blots out the world. And since I have seen pontoons loaded seven feet high vanish for two long seconds in the trough of really large waves (what looks were on the faces of Leachman and Kirschbaum!) from where I sat at water level, I would advise you to climb up for perspective. Otherwise, you will race back to town full of tales of "twenty-footers" on the local creek and make more experienced boatmen think your head is hotter than your kayaking skills. Even a fifteen-foot wave, the largest that I have seen, is some ninety feet from crest to crest.

But there are waves and waves; some five-footers I have seen we did not put our pontoons into, and others we ran air mattresses over. Constriction waves, tail waves, velocity waves, sand waves, haystacks, these are the gentler waves. The river has been given an excess of energy, respectively, by constriction, by acceleration over the declivity of a rapid, by excess flow requiring supernormal velocity to carry it away, by variations in bed friction when the river is at near-total bed-load capacity ("haystacks" is a general term loosely applied to all the above, and most properly applied to tail waves), and it surrenders that energy in a gently breaking series of waves. What is important here is that gentle break, variable and rarely splashing down more than a quarter of the wave's face. For the unsafe waves have a violent, large, steep and continuous break; these are breaking holes, and diagonal outwash from them are reflex waves. Reflex waves may also be set up off projections on the shore. The cause of these unsafe waves is a sudden, local and terrific over-steepening of the river's gradient (the river hits the rock which causes the breaking hole). This imparts to the water in the river an excess of energy which it must give up immediately below, in the form of a crashing wall of water. Or, in the case of reflex waves, in diagonal booming wings of water breaking at an angle downstream from the hole or projection. However it is gained, the river must give up that sudden excess of energy, and it does so with a violence delectable to watch and fierce to feel.

I can roughly define these waves by saying they break more than halfway down their face. On a clear river they show as pure white and physically stationary. On mud water they are stationary and look, from the violence of their break, very busy. Like a lizard nailed to a washboard, they are fixed but writhe constantly. They do not really have a crest of white water, like a haystack, but are a pulsing wall of it. Sheets of wavering water thunder from the crest into the trough upstream from them. Above about three feet tall they become an obstacle worth considering, for as you mount them you can be tossed all the way from the crest to the bottom: I saw a kayak pitched nine feet back down the face of the now defunct "Toilet Bowl" in Warm Springs Rapids on the Yampa, and even small rafts are vulnerable to this type of involuntary surf. If you must hit these (I advise against it until you are able to bring a few thousand miles of experience to bear upon them), the first strategy is to hit them as fast and hard as possible and try to brace through to the other side. This failing, you might attempt a trick that Kirschbaum, one of the best boatmen and kayakers who ever lived, told me he used on the high stage in Hell's Canyon many years ago— turn over and, upside down, brace in the solid water in the core of the wave. That solid water under there blasting on your paddle and body may tweeze you through. If not, you will come out of your boat and be carried beneath and past the wave.

It ought to be pointed out that very heavy rapids are by kayaking standards uncomplicated, as a rule. A mistake may be catastrophic, but it isn't so easy to make one when there is 500 feet of width in which to slip a 2.5-foot wide kayak. There are moments, of course, when one needs a good deal of power—trying to enter a giant eddy without stalling in the marginal whirlpools, hitting very heavy break, and trying to ski-jump large suckholes down to the point of no return. But in the main a mellow technique is advised; there is rarely the need for frenzy. You take note, again, of the oarsmen and their ways. Since direct, cross-stream motion is most efficient for getting the boat out of the current skein which leads to a hole, you can drift down on it broadside, and when ready take a few powerful strokes directly across the river, avoiding it. Even when you think you have had it, and are about to pitch from the crest,

143

remember there is usually a pad of water at the top of the rock causing the hole which flows upstream and to the sides; timing your strokes to the momentary pause the pad offers may give you the lateral impetus to sneak past the edge. You will find, if you try this on gigantic rivers with infrequent but disastrous holes, that it is a very pleasant, effective, and even rejuvenating technique. Who will have more strength for the sixth roll in a terrifying suckhole, he who has been paddling frantically all morning in a maze of nine-foot waves, or he who has bobbed through them taking only a few necessary lateral strokes? Having never kayaked waves more than about nine feet high, I must speak under the correction of men such as Chuck Carpenter and Walt Blackadar, but in my experience a kayak can be drifted broadside up immense waves; if there is a practical limit on its ability to do this I have yet to encounter it. This technique will save you power and speed for when you require it; it also inculcates that porpoise-like grace which gradually crops the imaginary terrors of the river, leaving only the real ones. The true heavy-water kayakers are not generally very good at racing, for they have never had to learn the fierce precision of the slalom course, but they have a reliability and style, a smoothness, which bespeaks not only absolute but justified confidence.

Suckholes

We have passed gradually into pretty advanced maneuvers. A kayaker will need to know how to get out of a suckhole. If he has entered it very quickly, as I mentioned before, he may shoot through the water below the fall which sucks back up into it and reach the point of no return, where part of the water boiling up from the depths of the hole slips away downstream and part roils back into the fall. If he makes the point of no return he may simply paddle away. If he does not reach the point of no return, and begins to bob about in the wash like a Ping-Pong ball in an airstream, there are a few strategies he may attempt.

But for now let us abandon the wretch in the hole, since willy-nilly he will be there in actuality long enough to learn irrefutably that the passage of time is subjectively perceived. By the time I have finished a paragraph or two upon the real and true name of the suckhole, and finally extract him, he will have endured seeming hours.

Saving the somewhat eristic matter of whether or not a plunge pool forms below the falls, the essence of a suckhole is not disputed; we all agree on the humping mound of water piled up by the rock, the fall down its back edge, and the recirculating wash below. We all agree you can die in them. Only upon the name is there dispute. A recent writer in American Whitewater has asseverated that the real and true names of a suckhole are "keeper" and "reversal," with "keeper" being the larger, dangerous type in which hair-ball kayakers delight to sport. A "suckhole," he maintains, is properly only a submerged pipe, crack, or crevice, into which a part of a kayaker's body may be inserted and then held by water pressure—killing him.

Unfortunately, I have been vitiated by the taking of a couple of courses in linguistics, and cannot tell this man he is wholly and recklessly incorrect.

I can, however, interpolate a little information on the historical usage of the term.

Now the earliest description of these features that I have encountered is in *Through the Grand Canyon from Wyoming to Mexico* by the Kolb brothers, a pleasant narrative of a trip in 1911, published in 1913, in which they tipped over in one of the features. They called it a "reverse whirl," citing the boatmen of the recent Alaskan gold rush as their source. Powell and his men developed no vocabulary for the feature, and I have found none in such of the narratives of the *voyageurs* I have encountered.

It is possible, I think, to state that on Western rivers, and in the talk of professional boatmen who are most familiar with them, the term "suckhole" is used as I have used it, and anyone using it for an invisible crevice will be thought incomprehensible. It is also true that "suckhole" as it is used in this book has not changed in meaning since at least the 1950's, when Sidell's Suckhole in Brown's Canyon on the Arkansas got its name. "Keeper" or "reversal," however, will be understood, though I think they are regional variants most used in the East. The beginner ought probably to learn the vocabulary of the area he will boat in, and be ready to define himself when he runs in other areas. It seems probable to me that standard terminology will gradually obtain as more Westerners encounter the incredible racing skills of the East, and more Easterners encounter the heavy water tricks the West has developed. Whether standard terms evolved by interchange among kayakers will be taken up by rafters I much doubt, so you may need to translate when dealing with them.

To return to our kayaker, stuck in the suckhole, it will be remembered that water is flowing past the hole on either side, and out of it beneath the surface. If he can plant a hanging brace in the moving water beside the hole, or reach past the point of no return for a brace, current will pull him out of the hole, though his brace may have to last many a long and aching second. This works for nice, sedate, man-sized holes, the kind that used to be called souse holes. Let us suppose a nightmare of a hole, a mineshaft whose shattered waters have a rainbow rising from their depths. Since the water passing the lateral margins of such a cavern may be several feet above the boiling surface of the wash, since a hole this deep is generally many feet wide, since the point of no return can be many rods downstream (I have myself traveled 150 feet underwater in one), the kayaker is in trouble. "Far better," as Edward Abbey says in *Desert Solitaire,* in a different context, "to have stayed at home in Albuquerque, drinking beer." There is one strategy which may work, though I have seen it fail as often as succeed. Grasping the paddle as if for a recovery roll, with one hand on the tip of a blade and the other on the shaft near that same blade, you

tip over and shove the other blade as far as it will go toward the bottom. Since far below in the deeps of the hole there is water moving downstream, the paddle will theoretically catch that water and the boat will be strained out by the pressure on that wobbling and tenuous blade. Now since it is maintained by very competent men indeed that a plunge pool forms below such a hole, and whether it does or not the water may be too deep to reach with that nine-foot paddle-and-arm combination, it is best not to plan to enter an immense suckhole relying upon this trick. If it does not work, you merely roll up and capsize until the hole sees fit to eject you. When you can no longer roll you bail out and swim for it, though a hole big enough to pull an expert from his craft will mock the mightiest crawl stroke of even a Mark Spitz. It used to be maintained, and perhaps still is, that the thing to do in such a case is to ditch the life jacket, swim back up the fall, dive under as it carried you down and swim out with the water far beneath the surface. In all but one situation, which I will treat in paragraphs to follow, ditching the life jacket is nonsense.

When you surface from such a swim you will have spent much of your strength before you even need it. You will likely have aspirated a lot of water and begun (at the *least* begun) to panic. A river large enough to produce such a hole will most probably be ornamented by no small rapids down below it, which you will have no ability to swim and no buoyancy to float. How shall your friends see you to rescue you, at least in the muddy water of desert streams, when you lack buoyancy and flush through the following rapids most of the time underwater? How shall you swim at all when you find that the flowing water at the bottom of the hole is not a rapid, smooth jet but a hammering millrace that pounds you, as I have been pounded, against the rocks on the bottom of the river, and may perhaps knock you out? Let us hope this nonsense about tiny life jackets ("Those big fat ones are *so* constricting I just can't stand it") and about ditching life jackets is not heeded, at least when you come to the descent of a big river or an extreme stage on a small one. Even in a nightmare hole you are better off in your boat, and if you must swim for it, better off in your life jacket. There are, to my knowledge, only two situations for ditching life jackets—when they hang up on a drift pile or the like and cannot be freed, and when they trap you in the wash below a man-made dam or an extremely regular ledge. Beyond these two situations, it is time to put an end to the nonsense about tiny life jackets and about ditching life jackets in holes. This is merely stupid for small, rocky rivers; it is pernicious for large, violent ones.

Waterfalls

There has been a lot of recent interest in kayaking waterfalls, and many a ledge once carried is now routinely run. This is really a case of *"Nihil novi sub sole."** Walter Kirschbaum used to tell tales of going across the French border to run a thirty-foot fall in his youth. It is a most exhilarating feeling; it can be the one of the easiest of moves, and one of the most dangerous. Only those falls should be run which have either so steep a river below them that there is no backwash below to trap and drown a boater, or a backwash so weak it cannot stem the efforts even of a swimmer. For it is not the height of a fall that determines its danger; very high, very safe falls may be produced on small rivers of the ledge-and-pond sort, where resistant cap rock covers friable strata. Such a ledge is quickly undermined by headward erosion and a deep plunge pool hollowed beneath it. A fall on such a river, at least at lower stages of water, will offer a gentle impact area with a puny backwash. In fact, many of the worst falls are only two or three feet high, but are tailed by such a violent backwash foaming up into the fall that they are almost certain death to enter. Man-made dams are often of this type. Diversion dams with their low, smooth flow of water over a lip claim many a life each year. They are, in fact, one of the only places on a river where a trapped man should give

*"There is nothing new under the sun"—Ecclesiastes (Ed. note).

any thought whatever to ditching a life jacket and trying to swim clear, for the moving water below the surface (except for the occasional reinforcing bar projecting up to impale you) is not complicated by a jagged riverbed. Better to take the advice of the many experts who refuse to run anything man-made.

There is one final hazard to the running of waterfalls that should be guarded against. Even when a fall has been scouted and has the requisite runout, there is still the matter of the boat's strength, or in particular, the strength of the foot brace. When a man drops fifteen feet into the water (or hits a rock going fast) his momentum must be absorbed mainly by his foot brace. If he breaks through it, one of the more terrible situations can ensue: He may slide far up into his kayak and lodge with little more than his head and shoulders showing above the coaming. He cannot roll, he cannot brace and he may be unable to extract himself because his hands can hardly be brought to bear on the coaming. If he tips over, life jacket or not, he may die in an awful claustrophobic drowning, with his friends unable to aid him.

Getting Pinned

Another of the nightmare situations is getting pinned broadside. The lore is just full enough of stories of boats wrapping around rocks, with their kayaker's legs crushed within, while the man's head is forced under upstream and the whole force of the current pins him in the boat he is trying desperately to leave. A few such tales attached to Widowmaker Rapid on the South Platte; a great boulder obstructs the channel just below a chute. The man who dumps in the chute and misses his roll pins on the rock. There can be but one strategy for such things; if you must hit them, lean downstream into them, away from the current, and as the current passes beneath you, catch yourself with paddle or hand. Then with a sort of hopping, pulling motion of the hand or with thrusts of the paddle, work around the side of the boulder. If you do pin broadside on a rock or a driftwood pile, and capsize upstream, you are in trouble. A roll, due to the force of the water, is beyond the capacities of all but a superman. It is probably best to get out of the boat and work around the rock. If it is a driftwood pile, do not allow yourself to hang up on or under it, but by scrabbling at sticks and logs either climb it or slither past it. Your boat will then be pinned. It may be possible, since a pinned boat is at first in a state of very delicate balance, to grab the end of your boat and pull it clear as you pass the edge of the rock. It may even be possible to climb on the rock and lift the boat clear. Probably you will have to rescue it from the shore, with the help of friends. At this point you will either bless your float bags for saving your boat intact, or curse your cheapness in not buying them as it breaks up.

Rhythm

I have made it seem, in describing a series of dangers and requisite countermoves, as if kayaking is a spasmodic series of instant saves from terrifying dangers, punctuating long periods of flat paddling. This is not so, but the techniques had to be printed. Actually the cruising of an expert is never a chain of frenzy and relaxation, never, even with a danger right below, a disjointed cluster of strokes with no relation to what has preceded them and what follows them. All the separate strokes you have learned in the pool are blended, woven together into a seamless and rhythmic descent. A kayaker should grow as lithe as the willows. You might see a man hurtling forward do an abrupt and potent back-paddle stroke which sets him, momentarily, broadside above a hole. Another quick back paddle to put him past the center line of the water entering the hole, and he is ready, with an arcing lean over the crest of the hole, to plant a reverse hanging draw in its wash and pull his stern over, straightening his boat to slip past the hole backwards. Or perhaps that reverse hanging draw will have been a reverse Duffek turn which drops his stern in the hole, spins him about and puts him ready to continue forward again. He might decide to

miss the hole forward, and again set up broadside above it with a leaning turn, then, linking more of those strokes, continue his lean and sweep his paddle through a long sweepstroke which simultaneously carries him past the hole and straightens him downstream for the next. Perhaps he will throw extra power into the sweepstroke, so it does not just straighten him from his broadside position above the hole, but turns him so far his nose enters its wash down below. Pitching his body then to the inside, he can do a forward Duffek turn into the hole and, facing upstream, chart a course or prepare to do some surfing. All this in seconds, all this with the grace of a salmon. Or, to vary the metaphor, there is an impression of avian power at work. There are the long, slow hooks and scrolls of eagles, the sharp fluttering of swallows, the steep wheeling of the hawks; the birds sign the air as the best of kayakers inscribe the water.

Surfing

Hi summo in fluctu pendent; his unda dehiscens terram inter fluctus aperit, furit aestus harenis.

These hang from the crest of the wave, while the gaping waves betrayed the bed to others; the waters boiled with sand.

—Virgil

The most graceful, most pleasant and probably most useless of a kayak's maneuvers is surfing, or ferry-surfing. If we posit a wave standing up steeply like its namesake, a haystack, and supply a kayaker resting high up in an eddy beside it who wishes to cross the river at this point, there are two ways to do it. He can do a Duffek turn out of the eddy, swing downstream, paddle at an angle across the current and through the waves, and do another Duffek turn into the opposite eddy (if he makes it); his course is a flattened S in shape. Or he can surf. He will paddle out of the eddy aimed steeply upstream so as not to be whirled away and plant his kayak on the upstream face of the wave. There is a moment

147

A number of techniques are illustrated by this photo. Once again the kayaker plants his brace in the solid water downstream from the froth. The high arm and cocked wrist indicate a Duffek or in this case an eddy turn. But this boater, as well as turning, is surfing; the velocity of the water and steepness of the wave permit him to aim rather widely across-river and still be carried clear across the stream to the feet of the cameraman without being swept downriver. By leaning downstream and angling toward the camera, he avoids a capsize and is pressed across the river to another gate out of the picture. Most surfing requires the kayak to be *aimed much more* nearly due upstream.
Photo by Roy Cromer

of pure stasis, of forces summed and exactly balanced; the boat hovers on the water like an eagle incising arcs on the sky. Gravity hurls him down the face of the wave into the base of the next wave upstream, and the racing water beneath him tries to rush him away downstream. These two forces, if he has done his work rightly, cancel each other, and he is lodged on the pulsing face of the wave beneath him. Should he back-paddle, he will be hurried away through the wave and down the river. Should he forward-paddle, or even lean forward, he will slip down the face of the

wave and plunge his bow deep into the wave upstream—this is pearling, from the surfers' term. Should he sink too deep into the wave upstream, an end-for-end or a pop-up is the result.

What he should do is start angled very slightly toward the shore he wishes to reach, and lean slightly toward it as well. Then, with gravity and water friction still pinning him in a water vise on the wave, this tiny adjustment of attitude will give the water purchase on the side of his boat opposite to the shore he would approach, and it will push him there. If the face of the wave is gentle, he may have to paddle to maintain on its face; if it is steep, he may have to back-paddle to avoid an endo. If his position is perfect, he may not need to lean at all, but may merely rudder with a paddle on one side or the other to swoop across the stream.

It is a sensation of perfect paradox: relaxation caused by roaring tension, stasis caused by canceling dynamisms; you are never more divorced from or in command of the river, and you are never more vulnerable. Your skill and power have been exerted to find a position in which skill and power grow more and more useless, and the outcome depends more and more upon the laws of physics and the whims of the Skag God who lives in the depths of the suckhole and beneath undercut cliffs. Despite the justifications a kayaker gives for learning to surf—"Suppose you have to rescue some guy on the other side and there's a 300-foot waterfall right below," and so forth—I think we all love it as the emblem of our sport. It is the moment of command and of surrender, of power and weakness, a moment of pure hedonism and pure justice, a worthless motion of a boat which is worthless, a purely existential moment without value beyond itself, with total value within.

The Endo and Pop-up

Let us deal with those physical rewards, if sought, or punishments if unsought, of surfing—the endo and the pop-up. If you break the stasis of your surf, schuss down the face of the wave and plant your bow deep into the back of the wave just upstream, what will happen? The water bending down from the crest of that upstream wave, ramming on the end of the boat, will carry it under deeper and deeper, until on a clear-water river there is nothing but a green-washed wavering bullet shape under the water, and on a mud-water river, nothing but rising silt-laden water covering the deck, pressing a belly in the spray cover, rising on your chest, rising on your chin. As the bow sinks and the stern rises, the boat stands forth proud and steep as an erec-

tion. If the kayaker leans back, if he back-paddles, if things have not gone too far, the buoyancy of the sunken bow will master the depressing force of the water and the boat will squirt out backwards, thump down on the river and wash downstream.

Now if the paddler should lean forward, paddle forward, or have selected a particularly strong wave, the snout of the boat will be forced straight down and swept right on downriver, beneath him. This is an endo. It can happen two other ways. If the kayaker has not planned it and is floating much too slowly up the face of a wave, he may lodge, surf backwards much to his eye-widening, stomach-cinching surprise, sink his stern and do an endo backwards, when the nose breaks from the water, blots out the wave, obscures the canyon, hides the sky and thumps down on top of him.

The second way to do an endo is to choose an appropriate suckhole. Since the water pouring over the rock causing a suckhole drops almost straight down, it will carry the nose under more efficiently than the water of a mere wave. To plant the nose of the boat in the falls is practically to demand an endo of the river. But, as it is a rock which has created the falls, so it is a rock beneath them awaiting the crash of the boat upon itself. Now if the curl of water over the rock is thick, the boat will strike that water and there will be no more than the usual problems of rolling in aerated water and getting out of the suckhole. If that hole is more a sleeper, and the water cushion on the rock is thin, a cracked or split rear deck will be the reward of such poor judgment.

On the High Stage

> . . . we were left to exercise our thoughts, by endeavoring to conceive the effect of a thousand streams poured from the mountains into one channel, struggling for expansion in a narrow passage, and at last discharging all of their violence of waters by a sudden fall through the horrid chasm.
>
> —Samuel Johnson, *Journey to the Western Islands*

Surfing out from the eddy in the background, this kayaker has planted his nose in the small breaking hole at the lower right, and is at the point of decision. By leaning back, he will do a pop-up, smack down on the river and be carried on downstream. Leaning forward will cause an end-for-end. The paddle is held ready for a brace to either side. *Photo by Roy Cromer*

All of the dangers of kayaking are increased running on high water; so, perhaps unfortunately, are the pleasures. A few words about what a high-water year can mean, and what it is like to kayak during one, may be in order. Now about one year in every three is a high-water year, and one in every fifteen is a great-water year. The year 1973 was the first great year I have seen in the Southwest, and according to older boatmen, 1957 was great too; 1974 in Idaho was a record year also, so the special hazards of high or flood waters are fresh in mind.

A kayaker is particularly vulnerable to the dangers of flood waters. This is because, given his love for privacy and penchant for derring-do, he will try to run small rivers in flood, and this is egregiously dangerous. In a real

water year, all the discharge of a large, or even a huge, river may be tumbling down the terrific gradient of a stream. Bushes, trees, shores, landings, all go under.

The water, except on certain undamaged drainages of the North, where it remains clear, is freezing and opaque with silt; a man who has fallen in it has only minutes of life, and but little more if he's wearing a wet suit. This is no exaggeration: When the water is below 40 degrees, one has a maximum of 15 to 30 minutes, depending on clothing and exertion, before the water sucks away so much heat that a man becomes unconscious. Long before unconsciousness his arms and legs are blunt clubs, and then cannot be moved at all.

Rescue must be practically instantaneous

if a man comes out of his boat. And rescue is most difficult. Because the bed of the river is rocky and the canyon narrow, the river cannot spread or scour to accommodate its flood; it must gorge up and accelerate to carry away the water. He who remembered a series of drops and useful pools on his favorite run may discover rapids four or five miles long: I have motored a fifteen-mile rapid in Cataract Canyon at a stage well below flood. Undermined by the suck of the flood, patriarchal trees topple into the water and break up; vast piles of driftwood from ancient floods slacken at the touch of the water and mottle the river with wood and scum; a paddle scarcely enters it. Railroad ties may drop from the crest of waves onto you; you share the current with trees a hundred feet long. Since the carrying power of water varies as the fourth or sixth power of velocity, great boulders are cracking and saltating in the bed. Sometimes, especially on smaller rivers, down logs lodge, damming the current; a man can be swept against them and pinned. Most dangerous are the great driftwood piles forming. Because the current passes through them, rather than rebounding as it does from rocks, a man may be pressed against them and held, or have his life jacket or wet suit catch on them.

The whole surface of the river, remembered as placid, is fretted with constant waves. Reflex waves and currents are set up off every projection on the shore and roll out toward the center of the river; a man can scarcely breast them if he seeks to swim ashore. Even the photographic memory of a first-class riverman for rapids is distressed, for some of the old rapids drown into ponds, some new rapids appear where nothing ever was before and some of the old ones are terribly changed. Old landmarks sink; recollected rocks thrust up great holes from far beneath the surface; familiar beaches and camps, deep beneath the water, are being cut away and perhaps rebuilt, perhaps not. In the worst of it, deer, dogs and great stiff-legged, bloat-bellied cows slip down the stream, revolving in stately dignity, incautiously

drowned above. Every rapid has a lash of tail waves which often pours over the lip of the drop below. Where once there were eddies adapted for rescue and play there may be none at all, and those few that exist are huge, and defended by powerful eddy fences.

Let us glance at a few figures. A flooding river's average velocity (merely the average) can easily pass ten miles an hour; some have been recorded just over twenty. Even at a mere ten miles an hour, a mile slips by every six minutes. In what seem moments, time rushing by as fast as the water itself, a capsized or injured kayaker can be miles away. As those minutes and miles pass, his strength is stolen by the icy water. The immense hydraulics of the river complicate the rescue. "High water," said Dellenbaugh, one of the primal boatmen, "diminishes the labor of passage, but increases the danger." Count on it; there will be five drownings or exposure deaths on the high stage for every one on the low.

But it is exciting, it is so exciting. A kayaker may enjoy his life on the river, but he only lives it on those rare crest stages when he is near to losing it. The best rule for flood stages is to stay off them. This cannot be stressed too much for the smaller rivers. If you do try any river in flood, try to catch it just after the peak; much of the driftwood will have piled up by then.

Keep it in mind that most rivers increase in difficulty by one to three grades when they flood. Splashy little intermediate runs on little rivers, whose gradient has never been accommodated to the power of a frequent large discharge, whose rocks have not known the attrition of millennia, can become torrents requiring a team of experts.

So, the final rule for heavy-water boating is to scout. Even when you are familiar with the river it is not the same river. Scout everything. If it is a river with a high gradient (over about 40 feet per mile continuously), this may mean you have to walk the entire length. But scout everything anyway. I have gotten into serious trouble by heedlessly thinking, "With the high water, I'll just flush through and everything will be over in a minute or two." Everything nearly was. If you are not an expert, if you cannot even recognize high water when you see it, forget it. For everyone who kills himself stupidly constricts the possibilities for those remaining; his epitaph is all too often a cluster of ill-considered and needless new regulations for those that remain.

Rescues

It is probably superfluous to remark that the best kayak rescues are those that are sketched in the rivers of the mind, and never need be made. With a reliable roll you will rarely burden your companions with the danger of saving you, your paddle and your boat. And a burden it is, for a kayak, as a rescue boat, is nearly worthless. In one you cannot, as Al Holland once did on the Middle Fork in his raft, snake an inadvertent swimmer into the boat, pin him to the floor with an unarguable foot, resume the oars and set up for the next wave with the loss of only one stroke. Usually you must approach a swimming kayaker (the novices, who need the most rescuing, are the most prone to panic) by gingerly offering the stern of your craft. Give a frightened swimmer a chance at the side of your boat and in his desire to grab at something he may roll you. On the stern he can exert very little torque. Let him grab the stern loop, and then begin to paddle laboriously directly across the river or, if there is close danger below, in the upstream ferry position toward the shore or an eddy. All but the most experienced of kayakers, once they catch hold of your boat, seem to drag their legs to the bottom of the river. Since they are vertical in the water, their drag on your boat is so great it feels like you are paddling in concrete; whole horsepower are lavished to slosh inches forward. Justly enough, when they do this they get their knees smashed. But in that interval between grabbing your boat and beginning to gabble excitedly about their tip-over ("I did an endo! Did you see? An end-for-end! God, did you see? It was . . .") and the time when they

get their legs up, it may be too late. I officiated, ill-humoredly, over the loss of a boat in Cataract Canyon in one such situation. So excited was the girl about her reverse endo that she could not bring herself to stow the chat about it and assist me with a sidestroke. After long seconds and pleas she was ordered to let the boat go over Satan's Gut so I could save her person.

So, such as they are, here are the rules.

The primary rule is, go as quickly as you can for an overturned kayak that is not twitching around; this means the man inside it is probably not conscious, since he is not trying to roll or bail out of it. You may have to abandon your own boat in order to get under water and lift the person's head into the air, and you have little more than 90 seconds to accomplish this. If he's a joker, and has been floating under there breathing from the inside of the boat, forget him on future river trips. Someone else may still want to boat with him, but your life is too valuable to risk on someone else's games.

In a normal rescue, when you are the rescuer, approach as I said and keep ferrying. You are in charge, you give the orders. If you must, let the rescued one go over the falls; the party will be stronger with only one lost than with two, and you will be in better position for the eventual rescue even if you must portage and lose time. Since it is nearly impossible to descend any real rapid with someone anchoring the tail of your boat, get rid of him, get through it, and then try again.

If you are the rescued, hang on to your paddle and your kayak. Leave it upside down; it will ship less water that way. Get upstream from the boat so it does not crush you between itself and a rock. Most kayakers grow furious at the thought of novices who run without flotation in their boat, for such a craft weighs half a ton, breaks up easily, can drag a rescuer where he would rather not be and can crush not only the owner, who deserves it, but the rescuer. A paddle that floats is a boon as well; not all do, but all can be made to with a little tape and Ethafoam.

Help your rescuer by sidestroking as much as you can. It is not really fair to tax his brawn to pay for your mistakes, and anyway he probably hasn't enough strength for the two of you. Take his orders instantly.

An abandoned drifting kayak can only really be rescued two ways. Put the nose of your boat at its center of rotation and paddle forward toward the shore. Try to shove it in an eddy. If it has a six- or seven-foot line attached to one end or the other, you may venture to catch it up with a hand against your paddle, tie it to the center of your paddle, or bite it with your teeth. With the line you drag the boat to shore. But I ought to point out that while many kayakers use such painters, and they are a convenience in rescuing, they can also be dangerous. First, they can accidentally tie the kayaker to his craft; a man drowned on the Snake in 1974 in just such a fashion. He and his boat passed on opposite sides of a bridge piling with a rope connecting them. And second, such a rope, if tied to the paddle of the rescuer, can jerk his paddle out of his hands.

A paddle to be rescued can be put against the forward edge of your coaming and tilted back over your shoulder; it is held by your chin. This is as awkward as it sounds. Or you can try to double-blade, by holding the found paddle right against your own with both blades parallel to yours. This is also awkward. Usually I just get as close as I can to the shore the kayaker has climbed out on and toss the blade over there; he can walk down and get it.

Real Danger

The true, high-grade rescues, with spent and broken bodies clinging to rocks upon which the torrent splits, or cinematic compound fractures à la *Deliverance,* have only one rule and one prohibition. The rule is to save life and forget equipment; the prohibition is never to tie a conscious man who is in the water or may be in the water to a rope. For if the rope should lodge or the person prove too hard to pull in, his body will become an aquaplane at the end of the rope, riding up to the surface and jetting down to the bed. If this happens and there is no remedy, cut him loose immediately, no matter what lies below. Men have swum Niagara but none has survived ten or eleven minutes of immersion.

As for the techniques of such rescues, I can say but little. Use your imagination, use the 25-foot lengths of nylon or polypropylene $\frac{3}{8}$-inch line you keep out of harm's way under your float bags, and use your first-aid books. Here are some suggestions. If a man is in a backwash and you have a rope to him, you will have to pull him out of it. But if his path lies through current, he will be swept to the end of the rope and swung like a pendulum until the rope is taut and pointed directly down the current; if the rope is fixed on the shore this should bring him close to the shore below, so have a man there ready either to wade out for him or to cast him a second rope.

When your man is ashore, treat his injuries and treat him for hypothermia (apply heat, not just warm clothes) and sit down for a long consultation on how to get him out of the canyon. Only when there is imminent danger of death, when a man's face is underwater or the water is icy cold or an artery is slashed, is there desperate need for speed. After that his chances will be much improved by your taking a long and exhaustive stock of all possible alternatives, from setting him in his boat, to getting a raft, or a car, or a helicopter, or a stretcher. To do this you will need expert assessments of his physical and mental condition, your own condition (nothing raises the rating of a rapid so much as the body of a friend on the shore above it) and strong knowledge of the terrain between you and help. You and your friends had better be prepared with such knowledge. You had better be prepared to be both leaders and followers in such a situation.

The psychological evaluations that have to be made after a rescue require finesse and perception. When you come to decide whether a man is capable of running his own boat out, it may be that his physical strength is fully up to the task. His mind may be, as mine has been on occasion, incapable of further travel. These are not imaginary terrors, to be glossed over or bullied into silence because you think it best for the man's future career that he get back on the water immediately and paddle through his envisioned terrors. After one accident his fear may breed others. If there is gentle water below, you may risk persuading him to re-enter his boat, when he is warm and has been talked to a good deal, but it is a risk and should not be thought of any other way.

RACING

When you have mastered most of the skills of kayaking, saving perhaps the heavy-water techniques, you may think of racing. Since a race injects another ingredient into the mix of self and river—competition—there are some who refuse to race. I was one, finding the idea of beating someone or being beaten a distasteful matter on the river. But on the Cache la Poudre River recently my views changed. Two old kayaking partners were competing. It had been some five years since we kayaked together and in the interval my skills had blunted, while constant racing had stropped theirs to a fineness unimagined in those earlier days. Ron Mason looked ever the more like quicksilver with a will; Roy Cromer ornamented the river. "I never learned to boat," was his remark, "until I began to race"; his performance was his proof.

Wildwater

There are two types of kayak racing—wildwater (also called downriver) and slalom. To descend a given stretch of river faster than anyone else is the goal of wildwater racing. It is practiced in the special boats I discussed at the beginning of this chapter. They balk and resist when turned, but in straight water they cleave the river like a blade does butter.

Most downriver races are relatively short, compared to the twenty-five to fifty miles a cruising kayaker can make in a day, for they are usually only four to seven miles long. An occasional and brutal race, like the famous

Salida Downriver, stretches to twenty-six miles. But the times that win are the shock. Four- to seven-mile races usually are won in about half an hour; the Salida run in two to three hours. Boats are numbered and started at regular intervals. The men who win these races regularly are supermen in my book; you need only paddle at full strength for ten minutes, then imagine doing so for two hours, to see why.

The best way to train for such a race is to paddle your boat as far and as fast as you can, for years. But, as we used to discover racing pontoons with the oars, it is brains which will prevail. For there are certain strategies which pay off in time gained and strength saved for the crucial roll in the last bad rapid. Obviously, one should hit no eddies; perhaps not so obviously, one should avoid large waves which ostensibly mark the best current. For it is extremely difficult to keep piling six miles an hour onto the current speed when the break of each wave stalls the boat. But on the lateral shoulders of the waves, between the crests and the eddy fence, there is pretty fast water and the chance to keep up the steady rhythm that gains time and saves muscles from poisoning themselves with lactic acid. This also keeps the boat relatively dry, an important consideration when there is no time to sponge out and one is adding eight pounds per gallon of water to a feather-light boat.

For similar reasons you should avoid the various hydraulics caused by rocks. There is an obvious eddy behind a suckhole; there is dead water behind a breaking hole; there is slow water downstream from even a deeply submerged rock. Only this last may provide an assist, for when the whole river is covered with obstructing waves, there may be a path, caused by just such a deeply submerged rock, where the waves are muted. All these things can be learned in a kayak, but they are easiest learned where you pay most for each mistake—at the oars of a raft, or preferably a pontoon. I could see that Roy Cromer had once learned that while a man could turn the

Threading the needle in a downriver (wildwater) race. Close inspection will show a narrow passage between the breaking wave behind the kayaker and the wave at the right center of the picture. Had he hit either of the two waves, his boat would have been buried by water and stalled, but by slipping between them he maintains his rhythm and thus his speed, justifying the name of his boat (IQ). This sort of precision is years in the learning, but it must be learned, for it, rather than brawn, wins wildwater races. *Photo by Roy Cromer*

great wallowing, wormy bulk of a 4,000-pound pontoon, it was better policy to let the river do it. His young competitors had not attended so rigorous a school. Minute current differentials they had never been forced to observe retarded their boats and accelerated his. Any boatman can benefit from a little cross-pollination by other craft; a wildwater racer may pick up some of the tricks that win his races from the most sluggish of all the river boats. Coupled to endurance there must be finesse to win.

Slalom

Knowing the currents thoroughly is also the secret to slalom races. To the simple velocity of a downriver race is added preci-

sion; you must not merely descend 800 meters of river quickly, but must pass through up to 30 gates. These are hung above the river some 3 to 10 inches, and are 3 to 6 feet wide. The green-and-white pole is passed on the right; the red-and-white pole is passed on the left. All the gates are numbered and must be passed in sequence. Some of them are upstream and some are reverse, through which you paddle backwards. On upstream gates you cannot see the number; on reverse gates you can, with a large "R" beside it. A gatekeeper watches each gate, assessing penalties, which are added to the total time, 10 for touching one pole from the inside, 20 for striking both from the inside and 50 for missing a gate or going through it the wrong way. A kayaker given aid is disqualified. Normally each kayaker gets two runs, each done in a sequence determined by drawing. So a typical good run might be 177, with 157 seconds elapsed and 20 penalty seconds attached; a poor one might be as high as 405, with 135 seconds elapsed and many gates missed or smacked. As in a downriver race, boats are started at regular intervals. A variant on the procedure is the team race, in which three kayakers must pass through one of the gates within fifteen seconds.

The new low-volume slalom boats have revolutionized slalom racing, while making the gatekeeper's job more difficult. Useless in heavy water for the very characteristic that wins races, these boats have low decks, so they can sneak under gates. In fact, slalom racers have developed a sharp backward lean against the back-brace mentioned previously, which will sink the whole stern of the boat under water at just that moment when it must pass beneath a gate. With a high-volume boat, a man must pass through a gate nearly straight on, or his deck will strike a pole. With low enough decks a man could, for instance, drift beneath both poles aimed 89 degrees to one side and still have passed through the gate "forward." If he passed under the poles at a 90-degree angle, of course, he would have missed the gate and would be assessed his 50 points. Since gusts of wind, splashing waves and clumsy spectators can all jog the gates, and since his calls may bounce a man out of the Olympics, the gatekeeper's is no happy lot.

Races vary in difficulty; they can be set up for novices or designed to torment experts. All that is requisite is a piece of water approximated to the skills of those who will race, with a lot of trees or rocks on the shore, from which to suspend lines across the river. After the lines have been ferried or thrown across and fixed, gate assemblies (which consist of a horizontal spacer bar with a number and two loosely hanging poles appropriately painted and attached to it) are slid out on the lines and their position adjusted by a second line attached only to the assembly. The second

line is then tied and the loose poles hang down near the water. One might plant a gate in a big hole for the experts; a modest eddy fence may be a sufficient obstacle for beginners. It is probably better to set a course just a little under the capacity of those running it, rather than over, since the idea of most of the competitors is to enjoy schooling themselves in precision.

And fine schooling it can be. A kayaker must know not only the currents, since in any tough race a quarter second may dump the 50 points on him, but the capacities of his boat. And this means not only what it will do but where it is, all of that lance-like unwieldy four meters, not just the part where he sits. And he must know where all of his body above the waist is too, for a man may have a gate clean, and by swinging his paddle an inch too wide, pick up the 10 points.

For a layman to watch a race is a matter of sudden beauties and an impression of considerable strain; the faces are all in a rictus of effort and the arm muscles stand out until both the component muscles of the biceps are revealed in strata. The boats wheel about in great curls across the river, suddenly arrest with a flick of the paddle and begin to battle back upstream against the current, like men battle to haul in an anchor, until they force an upstream gate and, on the instant liberated, slide across the river in a surf to the next gate. But for a lesser kayaker to watch a race among the experts is an education in possibility. You are constantly amazed that the old tub can leap through such hoops, perform such acrobatics; it surely never did at your urging. Even to a lesser kayaker each of the strokes has meaning: the tiny draw strokes that align the boat, just for a second, but in that second it twists through the gate; the odd angle of the strokes, with the upper arm momentarily high above the head to keep the paddle clear of the pole; a long wheeling curl of a surf which is not quite a surf since it ends up pointed downriver in time for a gate and yet not a Duffek turn since it gets the racer most of the way across the river before he swings on down the river; the new cross-bow draw stroke, done like a normal draw in the forward quadrant, except the drawing blade is swung clear across the deck to the opposite side, turning the boat and clearing the paddle for the gate. You get a new conception of power in a power stroke, in which the upper arm still punches forward but the whole body lunges forward, as if the paddle were not an object slipping through the water but was a solid block to be grabbed and pulled against.

The layman watching may, like the cub pilot in *Life on the Mississippi,* who is still able to respond to the beauty of a sunset without responding technically to the river reflecting and enhancing it, see more beauty than a kayaker who is watching virtuosity. But I expect, from having observed hundreds of dudes punching at buttons on their Instamatics, that the deeper appreciation is the kayaker's, whose aesthetic pleasure is sharpened by knowledge. He will have the same grasp of evanescent patterns being traced on the water, he will see the bobbing craft inset like gems in the chromed surface of the rapid, but it will be his also to see what the spectator cannot, the detail and the reason for it. Merely watching, a lesser kayaker feels his knowledge swell.

So I have dropped my distaste for racing. Clearly, when a man, faced by a rapid he would have counted it enough just to get through, not only runs it but tries to run the course set up on it, he returns magnified by the trial. All the future rapids he scouts and his image of them will be a hint closer to congruence. Having educated himself in accuracy he will carry fewer imaginary dangers and skirt more actual ones; he will bring sharpened judgment and vaster skills back from his racing. Nothing that schooled my old pards in such grace can be bad.

TOURING

Equipment

Some look upon racing as the perfection of their time in a kayak, but I think there are others who look to kayak touring for the finest days they spend in a boat. And touring is really pretty easy, the camping part at least, especially if you are an old backpacker. Many of the principles of gear selection and even of loading are the same. You can get a pretty good idea of gear from Colin Fletcher's *The Complete Walker,* but you get the best suggestions from Scott and Margaret Arighi's *Wildwater Touring.* The main determinants in gear selection are space, strength, warmth and bureaucratic regulation—never have understood how a party of kayaks carries an ax, shovel and bucket, but that's the law on some rivers at some times. But a kayaker, after he fulfills the requirements of the law, seeks light and compact gear. As he is at a lower altitude and probably will have warmer temperatures, he can usually go with even less than the Spartan accouterments of the backpacker. A minimum gear list for a brief hot-weather trip can fit as neatly into a sentence as a boat: sleeping bag or just a sheet, cup, pot, knife, spoon, matches, food and parachute cord. And the food itself (2,000–4,000 calories a day, depending on a person's size and the anticipated temperatures) need not be purchased from expensive stands in backpacking stores, but can come from the supermarket, which sells a number of cheap dried and freeze-dried foods at about half the backpacker's price. A man can even supplement his food with trout in the North Country and catfish in the desert, with the aid of a hand line.

But this list is a little abbreviated, since it presumes enduring the rain and wearing only a wet suit. For cold weather and water trips in early or late season you must add down and wool; two sets of clothes is plenty. Sharing a tent can be a pleasure worth the extra few pounds of weight. A rainsuit for camp in the rain, and a hat, boots and suntan oil with PABA in it for hiking are pleasant. A real camera is worth the weight; a little, light plastic jobbie is not. An Ensolite pad or shortie air mattress is crucial when it is cold. At the risk of confessing myself no true wilderness freak, I will remark that a good book is worth the weight—I have found that a skinny one with good notes in a language I do not know well provides for the most diversion with the least weight. When fire closures are in effect you will need a primus stove or the like.

This equipment, with a few individual additions to suit personal medical requirements and tastes (insulin, ties for glasses, spare glasses, tampons and so forth), should fit out each member. The group as a whole will need certain additional communal equipment: rescue equipment, meaning ropes and perhaps a hand winch; first-aid equipment, to wit: one substantial first-aid kit supplemented with an inflatable splint, prescription pain killers, monosodium glutamate for bee stings, a snakebite kit, aspirin and salt tablets. If you will be out more than three days you had better add some antibiotic tablets of a type no one is allergic to (if they are, anaphylactic shock may kill them in an hour or so), Lomotil for diarrhea and either calamine lotion or Neoxyn for poison ivy. A first-aid book is a good idea.

The party as a whole should have half a spare paddle per person; these must be carried on a raft or be of the breakdown type so you can stow them behind you or on your deck, by means of large rings cut from inner tubes. A spare life jacket is a good idea.

There must also be a repair kit. It should contain duct tape (a coated fabric tape), a couple of yards of fiberglass cloth and roving, at least a quart of resin with catalyst and eyedropper to measure it, four or five brushes, sandpaper, a coarse wood rasp, some waxed paper to stretch over the patch so it will cure smooth, Barge contact cement, epoxy glues, perhaps some acetone, and some little cans or paper cups to mix resin in. Somewhere there had better be a pair of pliers and a first-rate knife you could shave with in a pinch. I carry mine in a belt rig, but am inclined to think putting a sheath for the knife on the outside of a life jacket a good idea. For repairing foot braces a handful of nuts and bolts, an adjustable wrench and a small folding saw are useful.

The question arises, how are repairs made? Preferably they aren't; most dings and cracks can be taped with the boat tape or duct tape and will hold until you return. Massive contusions are repaired by sanding down to the fiber, mixing up resin, and sticking on glass pieces cut to size. Two or three layers are adequate.

Packing the Gear

From these basics one can expand at will through metal matches, sharpening stones, air-mattress pumps, full cans of beer and the like, until the boat wallows under the load and more experienced boatmen smile each night as it disgorges mounds of duffel. Now there are two problems to carrying the load—it must be positioned so as to hamper your maneuvering as little as possible, and it must be kept dry. Small .30 or .50 caliber ammunition boxes will keep things you need dry (check them in a bathtub first), but, being metal, they rattle about in the boat, digging divots out of your legs and back. I use them, if at all, only for items needing immediate access, like cameras. And tied in, they can wrap their cord about your legs and drown you unless you've a knife to cut free and are conscious to use it. The larger items can be put in special dunnage/float bags made by Whitewater Sports of Denver; your supplier should have them, and at about $27.50 a set they are well worthwhile. For after they are sealed, they are inflated by means of a tube. Army-surplus stores have heavy rubber bags—called wetpacks, black bags or blags—which also work but provide no flotation to speak of.

Now as to the packing of the boat, Dr. Gibbs, the mechanical engineer and boatman, informs me that the difficulty of turning a boat is governed by two power functions. First, difficulty will vary with the square of the distance between the boat's center of mass and a given weight. Load the heavy stuff as close to you as you can. Second, water resistance varies as the third power of the speed of rotation; water resistance is mostly a matter of draft, or wetted surface. So load it lightly.

And finally, load the heaviest items on the bottom and immobilize them, for they will help to ballast you.

How will it handle? Not well. It will likely have an extra twenty to thirty-five pounds in it, when five make a perceptible difference. It will be slow to start turning and hard to halt, the devil to accelerate and worse to stop. Well ballasted, it will be hard to capsize (*if* your gear is immobilized and does not slide around) and hard to roll. It will bite deeper in waves and take more dribbles through the spray cover. It will tire your arms and sharpen your wits, for it will not forgive you your follies as it has in the past.

¡ Arre Burro!

Now, barring certain difficulties I will discuss presently, it is probably easier to travel with a raft as support boat. Let *him* carry the beer, is the thought. But this is one of the difficulties. Kayakers seem to see the capacity of even a small raft as practically infinite, and to regard it and its oarsman as the party's pack burro. Only on the trip of a lifetime down Grand Canyon, when you have paid for the privilege, should you count on shifting your gear and your share of the communal items onto the raft.

The second cause of difficulty is the relative velocity of raft and kayak—a potential cause of more serious conflict than arguments about gear, for those the raftsman can solve simply by dumping your gear in the river. Even the most modest of kayakers can add a steady four miles an hour to the speed of the current; the sturdiest of raftsmen, persuaded to overcome his praiseworthy indolence, can move in bursts of nearly two miles an hour. He is not likely to want to, however. Over the course of a day a raft drifting at current speed drops miles behind a set of gung-ho kayakers. If the wind comes up, you will scarcely notice it, but the raftsman will be tortured. He must claw his way down the canyon against it. So it is a better plan to stop and play in rapids, giving him a chance to get a start on you, keeping the party together.

There can be very serious tension if you race ahead through the wind and ignorantly make camp just at sundown. He will be in well after dark, unless he decides to give you your deserts and leave you without food or shelter for the night; when he gets in you had better ply him with a few beers, let him off the cook crew and be very careful about making jokes about breezes. Only when you are on a regulated river is it fair to race to camp and sit him out, for then you are assigned camps and must (legally *and* ethically) use them, so it is his lookout to reach them. Even so, you have been having fun, while his steady rowing may, at least to him, begin to resemble work after the fifth unintermitted hour of it.

These differing velocities are dangerous in rapids, for there the raftsman will use the Galloway-Stone technique of rowing upstream. He will be going 3 feet per second slower than the current and you will be going full bore as much as 13 feet per second faster than the current. If you have a rapid 300 feet long, with a speed of 18 feet per second, you will require less than 10 seconds to run it and he will require 20. He must be more than half through it before you start, or you run the risk of fouling his oars or hitting his boat.

And collision between a raft and a kayak can be disagreeable. If you hit him nose-on or stern-on and haven't padded your tips, you can pass through the skin of his boat, blowing a section. Hit him properly, right on the diaphragm, and you blow two sections. Since many small rafts have only two chambers, if you get them both the boat will sink on the spot. Even if you don't, and merely blow one, the oarsman will have to spend odious hours sanding, scraping, sewing, gluing, drying and patching. Then he will have to pump it again.

On the other hand, if you are hit, especially by one of the big motored pontoons in Grand or Cataract Canyon, you will regret it. You will likely be bowled under; you run a fair chance of surfacing back at the propeller and getting "chopped." People have lost hands, severed at the wrist, to the larger motors. And the boatman doesn't know you are there; he has people distracting him and blocking his vision all the time. No matter what the Coast Guard regulations say, on the river little boats get out of the way of big boats. Kayaks are the littlest boats and get out of everyone's way. When the little ones insist on fancied rights of way and playfully see if they can push a big one on the rocks, they get motored and deserve it. Even if the big boats preferred not to hit you (and be sure that they will rather prefer to nail you if you are purposely getting in their way), they cannot generally help it; they are too sluggish. It is a case to warm the heart of a Christian or a liberal, for those who can help, must. The most agile of river craft, the kayak, must assume the burden of avoiding collision with all the others. For the times when you cannot avoid piling up, a bulbous mass of Ethafoam like a circus clown's nose at either end of your boat, attached with boat tape, will save the diaphragms of both the rafts and your friends.

General Considerations

A few tips. Do an overnighter before you head out for ten days with new equipment. Most trips run better if the food selection, utensil choice, packing and preparation are done communally. Unless you run with a set of good friends who are all fine woodsmen, it is well to regiment this, for there can be real trouble on a trip when nobody has to cook and everyone is supposed to, if one person will not carry his weight on the chores. Get everything clear before the trip, from how hard it will be to how expenses for food and driving and emergencies are to be shared. I have had no trouble with the simple policy that failures of equipment due to the equipment are the owner's expense, and failures that are a person's fault are under the "repair to the satisfaction of the owner or replace" understanding. The bigger the trip, and the less well-known its members are to one another, the more specific all this must be beforehand. For when they are not well-known, you have a greater chance of inviting some litigious jerk who looks to make his

court award pay for ten years kayaking, or some vapid spirit who has decided that since God made the air and the water common, He must have intended kayaks to be communally owned as well. Obnoxious as it is, you may even want to get this in writing; the formality of signing a bit of paper can be far less unpleasant than having your stove boat out of commission for months, and trying to get it patched with promises. See that you get the shuttle arranged; you can basically either pay drivers communally or do it yourselves, but get it arranged.

Before the trip a coordinator is a help. On the trip you may or may not want an official "leader," but it is a good idea to have the lead boat filled by a person who knows the run and has some of the party's finest water-reading skills. On more regimented trips there is a rule, and a good one, that no one passes the leader for any reason. There should be a sweep boat, preferably staffed by a man whose abilities at least equal the leader's. He passes no one, ever. Ideally he should carry some of the rescue equipment, the patch kit and the first-aid kit, but this is a burden. At least he should have the first-aid kit. He can drift down to a disaster easily enough, but it can be impossible, even with a good set of signals (not a must, but a damn good idea for a party that contains even one person who does not know the river), to get word ahead to a man heedlessly paddling the first-aid kit into the distance. Even if he gets the information it can be hours before he hikes back with the kit. So give some attention to keeping the party together and to working out some signals with paddle motions; it may seem Mickey Mouse until you find a brand-new rapid created by yesterday's flash flood, but then it can save a life.

Choosing the River

Selecting a tour can be most difficult. If you have a first-rate leader who knows the river, knows where to get information on it and permits to run it, and knows how to assemble a compatible party, you are set. If he is a really good man, he will know how to teach you the details so you can become a leader yourself, how to determine who is skilled enough and pleasant enough to invite, how to get it together, in short. If you do not have such a guide available, consult the Arighis' book or other guidebooks. Then select a river. You will have to get flow data on it from USGS Water Supply Papers for at least five years to get an idea of what possible stages you may face and therefore what times of year to think of trying it. You will need topo maps from the USGS, available in the West from the USGS, Distribution Section, Denver Federal Center, Lakewood, Colorado, 80225, and in the East from USGS, Distribution Section, 1200 South Eads Street, Arlington, Virginia, 22202, to determine the gradient and the type of country you will traverse, as well as possible escape routes. The Geological Survey will also know, or tell you who does know, what the flow is at the gauging station nearest your put-in, as the time approaches for your trip. Above all, write to one of the whitewater groups in the area for all the information they can give. Get a guidebook if they publish one. Write to the National Park Service, Forest Service or Bureau of Land Management if it is under their administration; they will direct you to the flow readings and best boating season, furnish maps and information, and give you information on permits. Write to professional outfitters who run the river; we professional boatmen are apt to be a little more reliable on paper than in person, or at least our bosses are. Of these various sources of information, a club in the area is probably most reliable. With a few notable exceptions, Park Service men drive pickups better than they drive boats, so their information tends to be a little overstated. One can hardly blame them; the Park Service and the Forest Service have lost so many suits to the estates of dudes claiming they should have been forbidden to go on the river, or the Park Service should have cut all tree limbs in camp that *might* fall, or should have had twelve-foot mildly electrified fences around hot springs so someone

wouldn't fall in, and so forth, that they are a bit leery. And they have had to pull a lot of devil-may-care, don't-bother-me-with-any-information-I'm-going-Down-the-River types out of so many places that they will feed you information a little on the overcautious side. Professional boatmen are indeed professional; they see the river through very competent eyes, as a rule. With the exception of a few young hippie types who are still scared and a few middle-aged old drunks with mercifully small local outfits who think any river is a picnic because they never ran anything worse than medium stages in Hell's Canyon or Desolation-Gray, they are pretty reliable. Many of the younger ones are fugitive kayakers. But they also look at their rivers from large and stable rafts. You get the best information from them by listening to a lot of stories and gradually getting them to compare the river you are on with a lot of others they have worked. This information, if you have a sensible source, should usually be upgraded a little; the river will likely be a bit bigger and rougher than he claims. But be warned. When that gleam shows in the eye, and you hear, "Why now, listen, son [or honey], lemme tell you there's rapids down in that canyon that'd crunch you the way a bass takes a crayfish," or "Hey man, hey, listen, there's some really heavy stuff down in there, I mean, really . . ."—then you may, if you are competent on rivers of the general size you are about to run, downgrade the information a little. You must simply judge your informant and second-guess his judgment of you, since it is not impossible he is, in the Western phrase, "packing your ass with sand." And be sure to find out what size boat he uses on the river in question. What he thinks of as a lot of maneuvering for his raft will be shot through with highways for your kayak, but what he thinks of as good waves and a fine ride may be water as large as you have ever seen. For what it is worth, an expert kayaker can get a kayak, so far as I have ever seen, through any rapid (not through any *place*) a pontoon can run.

In selecting a tour it is of very considerable

importance to find out the difficulty of the stretch of river you contemplate running. The river-rating scales, discussed in the first chapter of this book, should be consulted, and a rating either received from a whitewater group near the tour in question or guessed at from a contour map and the available record of flow. While on a single-day trip you may risk having people along who are not quite, for instance, Class III boaters when you are on a Class III cruise, it is a good idea on a prolonged tour to set the overall rating of the tour one grade below the skill of the participants. This is not just because you will encounter rapids a grade or so above the general rating of the tour, but because on a prolonged tour you want a margin of safety which the wilderness and the river may not give you. On a Class III tour a few boaters of Class IV and Class V will be useful in an emergency, not just because they can run the rapids of that grade which you will meet, but because they will probably have grown steady and cool in the years it took them to reach their level of ability.

As a general rule, I would point out that as a kayaker you will run rivers of a higher gradient than the rafts, and you will probably want more privacy than do the raftsmen. A raftsman tends to want, as does a kayaker, a good time on the river, but he is more physical than a kayaker is about his good times. Making the first descent of a miserable river may well mean so much to a kayaker that he can overlook his misery. And it should be pointed out that there are still first descents left within the continental United States to be made. Most of them require extensive planning and a team of experts, but they are there awaiting you. Of almost equal importance to a kayaker's intellectual enjoyment of a river is the remoteness and loneliness of a river. Kayakers, for instance, denied the first descent of the Grand Canyon, may well choose to run it in the winter, in order not to encounter anyone but their own party, and have the illusion of a first descent. While you should accord most consideration to match-

ing your abilities, by use of the rating system, to those required by the tour, you will be best pleased, as a true kayaker, by the lonely grandeur of a wilderness river.

SAFETY AND ETHICS

I have already covered a number of safety items and, while I have a few more yet to cover, I will point out that most of the matters which are called "safety" are also matters of ethics. I would differentiate the two by suggesting, rather roughly, that safety is a matter of preserving your health, while ethics is a matter of your responsibilities to your friends and those others with whom you share the river, in the past, present and especially future. You may, for instance, decide to go kayaking alone, and while this is a pleasure sometimes, it is something of a dumb stunt. It is not necessarily unsafe; that depends on the circumstances. But it is surely unethical, since you are risking not only the lives of those who may see you and decide to follow your example, but the lives of those who may have to come get you when you eat the load. You do not have their consent for that risk. It is unsafe, or more precisely, very prodigal, to kayak without float bags, and it is also unethical, since your rescuers can get into very serious trouble trying to save your wallowing boat. So I would offer these rules, not to save your life, the loss of which is mainly your business, but the lives of your kayaking partners and the feelings of your family; they are not yours to play with.

1. Do not boat alone.
2. Wear your life jacket, helmet and, if the water is cold, your wet suit.
3. Learn as much as you can about a river before and during the run. This means getting the assistance (and preferably presence) of someone who has run it, getting the flow and topo maps from the Geological Survey, scouting its major rapids, even walking its whole length if necessary, and perhaps in wild country like Alaska or Africa, chartering an airplane to scout it. You may have to learn to read

maps and become a fair lay geologist in the process, but you had better do it.

4. Do not exceed the limit of your abilities unless there is a good rescue spot below.

5. Keep the limitations of your fellow kayakers in mind.

With this last rule we are right on the frontier of ethics and safety. If, for instance, there is a strong, dumb, unskilled, competitive seventeen-year-old boy along, he may seek to run whatever you run, especially if you are a woman; you may thus have to order him not to, or more tactfully, carry rapids you could easily run and he could not. Orders may work if yours is a structured party, but since we kayakers are mostly prima donnas, they may not. I have seen a first-rate boatman pass what he thought his life's last chance at the only major rapid he had not run on the Green-Colorado system, because the pressure of his example might have impelled some less competent boaters into a rapid they could never have handled. Another caution applicable at this point is to avoid any sort of macho competitions. You are on the water, not to puff and strut your masculinity, but to descend the river safely and taste its secrets. He that carries a rapid is not chicken, not a coward, not "less of a man," but probably more of one, since he is using his judgment. He is the best judge of the relation between his abilities and the river. One hopes that the man who pressures others to run by insinuating that they are cowards will someday have one of those long, strength-sapping swims, and at the end of it know the fear we all have felt, when any water larger than a bathtub is terrifying, and all a man's will must be exerted just to get back in the boat. Then he will know, I hope, the shame of having scoffed at others just so reduced and humiliated and frightened as he then is. Better that he know this shame than cast up the debits of a friend's death in the ledgers of his conscience.

Beyond safety there yet remain ethical matters to be hinted at. A kayaker ought, as I remark in a following section, to be an active conservationist. He shares with hunters, hikers, climbers, bikers and mobile-unit drivers the obligation to pass through the landscape ruffling it as little as the winds. This means everything except feces and urine is to be packed out. Even used toilet paper should be packed out or taken right down to the river's edge and, fire regulations permitting, burned. The soil bacteria that digest feces do not attack the paper. All this may mean carrying a little in garbage bags, but it is important.

Most of the regulations which govern river use are sensible and should be obeyed. No committed outdoorsman can quarrel with litter regulations, or with the necessity of using an outhouse; these rules would not have been made if there had not been a problem with trash and sewage. The same is true of permit regulations and assigned camps. It goes against the grain to ask permission to use a river you know more about than the men who regulate it, but such rules hold the human erosion as low as it can be and alleviate the crowding many rivers already feel.

One matter which probably ought to be discussed is proselytizing. Some friendships and certain kayaking clubs have been strained about this matter already, it being the sentiment of some that we need as many new kayakers as possible, and the opinion of others that there are already more than enough. It is a double bind. Each convert is a voice to protect our shrinking stock of streams, and each convert adds to the human pressure on those remaining streams. And human pressure is a matter of consequence to kayakers. I have seen secret and lovely camps where the grass grew knee-high and down timber moldered in the woods turn into hard-packed basketball courts, have seen the arduous climb to a hidden waterfall become first a trail and then a hiker's freeway, have seen long vistas of beach sprout flowers of used toilet paper and waft off the stench of feces. Human erosion is no empty phrase.

But neither is it a phrase to claim we have saved certain rivers and will save yet more. I have thought through this bind as a professional river boatman for years and found no satisfactory conclusion. Many of the best and most devoted kayakers I know no longer seek converts. They will still be happy to teach if they are sought out, but only if the prospective convert seems to be material, not for a friend, nor even for a lover, but for a river pard. This is arrogant, though after all it is their skill which is sought, but then most dedicated kayakers, as I have hinted at before, do not think of the river as a vehicle for good times but as a sacred communion. They also think that a new and dedicated kayaker will be gentler to the river than any other type of boatman. Whether this is true or not (as a kayaker I of course agree, though as a raftsman I have some small doubts), kayakers revere their sport. If they teach, they share, not the ability to play a sport, but a part of their being. When the Forest Service planned to put picnic tables around Blue Lake, heart and source of the religion of the Taos Indians, the Indians were outraged and asked how the whites would enjoy their putting jeep roads and picnic tables in a cathedral; the feeling of kayakers for what they cannot help but think of as their river is the same.

So you must resolve this question on your own. If there is not a large stock of kayakers on a river, it may be lost to the dam builders. If there are many kayakers, and you have helped, even as these pages have helped, to recruit them, you may run the risk of losing your friends; you may even find it doesn't seem like the same river you once loved because of the crowds.

One final matter, not of safety but of ethics, seems to deserve some comment. We kayakers, as I have noted before, tend to be pretty self-righteous. We are not alone. A spirit of contempt has of late seemed to arise on many rivers, with kayakers sneering at oarsmen who sneer at those who use motors on the river. Having used all three modes, I feel justified in a comment. The skills involved are not at all disproportionate. A kayak *is* the purest craft, for what that is worth, but there are few kayakers who could not benefit from a stint on the oars under the tutelage of a really first-class oarsman. Those guys know things about current that very few kayakers have ever been forced to learn. And both groups might learn a great deal about timing and current from the man who must get $700 to $20,000 worth of motored equipment down the river unharmed, week after week, year after year. On river there is always opportunity to dissipate excess energy dealing with the water itself; there is no need to waste it maligning others.

THE KAYAKER AND THE LAW
The Lawman

The kayaker meets the law in three relations: being governed by it, aiding it and influencing it. The first of these, which also covers raftsmen and canoeists, is covered in the first chapter of the book. The list of applicable laws given there is by no means complete, and as these things vary from state to state, you will have to make some excavations before you know what you will be penalized for doing or not doing.

If you have discovered what laws apply to you, and have not followed them, you may meet the law in person: the game warden, the River Ranger, the River Patrol, the deputy sheriff. If you meet a River Ranger or the River Patrol, you are probably all right. These men have been down the river more than you have. If you get a ticket from them you have deserved it. You probably won't get a ticket from them unless you have gone out of your way to be unpleasant to them, or have violated the laws most prodigiously—killing harmless snakes and putting them in the ladies' outhouse, failing to wear a life jacket, and leaving fires burning qualify as violating the laws most prodigiously; so does brandishing or firing illegal guns. If you meet a deputy sheriff or a game warden, you may think that because you have been down the river and know what you are doing, and he has not, you can argue your way out of a ticket. You may think that because you are an expert and he has never seen the river from anywhere but the bank, you can talk him around to your point of view. Don't count on it. In fact, under most circumstances, don't even try it. If the guy were a kayaker he would be kayaking. Most kayakers agree that the only way to handle these people is to proffer a lot of "respect." If civil disobedience appeals to you, and it does seem to appeal to most kayakers, you may or may not beat the man in a higher court. Since most kayakers do as much starving off the river as on, the odds are you will not have the money to pursue your case. I'm getting old and a bit less impertinent, and find myself more and more inclined to obey the law. You take your choice and (perhaps) pay your money. At least, for your choice to have moral weight, you ought to know what the law is before deciding to disobey it.

Aiding the Law

You may be in the area when a rescue is required, and the law is incompetent for the task. The situation can be pretty complex. If you have been kayaking very long, you may have memories of deputies forbidding you to run, or friends chased all over the state and finally arrested by having Magnums jammed in their bellies for some piddling matter of a permit. You dislike all deputies for the capers of a few. The deputy, on the other hand, probably is far less rancorous than the kayaker; maybe he kicked a few guys off the river when it flooded five years ago, but it was his job and he has forgotten it. His attention is absorbed by the job at hand. And since usually the law is called to the river only for desperate matters, you can bet it will be a spectacular rescue. The deputy doesn't boat; his judgment may be rotten about the river. He may look at the deadly boil below a waterfall and think of it as relatively calm since it seems flat; he may try to wade across a Class II riffle, get swept away and beg you not to entrust your boat to such a torrent.

These situations all vary so much that I can only mention principles. Generally the person to be rescued is incapacitated; often he is dead. You may have to treat for shock. You may have to send for rafts since you cannot carry the man and dare not drag him. Very likely you will need to make a rope bridge and suspend a stretcher from it, so you had better learn your knots. Finally, you are the expert but they are the authorities, so you had better use your tact in order to get your opinions heeded. One good example of sense and competence will liberalize these deputies for kayakers yet to come.

Molding the Law

> . . . the Colorado runs its deep, silent, lonely course, too little understood, too little appreciated, loved by few, feared by many, and only a name to the multitudes who have never seen it.
>
> —Julius Stone, *Canyon Country*

The most important dealing a kayaker has with the law is influencing it. For the crisis period in molding or aborting pork-barrel legislation about dams is now upon us. A Wild and Scenic Rivers Bill which authorizes the study and perhaps eventual protection of some of the remaining rivers recently passed the Congress. The great bureaus of the government which specialize in the death of rivers, the Army Corps of Engineers and the Bureau of Reclamation, along with a rout of private power companies, have been repulsed with losses from their insane attempts to channelize Florida and dam the Grand Canyon (though plans are apparently being revived for the Grand Canyon with the energy crisis as explanation), and the Yampa and Green still run relatively free. But like an amoeba, a bureau will seep past an obstacle and ingest the next particle it finds; driven skulking from the Grand Canyon, it will ruin ten or a dozen little-known and lovely streams. We have the Grand Canyon still (thank Ourselves), but White Rock Canyon on the Rio Grande, which taught us when we were children, submerged in the fall of 1974. It will be long before we regain it, and till then we must scrape to find other rivers on which to teach our children.

165

And it is just the streams now most strongly attacked that are the most dear to a kayaker. They are not crowded like Hell's Canyon. They are lovely, they are close, they still permit the thrill of exploration, and by the dozen they are being stoppered up. Rarely run, their defenders are rare in consequence. Who is speaking for the upper Yampa? Who spoke for the Strawberry? The Rio Grande? The Chama? The San Juan? The Arkansas? The South Platte? The Blue? Few, for there were only few with the energy and knowledge to speak.

For six little projects, each requested by six avaricious and carefully coached local chambers of commerce, each equipped with mendacious cost-benefit analyses, each fitted out with built-in cost overruns, can more than overbalance one mighty spasm of empire building. And they draw a lot less scrutiny, which is important, given the sleazy doings of some of these bureaus.

Let us postulate an imaginary stream, the Rio Estiércol, to see how the problem is solved. Given a river meandering through broad alluvial plains all covered with trees, what is the solution? "What's the problem?" is the kayaker's question. But the solution is to deforest the plain (these phreatophytes "waste" a lot of water). Then put a city on the plain. It will be flooded, since flood plains are—that is how they are created. With no trees to hold the soil and retard the water, the city on the plain will be damaged. (Shall it be called Sodom? . . . or Gomorrah?) The solution is to straighten the channel. This accelerates the flow, so there must be a little more water in the river for the flood to come out of its banks. But the increased sediment load that the trees used to retain will now aggrade the river's bed. As the bed rises, floods of smaller and smaller volume can escape the straightened channel. The solution is to line the channel with concrete. This further accelerates the flow, so that anything that falls in must die, as I once saw a collie die in California. But then the river cannot scour to absorb its higher discharges, and must come out of

its banks to carry them. The solution? You must put in a dam upstream to store the "excess" water. But all that excess water is carrying a heavy charge of sediment from the deforestation. In fact, a relatively small logging operation on the South Fork of the Salmon in Idaho, once the source of some 30 percent of the state's salmon spawning, increased the sediment load 770 times. Fishing there was closed. Everywhere in the United States sediment loads are increasing exponentially.

But to get back to our dam. The city on the plain now has a trickle passing it, not a flood, excepting the oily effluents from its storm drains which pour into the channel after a rain. But the dam is filling in with mud—Lake Mead is said to have gotten one-half full in about thirty-five years. And, unfortunately, evaporation so reduces the water in the lake that our trickle out its base is getting saline. The solution? There must be more channels where the river collects salts upstream. The river needs more water to dilute the salts. We may obtain it either by modifying the weather, deforesting the upper basin or by building a series of dams, tunnels and canals and taking it from another river to ours. Busy, busy, busy. Thus we have the beginning, merely a few initial steps, at solving our river. The Rio Estiércol, now called the Steer Kill by its neighbors, who tell tales about how they saw a steer try to drink from it once and what happened to it, is now ripe for urban beautification; many millions await the task of turning it into an architect's idea of a river. Each solution, of course, engenders more problems, which engender more solutions. The river's balance, once skewed, oscillates back and forth with greater and greater swings. Each swing is dampened by taxation, which is to say by the creation of new projects and jobs. Each counter-swing creates yet more taxes and jobs as the old ones peter out. It is all most ingenious, and most vicious. And please do not think I fake this. I write nothing here which has not been either done or proposed. The ultimate solution, of course, is to plate the Rocky Mountains with plastic some 200 feet deep, and I proposed this some time ago, but the time was not then ripe for it. Since then, promising beginnings have been made at a number of ski resorts and I have the highest hopes for the future.

The point is made. A bureau with nothing to do collapses, given the monolithic structure of these operations, from mass wasting. Like a cancer, they must grow to survive; stasis to a bureau is death. So they must keep extruding these projects, getting them funded for studies, getting them authorized, getting them funded for construction, getting them funded for cost overruns, getting them funded for correction of little oversights like damming a limestone valley and finding the river then breaks through into a cavern system and vanishes, getting them funded for repairs and getting them funded for operation. There must be funds for propaganda too, so we may see little film strips telling us of how the "rampaging river" (Bureau of Reclamation engineers seem to have all the luck; I never yet in thirteen years saw a river rampaging, and would really like to, while they get to see them all the time and are inexpressibly pained by the sight) has now been "tamed," or "harnessed to its task of making the desert bloom." They are the Hydra. And we must, like Hercules and Iolaus, strike off the heads of these projects as they appear, and cauterize the stumps.

Now these bureaus have built up a good press. It is, as you will come to discover in your first battle to save one of your rivers, a reasonable compromise, arrived at by reasonable men, men with "tomorrow in their eyes," men wanting to avoid the chaos of today with plans for tomorrow, who wish to slaughter a river and drown its canyon in silt. But it is fanatics, "conservationists in their air-conditioned caves," spasmodically opposed to progress of any kind, men who want to turn back the clock and return us to Neolithic times, who would save a river. You will have to read, and maybe even indulge yourself in generating, a good deal of such rhetoric in trying to circumvent their plans. At base perhaps the two positions are not so far off. I gather from the folk songs and the silly plaques, the tales from old construction workers and engineers, that those who built the dams thought dealing with a river could turn a human into a Man. I gather from the fumes, the boredom, the vandalism, the noise and most of all the acres of litter, that a man-made lake cannot. With this the engineers might not agree, but that first position is most similar to a kayaker's. Yet an engineer or a worker, after his epic battle with the river, leaves not a river behind for other epic battles and other generations. As he ages, he will have mighty memories to thread through his old man's sleep, but what memories shall his sons have?

A kayaker, starting at that same position, has his battles and yet leaves the arena for the next man. When the engineer has done with the river, it will have irrigated acres and produced power, will have provided, in short, the adjuncts to a decent, placid, comfortable life. This is no small praise. But that same fierce joy the kayaker knows and the engineer may have known, will all have seeped away into farms and toasters, lawns and can openers. The difference is not just that the kayaker tries to obey Leopold's prescription that the highest recreations wear least on the resource base, but that the kayaker cannot accept man's being the only creature between heaven and hell that has rights. A dam is the solution to a river when man is the axiological measure. But when all things have their rights and duties, a river may not be a problem and may need no solution. When we have provided jobs and socially planned, when we have imposed our reason upon the hills and the water, what then? We will have centered the world upon ourselves, and will be surprised to find, once it is too late, that we are not such good architects as God was, and a world managed by men for man's interests is not so pleasant or intriguing a place as one run for itself, by itself. We will be rich, yet it will do us but little good to be rich in a human, tedious and defiled world.

Let us take a look at the men who supposedly leash up the Bureau and the Corps of Engineers, the men you will have to deal with in trying to save a river—the legislators. By their allocation of your money the rivers you love will be saved or blasted. It need hardly be stated that the best way to safeguard the river is to gain the power yourself. Next best is to elect a fellow kayaker, and barring that, to get a rafting friend and take your legislator down the river. It is only the most insensitive or the best-paid of men who can descend a river and then do it in.

It is just possible your legislator may be one who can. He may be "sympathetic," but he may be a "practical man." I never understood why practicality always means dams and never rivers, junk yards and never meadows, deadened souls and never joy, but it does seem that way. What this means generally is that your legislator, if practical, will see your river clapped up in tubes and nozzled into turbines. Seeing it flood, he will see neither cycles of time nor regeneration nor beauty, the gifts of the flood; he will hear no sermons in stones and read no books in babbling brooks; he has a gift of vision denied us kayakers, and can see through water, not to the fish in it, but to jobs, megavolts and votes. Seeing silt clogging the water, he sees neither the death and genesis of continents, nor even an indictment of some of the most prodigal farming practices the earth has endured, but mud. A great chocolate desert flood, freighted with continents, rolling down to the sea to build new ones, he will clean with the silt trap of a dam. But an icy pellucid stream he will warm with effluents and charge up with sewage. The man may be blind to the being of a river, but he has a pronghorn's eyes for his power.

This is where you "convince" him. A legislator's vanity (cowardice? practicality?) drives him to lead public opinion when he has been cowed into following it. He can be expelled from office for ranging either too far in front of or too far behind the electorate. Let us take an example. Lyndon Johnson and his Secretary of the Interior, Stewart Udall, a sort of fallen angel, both favored the Central Arizona Project in the late 1960's. Provisions in it would have dammed the Grand Canyon in two places. Only see them after they had plowed through the ensuing blizzard of a million letters protesting this. Then, you may be sure, they leaped to the defense of what had been successfully defended against them, and stood forth as the saviors of what they had been unable to destroy. Udall later confessed in a Sierra Club book that a Secretary of the Interior ought not to make decisions about land he had not seen, and Johnson's last act in office was to save Marble Canyon for future generations by proclaiming it a National Monument. Not a pleasant, but a very practical display.

The lesson and assignment are clear. We kayakers must be public opinion. Since, as a young Senator's aide told me, the majority of letters which come in each week are illiterate and unactionable, this is not such a task as it might be thought. The aide informed me that a matter of some twenty or thirty letters on a topic, if brief and cogent, would be brought to the Senator's attention by his staff. Happily enough, a tiny charge of intelligence can produce a laser beam of public opinion; those thirty letters are easily within the reach of two bright kayakers working for an afternoon. We speak out, whereas most of those we tend to think of as the enemy are dumb. And, if the letters do not merely state our position but also request the Congressman's, his staff will have to research the matter. A small club of dedicated kayakers can produce thousands of letters. The letters in turn can sway your Senator and, at least on a river in your state, this is the battle. The House and Senate are most unlikely to vote a project for your state against the wishes of your representatives, which in turn should be your wishes.

All of this requires something kayakers do very well and usually dislike—organization. You may, despite the purity we kayakers love to maintain, associate with fishermen, hunt-

Known only to the few who run it each year, this is a stretch in New Mexico's only Wild River. The Congress of the United States is available to save more such runs; when it proves stubborn, kayakers will have to convince state legislatures to set up their own systems. Without legal protection, no river is safe. Without boaters to convince them, few legislatures are apt to provide that legal protection. *Photo by Roy Cromer.*

ers, Sierra Clubbers, members of the Wilderness Society, and who not? You may need to set up a coordinating council which keeps all the conservation organizations in your state in touch, so as to alert them to the latest moves of government. Many organizations now are moving to set up Wild River Systems in their own states; they have passed from a negative reaction against what is done to them, to an asseveration of what they want to do. These are hopeful matters, if they can be moved quickly enough to outstrip the damming forces. They require vigilance, energy,

intelligence and research; they also require tact. This last, I think, is the hardest for us to learn. In these matters—surveying rivers, proposing them for inclusion in Wild Rivers Systems, monitoring bureaus, blocking pork-barrel legislation, and pollution surveillance and conservation education—kayakers are more fitted to lead than any other group on the rivers. Whether they take up duties in keeping with their abilities will determine whether not just their children, but they themselves, will have enough rivers left to kayak.

5 ARMCHAIR EXERCISES (or Living-Room Floating)

Books on Whitewatering

A book of this nature normally has a standard bibliography, and if this were a skin-and-bones work about hydrology, or floating techniques, or fishing, or geology, it might be best served with a dry list of "recommended reading." But if there's anything we three agree upon, it's that joining a river for a while involves a complex growth of skills, perceptions and pleasures. These don't present themselves by virtue of the act of floating on down a river; they gradually blossom after a combination of learning and seeing and doing. Reading is one way to encourage that flower.

The following is a selection of material that we've found contributes to growth in one way or another—with our comments.

Arighi, Scott and Margaret. *Wildwater Touring: Techniques and Tours.* New York: Macmillan Publishing Co., 1974.

An absolutely complete guide to arranging and safely completing a protracted kayak tour, written with sense and occasional humor. This book contains chapters on river selection, equipment, car shuttling, safety, and well-chosen words on the psychological factors of running a long tour. Its final section contains nine tours on six rivers in the North Country (the Rogue, Grande Ronde, John Day, Middle Fork, Main Salmon and Owyhee), complete with maps and comments. Some of the tours are adapted to the advanced novice, some to the team of experts. The two tours they describe that I have run are correct; there can be little higher praise. Their comments about water levels and safety are well taken. I do think they rate rapids rather high, but this is a picayune point. This is the sort of book whose recommendations, followed by a beginner, will permit him to grow old and sage enough to make just such niggling charges. The beginning tourer will find the book everywhere useful; the expert will appreciate its nine specific tours and copious lists of whom to write for whatever information on whatever topic he may need.   E.P.

Dickey, James. *Deliverance.* Boston: Houghton Mifflin Company, 1970.

A modern novel about a nightmare on a wild whitewater river. While this is by no means a recommended text on whitewater technique, it's a good yarn, with Dickey's past achievements as a poet coming through in the form of lyrical prose about the river. The book is also an excellent argument for observing the rule about always scouting ahead when you don't know what lies downriver.   N.S.

Fletcher, Colin. *The Complete Walker.* New York: Alfred A. Knopf, Inc., 1970.

No, this book doesn't discuss whitewater, but it does deal with backpacking equipment and that's what you'll want to carry when river touring. We recommend this particular guide because it's the most thorough book concerning the subtleties of backpacking gear that you'll find on the market. Besides being packed with detailed information and evaluation, it's fun to read. In his "Bedroom" chapter, Fletcher offers the following advice: "An experienced outdoorsman has suggested that I include in this chapter 'the ritual of getting to sleep in a bag,' and as he is my editor I suppose I had better attempt the task. My technique is to lie down, close my eyes, and go to sleep."   S.C.

Hesse, Hermann. *Siddhartha.* New York: Bantam Books, 1951.

Siddhartha is a novel written by Hesse in the 1920's about Buddhism and the spiritual growth of a man. The reason it is included here is that anyone who has read it and floats a river (or vice versa) makes an instant connection. That part of the book dealing with Siddhartha's years as a ferryman contains passages of description and philosophical reflection that are at once brilliant and vivid, subjective and objective; it's some of the most intriguing prose ever penned about a river. Once you've read it, Hesse's river—all rivers—keeps flowing through your mind. N.S.

Jenkinson, Michael. *Wild Rivers of North America.* New York: E. P. Dutton & Co., 1973.

While this book pretends, in part, to be an instructional work for the floater, its real worth lies in the historical/travel approach the author takes to rivers and, to some extent, the practical touring information it provides (put-in and take-out, points of interest, quality of fishing, etc.). Jenkinson has a keen eye for the whole landscape, painting word pictures that go far beyond the river shore to touch the hazy line of mountains seventy miles distant. He sees "stone and sand, thorn and sapless stem" on a vast sweep of desert near the Rio Grande, as well as the signs of a settlement: "TV aerials, higher than the crosses, as if to gather in greater blessings."

History is outlined with equal grace. Speaking about the original settlers along Idaho's Middle Fork of the Salmon, he writes: "Before long some men were raising families in the back country. Some say Charlie Bemis won his Chinese wife, Polly, in a poker game at Warren. Others claim this is untrue, that a mutual attraction developed while she was nursing pistol wounds he received from a feisty card dealer. At any rate, they got married, and together developed a ranch in the depths of the Salmon River Canyon."

The combination creates both a feeling and a perspective for the rivers he writes about. While this isn't strictly a whitewater book ("wild" rivers like the sluggish Suwannee are part of the text), it's a great companion for floaters that reads well on or off the river.   N.S.

Leopold, Luna P.; Wolman, M. Gordon; and Miller, John P. *Fluvial Processes in Geomorphology.* San Francisco: W. H. Freeman and Company, 1964.

An extremely technical book that makes for heavy wading in places, but a good place to look if you want to delve into hydrology and related fields (erosion, drainage patterns, sediment loads, etc.). Background in higher mathematics is recommended.   N.S.

Marisawa, Marie. *Streams: Their Dynamics and Morphology.* New York: McGraw-Hill Book Company, 1968.

This is a solid book about moving water, written in terms the layman can understand. The emphasis is on streams, not large rivers, and a great deal of the text deals with streams of the "Old Mill . . ." genre, but there

is still a lot of useful information for the floater.   N.S.

Robert E. McNair. *Basic River Canoeing.* American Camping Association, Inc., Bradford Woods, Martinsville, Indiana, 1969.

Basic River Canoeing was written as an instructor's manual for the Red Ridge College of canoeing in Pennsylvania. It's a concise book written in a rather stiff style, but the information is solid and helpful.

The text is aimed primarily at folks with open canoes, although there is a chapter entitled "Slalom Canoes Are Different." This describes the idiosyncrasies of C-1's and C-2's and goes on to explain in detail the technique of the Eskimo roll—the process of righting a decked canoe with your paddle when you find yourself floating upside down in a river.

Within the other chapters you'll find pointers on equipment and clothing, paddle strokes, reading whitewater, river tactics, safety, rescue and strategy for a hypothetical river. There are many line drawings included which are particularly instructive in the chapters on reading water and river tactics.

The textbook flavor of *Basic River Canoeing* doesn't make for lively reading, but it's clear and up to date, a good guide for both teacher and student.   S.C.

Morris, Dan, and Strung, Norman. *The Fisherman's Almanac.* New York: Macmillan Publishing Co., 1971.

A pocket-sized book (with waterproof covers) that lists every game fish, and how to catch them, in salt and fresh water. Includes information on tackle, fishing techniques and best times to fish. A good guide for the novice or casual angler.   S.C.

1,000,000 Miles of Canoe and Hiking Routes, Ohio Canoe Adventures, Inc., 5128 Colorado Avenue, P. O. Box 2092, Sheffield Lake, Ohio, 44054.

If you enjoy sitting around dreaming about next season's canoe trips, this catalogue will drive you nuts. It has hundreds of listings that range from canoe trail maps to detailed guides covering rivers throughout the United States and Canada. The catalogue costs a dollar, but you'll probably spend more once you discover what's available. S.C.

Pirsig, Robert. *Zen and the Art of Motorcycle Maintenance.* New York: William Morrow & Co., 1974.

What have Zen and motorcycles got to do with floating? Well, nothing—-and everything. Pirsig's concise, cogent perception of the underlying relationship between rational technology and mystic experience fits when you're dealing with boats and rivers too. N.S.

Porter, Eliot. *The Place No One Knew: Glen Canyon on the Colorado.* Ed. David Brower. San Francisco: The Sierra Club, 1966.

They closed the gates in 1963. In June of 1964, the mouth of the Dirty Devil River was well under the waters of the lake, and the rising water drowned another two feet of the canyon while we slept. The beauty we younger boatmen never saw was under even then, and the ten ensuing years of the thousands it will take before it surfaces again have only brought home the magnitude of the loss. It is, I guess, a little like being married and contented and suddenly finding that one woman you had longed for, too late, too late. But we have divorce to rearrange our marriages; we have nothing to resurrect Glen Canyon.

This book is the greatest text for conservation our century has seen. Porter, in sequence a physician, a teacher and a photographer, proves himself a first-rate stylist in his chapter on geology. His nature photography has but two rivals in American history, Philip Hyde and Ansel Adams, and to my

knowledge Adams did not get into the canyon before it was dead, and Hyde's photographs are not widely desseminated. The photographs, though able to stand alone and deliver their message eloquently, are ornamented by the text. Not only is Porter's chapter on geology of the first caliber, but the selections from Dutton, Thoreau and Stegner come up to standard. And that standard, as anyone who glances at the photographs will attest, is very high indeed. In the age of advertising, superlatives are stale, but I risk saying no finer Sierra Club book has been done, no finer photographs of the canyon country have been taken and no finer canyon now exists. Parts of the beauty I never saw, exist still, on other rivers, but the whole is gone, with nothing left but a scummed lake reticulated with whining power boats and this mighty book as stele. The book stands, and will stand, the monument to our dereliction of duty. Some of us were ignorant, some lazy, and our responsible representatives were corrupt, unimaginative or uninformed. So striking is the book that it lifts a boater out of his customary and proper detraction of the Bureau of Reclamation, which was the death of Glen Canyon. Mere resentments, blames and exculpations shrivel beside the loss the book commemorates. It is not so much that we are all diminished by the loss, as that we were all diminished before, or it could never have been suffered. This book—symbol, tombstone and monition—belongs in every boatman's library. It will keep him worthy of the trust the river confers upon him.   E.P.

Powell, J. W. *Down the Colorado: Diary of the First Trip Through the Grand Canyon.* Ed. Eliot Porter. Promontory Press, no date or city given.

This is a rather extensively abridged version of Powell's narrative of the first expeditions down the Green and Colorado river system in 1869 and 1871–72. First published in *Scribner's Monthly* in 1874–75, it was later done as a book (still reprinted) under the title

Explorations of the Colorado River of the West and its Tributaries (1875). This particular version of the narrative is supplied with Porter's photographs; they are, with the exception of a little of Adams' and Hyde's work, the best ever done of the canyon country. There are also quite respectable black-and-white wet-plate photographs taken on those first expeditions, and illustrations done by the early artists. A book of singular beauty.

Powell's text is well cut. None of the important and well-memorized incidents are missing. Powell himself writes that funky and highly literate prose of a nineteenth-century scientist; he is not so good a writer as two of his geologists (Dutton and Gilbert) and one of his men (Dellenbaugh), but this is still high praise; most modern scientists do not write as well. And the account is a classic of adventure, danger and devotion to science carried to success through a wilderness of canyons, a booming of rapids, a shrinking of provisions, several desertions and an Indian massacre. Powell, however, though one of the great minds of his century in America and a sort of catholic genius whose contributions to a half-dozen fields are fundamental, was writing to sway the public; his account is not strictly accurate, as historians and boatmen have known for years. His writing is not the less for it. Anyone wanting more accuracy can consult Dellenbaugh's *A Canyon Voyage,* a narrative of the second expedition; his facts are more accurate and his writing is better. Anyone wanting to know more of Powell and his setting will see Stegner's great *Beyond the One Hundredth Meridian.* But all those who have unavailingly punched a shutter in the canyon country will want to see how the master has photographed the same land, and those who have fallen under the enchantments of the great desert rivers of the Southwest will want the words of their pioneer.   E.P.

Pringle, Laurence. *Wild River.* Philadelphia: J. B. Lippincott Company, 1973.

Wild River does an excellent job of explaining the interrelated ecosystems that occur in conjunction with a river that's been left to function naturally, tying the autumn leaf to the mayfly nymph, to the trout and to the trees along the bank. This isn't a book about whitewater per se, but being exposed to Pringle's understanding of and love for moving water is a good beginning for any float. Another good exposure lies in his arguments to preserve what wild rivers we have left.   N.S.

Rent-a-Canoe Directory. Grumman Boats, Marathon, N.Y., 13803, 1974.

Here's a free 19-page booklet that lists places in the United States where you can rent canoes. Every state is covered, plus five rental locations in Canada. This is a good source of information when planning a trip far from home where lugging your own canoe along might be a nuisance.   S.C.

River Guide's Manual. The American River Touring Association, 1973.

This is a practical book essentially about rafting, written as a text and handbook for ARTA's boatmen. While much of the information is presented in outline form, you still learn a great deal by implication. Then too, the form functions as a thorough and easy-to-follow checklist for all phases of a raft float, from the condition of the battery on the shuttle car to the physical condition of members of the party.

There are classics of understatement contained herein. For example, under "when paddling a raft": "paddle commands: (1) forward, (2) right turn, (3) left turn, (4) back paddle, (5) stop, (6) paddle 'at will.' Tone determines urgency!" No doubt.

And advice has a sense of humor that indicates the adviser has been there before. Regarding the procedure for freeing a pinned raft, the manual lists step-by-step maneuvers (a) through (g) that start with shifting the weight of the passenger load and finish with an admission of defeat: "line everything to shore and leave a note . . ." The topic ends upbeat, however: "(h) come back in a week and try again, (i) Good Luck!"

It's a small book (50 pages) and is easy to carry with you. That's where it will do the most good—as an instant reference, there, whenever you need it. The price is $2.50. N.S.

U-Paddle Canoe Service. Hudson's Bay Company, Northern Stores Department, 77 Main Street, Winnipeg, Canada. (Free brochure.)

That's right, "the Bay" is keeping up with the Hertzes by offering this modern service, but it's still in the tradition of the *voyageurs.* For example, their canoe routes include a journey from Yellowknife to Baker Lake where you'll paddle 800 miles across the Northwest Territories. Or you might prefer the Fort Providence–Inuvik trip; that's just 700 miles.

This service is available only to experienced canoeists. Rental rates are $50 per canoe per week, and there's a two-week minimum. You'll be supplied with a 17-foot Grumman canoe equipped with carrying yoke and three paddles.

The latest word from "the Bay" is that due to the popularity of this service, reservations have to be made at least six months ahead of your trip. They'll also want a 50 percent deposit to confirm reservations. S.C.

Urban, John T. *A Whitewater Handbook for Canoe and Kayak.* Boston: The Appalachian Mountain Club, 1974.

This is the standard how-to-paddle manual, and well deserves its position. It contains chapters on reading water and picking courses through it, plus descriptions, drawings and photographs of the various strokes. It has little information for the use of a touring party, and should rather be considered an aid to gaining the skills you will later use on the tour. The book betrays, it seems to me, a "little water" bias, even as my pages betray a "big water" bias. Some of the technical information on ledges and rock gardens is applicable mostly to the East and some of the terminology ("white eddies") is unfamiliar to me. Different strokes for different rivers. The author's sense, style and liberal illustration make this an important purchase for a beginner and a useful one for someone more advanced. E.P.

Walbridge, Charles. *Boatbuilder's Manual.* Wildwater Designs, Inc., Penllyn Pike and Morris Road, Penllyn, Pa., 19422.

This 64-page book is indispensable for the boat builder. It contains exhaustive data on materials selection, equipment, safety in construction, construction tips and what not. The only thing missing could not be put in— a discussion by name of what design to pick. For the hot racing craft of one season are the tubs of the next, and one man can scarcely keep up with the supersession of Duffeks by Mendestas by Vertexes by Lettmans by Prijons by who knows what. You will have to choose your own model of kayak or canoe, but after that choice Walbridge is ready to help with everything else. Probably the boat maker will never spend $3 in a better cause. E.P.

Epilogue

The Beartraps of the Madison (Montana). *Photo by N. Strung*

Two Prayers

There once hung a prayer in the musty cabin of a boat owned by a crusty old seaman I had the good fortune to know.

"Lord, I am so small, and the sea is so big," was the supplication, stark and beautiful in its simplicity.

Each time I slide my raft off the bank and slip into the swirling currents, I remember that prayer. I am at once aware of the power and majesty of the river, of the white adventure that lies downstream and the very real dangers. I am nothing but an ant swept along on a popsicle raft, and the tight, nagging knot in my stomach, a combination of awe, humility and deep respect, is my constant companion through every rapids.

"Beauty in front of me, beauty behind me, beauty above me, beauty below me, there is beauty all around me," drifts along too. It is a Hopi Indian prayer that strikes a mental chord in perfect harmony with what I see: the jade green of deep, quiet pools, the pinpoints of sun glare dancing on ripples like candlelight on fine silver. I have marked the shades of pink and purple mountains slowly dimming at sundown, seen the world turned blood red in a fiery dawn and watched finger-like clouds blossoming burgundy to rose, then brilliant yellow, reflected in the mirror of the river.

There is beauty all around.

From the universal design of drainages to the magic work of erosion; to the colors, the rocks, the seasons of shifting water and the crystal droplets leaking from a paddle blade—a river is unique.

Yet some men in their questionable wisdom seek to destroy that uniqueness.

Virtually every free-running river in this country has been mapped and surveyed for eventual damming, and one by one they fall choked by a collar of cement, to drown in their sediment.

It is reasoning I have never quite understood. Flood control was the initial cry; now it's power. That there is a need for both is undeniable, but it's also undeniable that our most beautiful rivers, because of their gradient, because of their youth and because of the wild, untamed country through which they flow, carry a great amount of sediment.

Put a dam across this kind of river, and the sediment filters out. Dirt, rocks and rubble fill the flooded valley, eventually creating a shallow lake capable of neither power efficiency nor flood control. A hundred years is the life given to most impoundments; what then? In that minute span of geologic time the intricate face that nature has carved into the land has been radically altered forever and now, for no good. Once a dam is built, it will never be removed—by man at least. Only a catastrophe—an earthquake or land upheaval of proportions beyond the scope of human imagination—would set things right again, with incredible human suffering.

Does that sound far out? Perhaps it does, but as I build experience upon experience in that world that exists beyond doorsteps and cement sidewalks, I perceive in natural order a terrible power to overcome the puny mechanizations of man when they go too far.

It has taken water running downhill eons to create the complex system of drainages and streams and rivers, and that system is surely balanced against other systems which, in total accord, make up the clockwork of the universe. It is more than conceivable that by tampering with one of the gears, we'll reach a point in our collective arrogance where it will no longer work, and the rest of the machinery will be thrown into a cycle of readjustment. Nature will slap back.

It has been posited that we are throwing so much pollution into the atmosphere that we're altering the intensity of sun rays the earth receives. All life depends on the sun. How far can we tamper with the amount of sunlight reaching the earth before nature makes a readjustment, and what will it be?

The level of pollution in our oceans is changing the response of plankton, tiny plant organisms that create most of the oxygen we breathe. How far can we push that gear out of alignment?

Several of the big impoundments in the Southwest lose incredible amounts of water through evaporation. Now great stretches of water face the sun. The effects haven't been fully analyzed, but changes in weather patterns are a possibility, and surely, the ecological balance that once existed along a free-flowing river has been disrupted.

How many more dams can we build before nature slaps back?

Much of this is hypothesis, but nonetheless, nature has the ability to make the workings of this planet conform to her plans, not man's. And the damming of rivers is nothing short of an atrocity to natural order.

If the dam builders reject that notion, there's still the aesthetics of the river. We must preserve what is left for us, and for future generations. So we all can know more about rivers and canyons and the wonders of water than a concrete plug and a surging afterbay. So some valleys can go through their seasonal cycle, nourishing life. So those of us who care can feel spray on our face, and know the thrill of wild, white water.

Let us be humbled and full of awe. Let there be beauty all around us. Amen.   N.S.

Appendix

Boat-Building Materials

Shop Equipment

Plastic sheeting, to protect the floor.

Sawhorses, to suspend the molds.

Large and small coffee cans, clean, six to eight of each, for mixing resin.

Measuring jugs, to measure resin.

Eyedropper or graduated cylinder, to measure catalyst.

Measuring tape, for cutting the glass.

Large (4′ x 16′) plywood or cardboard sheets, for cutting the glass while keeping it clean and unwrinkled.

Fans, for ventilation.

Heaters, to help cure stubborn lay-ups and to maintain a standard temperature.

Air thermometer, to give you an idea how much catalyst to use; the resin system is very heat-sensitive.

Power drill, several bits for foot-brace construction, end holes for grab loops; use it also for mixing the resin with the catalyst using a piece of coat hanger bent into a *T,* and sanding disks.

Saber saw, useful though not essential for trimming foot-brace blocks, if you use them; get fine blades.

Hacksaw (same use as saber saw).

Wood rasp, to be ruined—you may need several or replaceable blades—for roughing the seam areas.

Knife, like a razor and likely to be ruined, for trimming the lay-up when it has set firm.

Scissors, several large pairs for cutting the glass.

Sandpaper, at least a dozen coarse sheets for roughing areas that have set hard and need attachments; if you have to work on the mold, extremely fine wet paper is required.

Brushes, one very good and clean for the mold release, and a dozen cheapies to be ruined and scrapped, for the resin.

Squeegees, for resin work, although inferior to plasticators.

Plasticators, wedgies for resin work, from auto-parts stores; get three or four.

Rollers, about three of the 3- to 6-inch width, for resin.

Stick or broom handle, about 4 feet long, with a nail driven through one end and a cheapie brush taped to the same end, both protruding past the end of the stick at about a 45-degree angle—for installing the seams.

Clamp or trouble light with substantial cord, for seeing the seams you are doing; it clamps in the coaming area.

Rubber mallet, tongue depressors, for getting the boat out of the mold.

Boat Equipment

Molds, flanged so they can be bolted together.

Carnauba wax, several coats in the mold to smooth it and help with the release, and several coats on the boat to fight sun rot.

Mold release, self-explanatory and crucial.

Resin, three or four gallons; the less you can use and still saturate the glass, the lighter and better the boat.

Catalyst, should come with the resin; get your air temperature, follow the directions and don't mix much at first.

Coloring, should be supplied.

Acetone, solvent; store it carefully; there have been fires.

"Glass," whatever types of glass, glass tape for seams, roving, PRD, S-glass, polypropylene, Dynel, nylon, you decide to use after consulting Walbridge's book and the experts in your area. It is easiest to have it cut slightly longer than the boat (5 yards being just a bit too long), with the center line marked on the glass and the mold, and both ends of the glass rolled up (*never* fold it) to these marks. The glass layer, which looks like a papyrus scroll, can then be

179

put into the mold with the center lines matching, then gradually unrolled, and worked out to either end.

Cab-o-sil, a fiberglass dust you can thicken up your resin with to help in uncooperative places like the ends and the coaming; usually unnecessary.

Epoxy cements, many uses.

Barge contact cement, for attaching some foot, knee and hip brace systems.

Ethafoam, for certain bracing systems.

Safety Equipment

Protective clothes, overalls or a garbage-can liner made into a poncho; will be ruined.

Rubber gloves, to be ruined; about six pairs.

Hairnet or, better, swimming cap, avoids fiber hair, especially when seaming.

Barrier cream, at the openings of your clothes, keeps some of the irritating dust out.

Respirator, best is the cartridge type with filters; next best is a simple screen type that keeps the dust of a sanding operation out of your lungs, where it can kill you; of crucial importance.

Index